THE ACHIEVEMENT OF
GRAHAM
GREENE

THE ACHIEVEMENT OF
GRAHAM GREENE

Grahame Smith

Senior Lecturer in English Studies
University of Stirling

THE HARVESTER PRESS · SUSSEX

BARNES & NOBLE BOOKS · NEW JERSEY

First published in Great Britain in 1986 by
THE HARVESTER PRESS LIMITED
Publisher: John Spiers
16 Ship Street, Brighton, Sussex
and in the USA by
BARNES & NOBLE BOOKS
81 Adams Drive, Totowa, New Jersey 07512

© Grahame Smith, 1986

British Library Cataloguing in Publication Data

Smith, Grahame
   The achievement of Graham Greene
   1. Greene, Graham—Criticism and interpretation
   I. Title
   823'.912   PR6013.R44Z/

   ISBN 0-7108-0604-X

Library of Congress Cataloging in Publication Data

Smith, Grahame.
   The achievement of Graham Greene.
   Bibliography: p.
   Includes index.
   1. Greene, Graham, 1904– ——Criticism and interpretation.
   I. Title.
PR6013.R44Z85 1985   823'912   84-28310
ISBN 0-389-20562-1

Typeset in 12 point Garamond by M.C. Typeset, Chatham, Kent
Printed in Great Britain by Oxford University Press

For Matthew, Helena and Dan

Contents

CHAPTER ONE

Introduction

He came over the top of the down as the last light failed and could almost have cried with relief at the sight of the wood below. He longed to fling himself down on the short stubbly grass and stare at it, the dark comforting shadow which he had hardly hoped to see. Thus only could he cure the stitch in his side, which grew with each jolt, jolt of his stumble down hill. The absence of the cold wind from the sea that had buffeted him for the last half hour seemed like a puff of warm air on his face, as he dropped below the level of the sky. As though the wood were a door swinging on a great hinge, a shadow moved up towards him and the grass under his feet changed from gold to green, to purple and last to a dull grey. Then night came. (*The Man Within*)

Begun in 1926, when he was just under twenty-two, and published in 1929, Greene's first novel announces in its opening paragraph the arrival of a new voice in English fiction. The book as a whole may disappoint – its author certainly feels so – and yet one is grateful for his decision to reprint it as, in the words of his Author's Note to a later edition, a 'gesture towards his own past, the period of ambition and hope.' And this first paragraph fascinates because of its revelation of a characteristic range of the stylistic and thematic preoccupations which will be central to Greene's career. These preoccupations will vary and deepen with the demands of increasing literary skill and richness of experience; there's no question of deadening repetition, a procession of novels more or less identical. The opening of *The Man Within* is simply the guarantee of a mind and artistic sensibility strong enough to have its own vision and modes of expression even from an early stage.

1

The passage is strongly pictorial in a way that will come to seem characteristic, but with the vividness of a moving picture not a static composition. Greene testifies, in *The Other Man*, to experiencing his descriptive writing as a form of movement, that of the recording, and transforming, eye roving like the film camera.[1] The man himself moves, but so also does the wood, swinging on its hinge, and the shadow coming up to meet him. Simile, the bane of Greene's early style, and a never-abandoned staple of his later writing, reinforces the sense of movement by making the wood into one of the key images of his oeuvre, a door. Finally, the passage is permeated by that atmosphere of 'something weary and hunted'[2] which will recur with undiminished interest in novel after novel as patterns of pursuit unfold, hunter and hunted changing places with dazzling virtuosity.

Greene's grand theme of the self divided, whether as jealous lover, drunken priest, double agent, to name only a few variations, is clearly present in the novel's epigraph from Sir Thomas Browne:

> There's another man within me
> that's angry with me.

To sound thus early the discord of a conflict that will remain a constant in his writing suggests that its seeds lie in Greene's own experience; an acknowledgement of the usefulness of biography that this book accepts in assisting its major purpose of literary criticism. Only a self-defeating purism would ignore the help proffered by such a richly self-documented life as our author's. In a review of some critical works on Wordsworth, Marilyn Butler expresses a commonsense view of literary study in a neat sentence: 'For most students, and such general readers as survive, the readiest approach to a writer is still a blend of biography and of the 'close reading' of a limited, knowable selection of the poet's oeuvre.'[3] My reading of Greene may, then, strike some as old-fashioned although it is not written in ignorance of current theories of literature and the debate concerning the nature of literary study that rages at the moment. I simply doubt the usefulness at this stage of, say, a structuralist analysis of a writer who has not been overburdened with critical enquiry, in recent years at least. Also, to alienate possible sympathizers from the first full-length study of what looks increasingly like Greene's complete output would be peculiarly disappointing given the special nature of that output as I shall present it in what follows. If, as I believe, Greene's popularity is an important element in his total achievement, it would be an irony indeed to subject his work to approaches understandable only to professional literary critics.

If knowledge of the life does help us to understand the work better, the reader may welcome a few dates and facts as a starting-point:

1904 Born in Berkhamsted, a small and prosperous country town close to London. Attended Berkhamsted School, an English public school for middle- and upper-class boys, where his father was headmaster.

1920 Period of psychoanalysis after unhappiness at school and various attempts at suicide.

1922 Balliol College, Oxford where he edited the *Oxford Outlook*, wrote poems and film reviews, and studied modern history.

1926 Period in Nottingham as journalist on the *Nottingham Journal*; conversion to Roman Catholicism initiated by his future wife being a Catholic.

1927 Sub-editor on *The Times* which he left in 1929.

1928 Married; eventually one son and one daughter.

1930 Struggling to establish his career as a novelist with earnings supplemented by literary journalism and film reviewing for *The Spectator*.

1935 Journey across Liberia in West Africa.

1938 Journey to Mexico to investigate government persecution of Roman Catholic church.

1941 War service, in intelligence, in Sierra Leone, West Africa.

1951 Post-war travels as a journalist to world trouble spots: the Emergency in Malaya, 1951; four winters in Vietnam reporting the French war, 1951–5; reporting the Mau Mau episode in Kenya, 1956.

1958 Visit to a leper colony in the Belgian Congo.

One or two of the bare facts listed here may help to counter one-sided views of what is a highly paradoxical life. (Greene's future biographer, Norman Sherry, has the exciting, if difficult, task of attempting to resolve these paradoxes). One would have to look far among important writers to find a more adventurous and well-travelled life than Greene's. This way of life, as well as its related journalistic activity, undoubtedly served to make him a fairly well-known personality in the 1950s and 1960s. Greene never courted fame, if that's not too strong a word, of this kind; his aversion to appearing on television and to giving interviews is well known. And yet the degree of exposure he was afforded can hardly have hindered the sales of his books while, more damagingly, creating a view of him as a writer whose dominant interests were *reportage* and the local colour of exotic settings. It would be fatally easy, in fact, to be drawn to the rich texture of Greene's external life forgetting that for him, as for any writer, the inner life is the creatively important area of experience. For all its vivid detail, for example, *Journey Without Maps* is more of a journey into the heart of the self than into the heart of Africa.

The sheer volume of Greene's autobiograhical writing helps to make this point. *Journey Without Maps* (1936) and *The Lawless Roads* (1939) may seem to fall into that category of between the wars travel writing chronicled by Paul Fussell in his book *Abroad*,[4] but their insights into Greene himself are for me much their most important aspect. The English setting of the Epilogue to the *The Lawless Roads* might tempt one to parody Marlowe's Dr Faustus on hell, 'Why, this is Mexico, nor am I out of it,' for 'Mexico is a state of mind.'[5] The violence Greene met everywhere in Mexico becomes a paradigm for a brutality widespread in the years immediately before the second world war, a phenomenon which has its roots in spiritual blankness for Greene, as well as in social deprivation. His travels become, then, an encounter between two states of mind, his own and that of the physical setting he explores. A link to a more conventional form of autobiography is provided by the overall title of his two African Journals (the 'Congo Journal' and 'Convoy to West Africa'): *In Search of a Character*. It seems clear that Greene himself regards his journeys at least partly as exercises in drawing a map of the self. His responses to an exotic and alien setting help to define the personality that does the responding. With *A Sort of Life* (1971) and *Ways of Escape* (1980) we move into more or less familiar autobiographical territory. But although Greene has been generous with insights into his personal life, we can note a major difference between these last two books. In the first, Greene is bravely prepared to relive the pain of childhood and adolescence, recreating in the process the texture of his inner life in copious detail. An honourable concern for the 'copyright of others' lives'[6] inhibits *Ways of Escape*, however, so that it becomes something of a chronicle of external events, the novelist in danger of disappearing behind the activities of the journalist and man of affairs.

Greene's engagement with public events is, though, an important strand in his life; if nothing else, it has prompted him to travel the world, acquiring in the process an enviably wide knowledge of international politics in the twentieth century. A Catholic convert with left-wing sympathies was bound to be something of an outsider in the England of the 1930s. And yet, despite its limitations, this vantage point may well have given him a heightened sense of the political and social tensions of that era. During his period on *The Times* Greene flirted with the anti-General Strike sentiment of his middle-class background, but the horrors of Depression poverty and unemployment rapidly infused him with a sympathy for the underdog that has remained a constant in his life and career. Catholicism complicated Greene's feelings about the Spanish Civil War into a more interesting response than the routine left-wing gestures of the day, but the evils of Nazism left no room for complexity, only an intensity of loathing. Unlike some other left-wing writers and intellectuals of the 1930s, Greene became neither a cold warrior nor indifferent to politics once the war was over. He has steered his own distinctively non-communist, anti-authoritarian course since then, castigating American imperialism, and supporting human rights wherever they have been violated. Even in recent years, at an age when most men are well and truly retired, apparent illegalities on his own doorstep have roused him to attack 'The Dark Side of Nice,' the sub-title of *J'Accuse* (1982).

This aspect of Greene's life is important enough to demand comment and I shall elaborate on it, whenever this seems necessary, in the discussion of specific novels. At this point, however, I want to isolate some of the master images and so preoccupations of Greene's inner life in the spirit of his own distinction between life and art in *The Other Man*: 'I consider that in spite of the prevailing chaos, my life is a relatively coherent whole, at least in so far as my books are concerned.'[7] The books, too, are a form of life just as much as the journeys to Indo-China, and the rest; for our purposes, indeed, much the most important. *The Man Within* can help us again for, as early as the opening paragraph of Chapter Two, we find the following:

> Over a toppling pile of green vegetables two old women were twittering. They pecked at their words like sparrows for crumbs. 'There was a fight, and one of the officers was killed.' 'They'll hang for that. But three of them escaped.' The vegetables began to grow and grow in size, cauliflowers, cabbages, carrots, potatoes. 'Three of them escaped, three of them escaped,' one of the cauliflowers repeated. Then the whole pile fell to the ground, and Carlyon was walking towards him. 'Have you heard this one?' he said. 'Three of them escaped, three of them escaped.' He came nearer and nearer and his body grew in size, until it seemed as though it must burst like a swollen bladder.

This is, of course, a dream, an aspect of his fiction Greene creates with an authority apparent in both vividness of detail and a sense of total believability. The authority stems from direct experience. His period of psychoanalysis in adolescence led Greene to keep a dream diary (a habit to which he has returned in old age), the treatment itself concentrating on the discussion of his dreams. Dreams have thus played a central role in his life and also, largely unremarked, in his work. Novel after novel contains dreams which are fascinating in themselves and organically related to theme and character. Out of an embarrassment of riches one might choose Chapter Five, 'Between Sleeping and Waking,' of the first book of *The Ministry of Fear* as Greene's finest excursion into the dream world. It can only be fully appreciated, naturally enough, in the context of the novel as a whole. Some of the deepest levels of the protagonist's inner life surface in it with an almost unbearable pain and horror, but Greene also shows a remarkable insight into the mechanics of dreaming as Rowe drifts fitfully in and out of consciousness: 'He had worked the dream to suit himself, but now the dream began to regain control.' Greene's ability to unify a fictional dream with the world of the novel as a whole is perhaps related to his belief that dreams also have a kind of unity: 'I've discovered that dreams are like serials—the instalments sometimes carry on for weeks. At the end they form a whole.'[8]

Dreams, and their associated worlds of fantasy, form a link with what I've already called the master image of Greene's oeuvre, the door. This clearly relates to the green baise door between the countries of school and home at Berkhamsted, the most important creative transformation of which I analyse in my discussion of *The Ministry of Fear*. It recurs times without number, making an appearance, for example, on the first page of *The Lawless Roads*:

> Two countries just here lay side by side. . . . You had to step carefully: the border was close beside your gravel path. . . . If you pushed open a green baize door in a passage by my father's study, you entered another passage deceptively similar, but none the less you were on alien ground.

Greene's ejection from the Eden of a loving home circle into the fart-ridden hell of dormitory life parallels Dickens's abandonment to the blacking factory, both being marked by a sense of betrayal and degradation. Greene, though, risks appearing as the poor little rich boy in this episode liable, like Stephen Spender, to have stones thrown at him by those who would have found his hell a heaven. The sheer power of Greene's writing rescues him, however, convincing us that for that boy in that place life was indeed intolerable. And the fascination and resonance of the door image stems from its importance in Greene's inner life long before this 'rational' cause of unhappiness. Significantly enough, the best clues to this earlier occurrence are found in that supposed travel book, *Journey Without Maps*, where Greene writes of 'the earliest

dream that I can remember . . . this dream of something
outside that has got to come in. The witch, like the masked
dancers, had form, but this is simply power, a force exerted on
a door.'[9] The later dream he 'used to have almost every night
when I was small. I was walking along a dark passage to the
nursery door. Just before the door there was a linen-cupboard
and there the witch waited, like the devil in Kipangblamai,
feminine and inhuman.'[10] As with dreams, so the image of the
door recurs in Greene's work too often to be counted,
sometimes as part of a simile, say, of no great significance, but
on occasion conveying an insight of central importance. One
senses the cumulative power of the image even without
knowledge of its genesis which, as I've suggested, lies in a
triple range of associations from Greene's buried life.

Dreams and doors lead us, with an apparent inevitability, to
frontiers and boundaries, for there is an underlying unity
between the master images of Greene's writing, a unity of the
kind he claims to exist between the fragments which make up
the ultimate continuity of his dreams. Greene has tended to
stress the obsessive nature of creative work, his own and
others', but obsessions may acquire an interest, as well as
dignity, if they have some connection with the daylight world.
Just as the green baize door provides a rational explanation for
Greene's childhood misery, Paul Fussell's *Abroad: British
Literary Travelling Between the Wars* gives objective substance to
his evidently deep-seated concern with the idea of borders.
Fussell discusses the 'general sense of frontiers as menacing
which forms so large a part of the imagination between the two
World Wars':

> The anomalous 'front' of the Great War, that appalling line of
> wandering smelly ditches demarcating the border pro-tem
> between Allies and Central Powers, helps establish for the
> succeeding two decades the idea that a frontier is not just absurd
> but sinister . . . But the New World has its nasty frontiers too,
> as Graham Greene discovered in Mexico in 1938 . . . and [he]
> observes 'It is before you cross a frontier that you experience
> fear.'[11]

Fussell's observations here connect with his brilliant work on
the first world war, *The Great War and Modern Memory*, in

which he demonstrates how images of the war permeated the consciousness of a generation, passing into the common usages of language itself. Greene clearly participates in the public dimension of this phenomenon—his novels are filled with images of battle—and this adult level of awareness is revealed in his 'love for the landscape around Berkhamsted' which centres on its special position 'on the very borders' of suburbia and real countryside, a conjunction which has the 'excitement of a frontier.'[12] Again, although Greene draws attention to moments in his life with an apparent prophetic quality, he passes over the possible 'clairvoyance' in his writing of an early unpublished work, *Across the Border*, 'an African story.'[13] For it is in the record of his real African journey that we find some of the most clearly personal uses of the image:

> And yet all the time, below the fear and the irritation, one was aware of a curious lightness and freedom; one might drink, that was a temporary weakening; but one was happy all the same; one had crossed the boundary into country really strange; surely one had gone deep this time.[14]

This going deep is unmistakably into the self, and the central significance of the African journey for Greene's inner life lies in its reworking of the experience of psychoanalysis in another form. For some, there may be an element of Conradian mumbo-jumbo in Greene's attitude to Africa; analysis of the possible overtones of racial superiority in *Journey Without Maps* is, however, no part of my purpose here. The important border Greene crosses in his journey is from the conscious into the unconscious life:

> But it was only fair, I suppose, that the moments of extraordinary happiness, the sense that one was nearer than one had ever been to the racial source, to satisfying the desire for an instinctive way of life, the sense of release, as when in the course of psycho-analysis one uncovers by one's own effort a root, a primal memory, should have been counter-balanced by the boredom of childhood too . . .
> I sometimes wonder whether, if one had stayed longer, if one had not been driven out again by tiredness and fear, one might have relearned the way to live without transference, with a lost objectivity.[15]

Greene didn't stay long enough for this transformation to take place, supposing it were possible; if he had, one doubts if he would have continued to be a writer. Returning to the fragmented world of modern commercial civilisation meant the return to a moral and spiritual landscape where frontiers and borders have continued to exert a profound fascination. Uneasiness and excitement are the hallmarks of this fascination, qualities indicated by a question on the first page of *The Lawless Roads*: 'How can life on a border be other than restless?'[16] Greene's sense that crossing a frontier may change his life is rooted in the depths of his personality. Home, school, psychoanalysis, all involved different selves in a constant process of movement across the lines dividing one world from another. Yet there is a more light-hearted side to this, a pleasurable uncertainty that we're all capable of experiencing:

> The border means more than a customs house, a passport officer, a man with a gun. Over there everything is going to be different; life is never going to be quite the same again after your passport has been stamped and you find yourself speechless among the money-changers.[17]

Greene's version of this experience may have a special intensity, but the preoccupations I am cataloguing in this chapter are not merely isolating eccentricities; as part of the common stuff of human life they are essential raw material for the writer.

Even a cursory examination of Greene's work reveals the centrality of his theme of betrayal. Sex, religion and politics form a triangle united by different forms of treachery. Dr Plarr's cuckolding of Charlie Fortnum, in *The Honorary Consul*, is only one of the most recent, and painful, examples of sexual deceit; Scobie betrays God in killing himself; Maurice Castle is a traitor to his country in *The Human Factor*—the examples could be multiplied almost indefinitely. Again, the heart of the ulcer lies in childhood and, as before, we can unravel two levels of suffering, one pre- and the other post-conscious. Greene analyses in detail the forms of betrayal he experienced as a schoolboy in a school where his father was headmaster, but he leaves implicit the recognition of parental deceit which lies behind his evocation of the Eden-like bliss of his early childhood. As so often with writers of his generation, we're placed under the spell of a glowing Edwardian family life:

> The clouds of unknowing were still luminous with happiness. There was no loneliness to be experienced, however occupied the parents might be, in a family of six children, a nanny, a nurse-maid, a gardener, a fat and cheerful cook, a beloved head-housemaid, a platoon of assistant maids, a whole battalion of aunts and uncles, all of them called Greene, which seemed to bring them closer, and invariably at Christmas that old bachelor friend who in those days formed part of any large family gathering, a little mocked in secret by the parents, a little resented in secret by the children. The six birthdays, the Christmas play, the Easter and the summer seaside, all arrived like planets in their due season, unaffected by war.[18]

Greene loves and admires the memory of his parents, but he would hardly be human if he did not feel them to be in some way responsible for this idyll coming to an end. When the clouds of glory did disperse he found himself in Greeneland for the first time, a world not peculiar in its seedy cruelty, but for him an image of the human condition as he has consistently experienced it in different places at different times. As Greene presents his move into the upper school in *A Sort of Life*, the resulting tensions have the logic of inevitability. He succeeds, yet again, in convincing one that his plight was not simply special to him, but only what was to be expected given the circumstances:

> I had left civilisation behind and entered a savage country of strange customs and inexplicable cruelties: a country in which I was a foreigner and a suspect, quite literally a hunted creature, known to have dubious associates. Was my father not the headmaster? I was like the son of a quisling in a country under occupation. My elder brother Raymond was a school prefect and head of the house—in other words one of Quisling's collaborators. I was surrounded by the forces of resistance, and yet I couldn't join them without betraying my father and my brother.[19]

The broad outlines of this situation are familiar enough from general human experience. An extra dimension—apart from Greene's own temperament and sensitivity—was provided by some unlooked-for twists of the knife. The housemaster in his first year added 'to my inextricable confusion of loyalties' by turning out to be 'my godfather, mysteriously linked at my birth to look after my spiritual well-being with that formidable gouty Colonel Wright of Number 11, who owned the chamber-pot in the dining-room cupboard.' And this unhappy coincidence was reinforced by the fiendish 'Carter who perfected during my fourteenth and fifteenth years a system of mental torture based on my difficult situation. Carter had an adult imagination—he could conceive the conflict of loyalties, loyalties to my age-group, loyalty to my father and brother. The sneering nicknames were inserted like splinters under the nails.' Greene feels that the relationship between the 'torturer and the tortured' would have allowed him to deal with Carter if it had not been for the betrayal of Watson: 'Watson was one of my few friends, and he deserted me for Carter . . . with his defection my isolation had become almost complete.'[20]

We can discern the outline of the future development of both man and writer in all this. Greene's conversion to Roman Catholicism, prompted by meeting his future wife and accomplished on purely intellectual grounds of conviction, has always seemed something of a biographical puzzle. One explanation may be a predisposition to a religious belief through the way in which his earlier life appears to enact a secular version of the Christian story. Expulsion from Eden, mental torments of hellish intensity, betrayal, and the sense of having been born again into a better life through psychoanalysis, however temporarily, may well have played their part. One certain result of these experiences was to turn him into an 'invisible watcher, a spy on all that went on, and so I moved restlessly among the bushes on the edge of the Common, watching for an enemy, ready to retreat unseen into the depths, like the *franc-tireurs* of Henty or David Balfour pursued by red-coats or Buchan's Hannay.'[21] The novelist as spy, the secret observer of human experience, has remained one of Greene's most constant images of the creative writer. To this heady brew may be added what he calls his innate penchant for secrecy' and a love of practical jokes, one particularly finished example being his deception of the distinguished writer, Elizabeth Bowen:

> My last evening I gave dinner to my friend, Elizabeth Bowen, who had come to Vienna to lecture at the British Institute, as a guest of the British Council. I took her afterwards to the Oriental. I don't think she had ever been to so seedy a nightclub before. I said, 'They will be raiding this place at midnight.'
> 'How do you know?'
> 'I have my contacts.'
> Exactly at the stroke of twelve, as I had asked a friend to arrange, a British sergeant came clattering down the stairs, followed by a Russian, a French and an American military policeman. The place was in half-darkness, but without hesitation (I had described her with care) he strode across the cellar and demanded to see Elizabeth's passport. She looked at me with respect—the British Council had not given her so dramatic an evening. Next day I was on my way to Italy.[22]

The whole incident is deeply characteristic of Greene, involving as it does a form of betrayal, harmless in this case, but it is also a perfect little embodiment of his conception of the creative act. Guile, craft and secrecy combine to make a little fiction, a tiny narrative which is revelatory of character in Miss Bowen's naivety (through the British Council a dig seems intended at the intellectual world he finds 'academic and sometimes a shade pretentious'[23]) and the narrator's amused sense of superiority.

It is pleasant to approach the end of this chapter with a joke lacking in any real cruelty, because so much of Greene's inner world is filled with painful conflicts. Suffering and betrayal demand relief of some kind and this is to be found in his central positive image, and perhaps his most important key word, 'peace'. It makes its first appearance on the fourteenth page of *The Man Within* ('He must be terribly alone . . . but there's the peace of God in his face.') and echoes through everything he has written since. It takes many forms, from the peace which passeth understanding of traditional Christianity to the domestic quiet longed for by Maurice Castle in *The Human Factor*. The search for peace is a journey that can only end with death and so we do not often see his characters enjoying it. But if its attainment is endlessly postponed, the pursuit itself adds dignity to the apparent shapelessness of human existence, that dimension of something more than the mundane which elevates life to a plane of real seriousness. To be serious—as well as amusing, interesting and exciting—about the human condition is a sign of the distinguished popular writer, an honourable title that Greene fully earns through the skill with which the preoccupations I have traced in these pages are embodied in art.

NOTES

The following abbreviations are used throughout: SL—*A Sort of Life* (Penguin, 1974); WE—*Ways of Escape* (Penguin, 1981); OM—*The Other Man:Conversations with Graham Greene* by Marie-Francoise Allain, trans. from the French by Guido Waldman (London: The Bodley Head, 1983).

References to quotations are given in the text in brackets following the passage cited; Greene frequently divides his novels into books and parts as well as chapters and these are indicated where appropriate.

1. OM, p.132.
2. *Stamboul Train*, Part One, Ch. 1.
3. *London Review of Books*, July 7–20 1983, Vol. 5, No. 12, p.18.
4. Paul Fussell, *Abroad:British Literary Travelling Between the Wars* (Oxford University Press, 1980).
5. *The Lawless Roads* (Penguin, 1981), p.244.
6. WE, p.10.
7. OM, p.17.
8. OM, p.150.
9. *Journey Without Maps*, (London: Pan Books, 1948)
10. *Ibid.*, p.111.
11. Fussell, *op. cit.*, pp.32–3.
12. SL, p.79.
13. *Ibid.*, p.132.
14. *Journey Without Maps*, p.124.
15. *Ibid.*, pp.148–9.
16. *The Lawless Roads*, p.13.
17. *Ibid.*, p.23.
18. SL, pp.52–3.

19. *Ibid.*, pp.54–5.
20. *Ibid.*, pp.57 and 60.
21. *Ibid.*, p.65.
22. OM, p.35 and WE, pp.99–100.
23. OM, p.148.

CHAPTER TWO

The Entertainments

SECTION A: THE ENTERTAINMENT AS A GENRE

Perhaps the feature of Greene's work which marks it off most decisively from that of his twentieth-century predecessors is the commercial and artistic success of his entertainments. The achievement rather than the intention is the distinguishing factor. Several of the high priests of modernist fiction—James, Conrad and Lawrence, for example—made conscious attempts to reach a wider public. However valuable in refining the techniques of his later fiction, James's flirtation with the stage was, however, a painful fiasco. Conrad, in collaboration with Ford Madox Ford, produced historical novels of monumental absurdity. And Lawrence's attempt to rival the success of Arnold Bennett with *The Lost Girl* remained too resolutely Lawrentian to be the money-spinner he had hoped for. With the partial exception of *The Lost Girl*, these works have been consigned to the limbo of artistic failure, a fact which crucially affects our perception of their creators. With Joyce and Virginia Woolf, these writers appear to belong to a world of artistic purity uncontaminated by commercial values and so take their place in that pantheon of modernist martyrs, entry to which is secured only by a total dedication to formal rigour of an extreme kind. Picasso did, of course, make a fortune; Stravinsky showed the keenest appreciation of his financial value; and the letters of Joyce and Lawrence reveal a perfectly legitimate desire to secure their financial due. These facts notwithstanding, a rejuvenated Romanticism insists that such figures be seen as suffering in every possible way, above all, perhaps, because the cult of modernism is associated with unpopularity.

16

How is it possible, within this context, to explain Greene's turning to such a popular form as his entertainments? Economic circumstances were clearly a factor. After the promise, and modest success, of *The Man Within* Greene's career plunged disastrously with two novels which he has resolutely refused to reprint. *Stamboul Train*, his first entertainment, was an evidently painful attempt to rescue himself and his wife from a desperate situation, a process which involved a turning away from earlier heroes: 'Never again, I swore, would I read a novel of Conrad's—a vow I kept for more than a quarter of a century.[1] But personal pressures and a revulsion from earlier writers are not enough to account for such a specific change of direction. I shall argue later that Greene's involvement with the cinema is of central importance to an understanding of his achievement, and the connection between the world of the entertainments and certain types of popular film is one I shall touch on in the next section. For the moment a more pervasive, and personal, point is relevant, which is that the whole temper of Greene's mind and personality is not wholly out of tune with popular, commercial even, aspects of modern culture; anti-commercialism is, however, almost axiomatic for such figures as Lawrence and Conrad. T.S. Eliot evidently loved Marie Lloyd and the English music hall, Lawrence his seaside concert-parties, but these interests are faintly self-conscious, like a philosophy professor's enthusiasm for football. Moreover, whatever their personal differences, in belonging to the modernist movement they are associated with an outlook which sees modern commercial entertainments as hopelessly corrupt and corrupting. Only Joyce, perhaps, of the writers of the period is prepared to accept this world without moralistic and apocalyptic condemnation.

Greene's feel for such matters is quite different. In a brilliant little review of a biography of G.K. Chesterton he remarks: 'When we love we hoard a scrap of dialogue, a picture postcard, a foreign coin, but "these foolish things" must be excluded from a biography which is written for strangers.'[2] The easy unselfconsciousness of this reference to a popular song reveals a mind which enjoys harmonising widely different aspects of experience. This should not, of course, delude us into forgetting that Greene sees many aspects of modern life as brutal and disgusting. But, and this is the important distinction, he doesn't seize only, or even mainly, on the commercial aspects of contemporary culture as his target. Writing from a religious centre, Greene's concern with questions of good and evil differs radically from the tradition of moral and social criticism associated with, for example, F.R. Leavis. Within that perspective, Matthew Arnold's prophecy that literature would take the place of religion has been fulfilled. Accordingly, the forms of art and entertainment associated with urban, industrial civilisation—film, jazz, radio, television, popular songs, and so on—are condemned root and branch because any divergence from the severest standards of high art represents a fundamental betrayal of the human spirit. Despite their mutual hostility, this strain of thought links Leavis's school with the rejection of popular culture by Marxist intellectuals in the 1930s, illustrated by Christopher Caudwell's reported belief that 'slaves cannot produce art . . . Caudwell, of course, dismisses jazz categorically.'[3]

Greene's response to the world is so fundamentally different from that of Leavis and the Marxists that his move towards the entertainment involves no lowering of artistic standards. Indeed, W.W. Robson believes that this is where his 'best work' is to be found.[4] If, as Greene claims, he is not a Catholic novelist, but a novelist who happens to be a Catholic, it is equally legitimate to see him not as an entertainer, but as a novelist who happens to write entertainments. In a later section I shall try to demonstrate that *The Ministry of Fear* is one of Greene's masterpieces, an entertainment-novel whose exciting form coincides precisely with its theme. For the moment, however, some discussion of the form itself is in order, if only to clarify the precise nature of Greene's achievement within it. Jerry Palmer's *Thrillers*: *Genesis and Structure of a Popular Genre*[5] is useful here although, interestingly, it contains no mention of Greene himself. In defining his genre, Palmer touches on ideas which are important for this chapter but which also reveal how fundamentally Greene differs from the writers with whom Palmer is concerned. For Palmer, 'it is the element of conspiracy which is . . . the

distinguishing feature of the thriller as a genre . . . the world
that the thriller portrays is a paranoid world.'[6] The conspirato-
rial element in Greene's entertainments is too obvious to need
detailed examination, above all the image of a hunted central
figure being conspired against by a hostile world. Paranoia—a
term taken, of course, from abnormal psychology—is used by
Palmer in a sense that has achieved wide recent currency,
especially in film criticism related to the so-called *films noirs* of
the 1940s American cinema. A passage from a recent history of
film demonstrates the similarities between this cinematic
world and that of a work such as *The Ministry of Fear*:

> Theirs was a nightmare hallucination full of indecipherable
> complications, a pervasive sense of threat, and fear and
> helplessness in the face of enigmatic human malevolence. The
> protagonists are typically trying to comprehend the incompre-
> hensible motives that exist within their subterranean world; they
> are trapped, seeking to find their way out of a tortuous labyrinth
> of unpleasantness, violence, and evil.[7]

Arthur Rowe's involvement, in *The Ministry of Fear*, in the
'murder' of Cost, being used for his own destruction in
carrying the suitcase of 'books', and the loss of identity from
which he inches unwillingly towards self-knowledge—these
amount almost to a distillation of *films noirs*.

From a strictly novelistic standpoint, the roots of the
paranoid view of modern urban existence lie deep in classic
nineteenth-century fiction, especially in Dickens and Dostoevski, both of whom deploy human bafflement in the face of
the bewildering complexities of city life in a form that
approximates to the detective story. *Bleak House* and *Crime and
Punishment* both contain detectives who painstakingly unravel
mysteries which are, ultimately, insoluble. The personal
mystery surrounding Esther Summerson *is* soluble, but the
problem of city life itself remains, as does the all-enveloping
miasma of the law. The burden of the mystery is shifted
brilliantly by Dostoevski from the question of who committed
the crime to the reasons for its commission, a difficulty outside
the moral and spiritual remit of Raskolnikov's pursuer, Porfiry
Petrovitch. Both novelists manipulate, to profound effect, a

setting of shadowy darkness, of narrow streets and towering tenements, of hysterical extremes of emotion. In doing so they create a world in which the innocent suffer—Jo, the crossing sweeper, of *Bleak House* and the girl drugged and raped in *Crime and Punishment*—and in which the good seem powerless to effect a more than local amelioration. This tradition of urban horror is extended by the Conrad of *Under Western Eyes* and *The Secret Agent* to the creation of paranoia on a scale beyond national boundaries, an achievement which helps Greene, in Robson's words, to turn 'the thriller into a genre which uses the modern international world as the material for art.'[8]

Greene modestly, if accurately, disclaims his right to a place in such mighty company, although there is nothing absurd in discussing him at this level. On the other hand, his very omission from *Thrillers* marks an accomplishment quite beyond that of Palmer's subjects. Greene is simply too large for Palmer's definition of his genre, as when he remarks that what 'the thriller asserts, at root, is that the world does not contain any inherent sources of conflict . . . for the world is basically a good place.' In other words, the conspiracy which Palmer sees as crucial to his form is criminal, local, and remediable by the 'courageous intervention . . . [of] one man who thereby saves the Western way of life.'[9] Greene is not, of course, greatly enamoured of the Western way of life and in the face of this trivial view of experience he stands revealed as a novelist, a true writer, whose vision accepts the opacities of a complex modern world and whose protagonists are recognisably human in their frailty rather than the faultless knights-errant of a contemporary fairy-tale. Greene's status is clarified further by a comparison with Raymond Chandler who is often said to add grace to the thriller/private detective form. This may well be true, and Chandler's world is undeniably amusing in its hard-boiled, wise-cracking way. But a moment's consideration should be enough to acknowledge that Greene operates on a totally different level of seriousness. The form of *The Ministry of Fear* has a breathtaking complexity which outdoes conventional thriller writers at their own game, but this technical virtuosity is in the interest of a theme and meaning that repay real thought.

One final explanation may be offered for Greene's unforced acceptance of a popular form, one that suggests he is very much a man of his own time. In an attempt to reassess a now almost forgotten writer, Patrick Hamilton, P.J. Widdowson remarks on the tension between realism and experiment in the novel of the 1930s and suggests that any 'reconciliation of these approaches, in the English fiction of the 1930s lies in the work of Greene, Isherwood and . . . Patrick Hamilton's *Hangover Square*.'[10] Such a move towards fictional realism is explicable both in terms of a reaction away from the innovations of the great early modernists and as a response to the more socially oriented concerns of a world whose intellectuals were preoccupied with the rise of fascism abroad, and poverty and unemployment at home. Greene experienced his own specific form of this move from the private to the public related to his own personal concerns:

> My professional life and my religion were contained in quite separate compartments, and I had no ambition to bring them together. It was 'clumsy life again at her stupid work' which did that; on the one side the socialist persecution of religion in Mexico, and on the other General Franco's attack on Republican Spain, inextricably involved religion in contemporary life. . . . A restlessness set in then which has never quite been allayed: a desire to be a spectator of history, history in which I found I was concerned myself.[11]

For sensitive writers, however, this change of direction did not lead to the wholesale rejection of the achievements of the recent past. What it did mean, for this later generation, was a recoil from the extremer forms of experiment such as stream-of-consciousness. Greene has made his own additions to two central features of fictional innovation: Jamesian point-of-view, and Conrad and Ford Madox Ford's use of the time shift, the disruption of conventional chronology. But there is no evidence that the move from the wilder shores of experiment in the 1930s was any great loss to him. Greene has always been markedly uneasy in the Joycean territory he inhabits briefly in, say, *England Made Me* with its attempts to capture the flow of Kate and Anthony Farrant's consciousness.

The cast of Greene's fictional temperament, the pressures of his personal life, and the historical forces of the period conspired to lead him to a form which may have damaged his status in academic criticism, but which ultimately created for him a large and admiring public.

SECTION B: *STAMBOUL TRAIN*

It seems entirely appropriate, then, that Greene really got into his stride as a writer with the first of his entertainments, *Stamboul Train* (1932). Encumbered by debts to his publishers and appalled by the realisation that he had entered a dead end with his early romantic fictions, he faced nothing less than the restructuring of his career. In this desperate impasse, 'for the first and last time in my life I deliberately set out to write a book to please, one which with luck might be made into a film.'[12] This crisis no doubt coloured Greene's impressions of the novel, and the experience of writing it; both are almost uniformly grey. He managed a brief train journey to Cologne to collect material, but his main imaginative resource was playing a record of Honneger's *Pacific 231*, in its day an avant-garde evocation of railway travel. Neither helped to alleviate his feeling of writing 'with a sense of doom,' an aura almost of horror that explains his later inability to reread the novel: 'The pages are too laden by the anxieties of the time and the sense of failure.'[13]

One can only think, however, that Greene's personal difficulties had the effect, like the prospect of being hanged, of concentrating his mind wonderfully, for a major impression produced by *Stamboul Train* is of creative joy. The subject matter may be sombre, but it is embodied in an unfailingly inventive form, above all in the incisiveness of the novel's structure. *Stamboul Train* is built around the effectively simple device of five parts, each named for a station on the journey: Ostend, Cologne, Vienna, Subotica and Constantinople. This domination of setting by a train permits Greene many deft touches in the introduction of his characters and the creation of atmosphere. Coral Musker, the pathetic chorus girl; Myatt, with whom she has the briefest of affairs; Mr Opie, the cricket-mad clergyman; Dr Czinner (alias Richard John), the

communist refugee returning to a failed uprising—we meet
them all in a series of fragmentary sections that have an effect
of cinematic cutting: the change in point-of-view from Coral
to Myatt may serve as an example:

> But it was no one she knew; she was back in the unwanted,
> dreaded adventure of a foreign land, which could not be checked
> by a skilful word; no carefully-measured caress would satisfy the
> approaching dark.

> The train's late, Myatt thought, as he stepped into the corridor.
> He felt in his waistcoat pocket for the small box of currants he
> always carried there. . . . At the end of the corridor a girl in a
> white mackintosh turned and gazed at him. Nice figure, he
> thought. Do I know her? (Part 3, Ch. 1)

Later, snatches of conversation catch the ebb and flow of
impermanency, the rise and fall of noise, characteristic of a
railway restaurant-car:

> 'I've never been able to understand. What can a woman like that
> *do*?'

> 'Ask them, haven't they got a Guiness. I'd just fancy a Guinness.'

> 'Of course. . . . Take Hobbs and Sutcliffe . . .'.

> 'Kisses. Always kisses.'

> 'But I don't speak the lingo, Amy.' (Part 3, Ch. 2)

At a moment of that 'sudden concerted silence which is said to
mean that an angel passes overhead' this hurtling island of
humanity remains full of noises: 'the tumblers tingled on the
table, the wheels thudded along the iron track, the windows
shook and sparks flickered like match heads through the
darkness.' During this 'human silence' a rapid succession of
inside views deepens our sense of the characters while
simultaneously enforcing their isolation—Czinner, whose
political idealism is tinged with vanity; Peter with his
furtively dirty thoughts of Coral; Myatt fretting about

business; the novelist Savory, indulging for once a serious concern for his craft; Grünlich debating his chances of escape; Coral worriedly anticipating her night with Myatt. The waiters' cries of 'Braised chicken! Roast veal . . .' break the 'minute's silence' and attempts at communication resume, from Opie's fatuous, 'I find the Hungarians take to cricket quite naturally.' to Coral's desperate, 'I love you.' (Part 3, Ch. 2) In short, *Stamboul Train* embodies a wonderfully evocative sense of railway travel.

The consummate ease of this first venture into the thriller shows Greene far outstripping existing, and later, practitioners of the genre. The novel's tight structure, its crisp introduction and rapid sketching of characters, the excitement and suspense of, say, Myatt's hair-raising drive to rescue Coral—all reveal a mastery which enforces the sense that in discovering the genre Greene is discovering himself creatively. Added to this is a level of writing quite beyond that of his supposed rivals. ('The great blast furnaces of Liège rose along the line like ancient castles burning in a border raid.' Part 1, Ch. 2) But—despite the book's genesis in its writer's desperate need for success—Greene the novelist is present here also. And this is not a matter of seriousness breaking out willy-nilly; seriousness is entwined with the novel's excitement and comedy in a satisfyingly unified way. At an obvious level, the introduction of Grünlich is a classic example of the thriller's abrupt transitions of character and setting, an apparent irrelevance which is later seen to lock into the work's larger pattern. Consciously or not, Greene must have felt a need to vary the novel's setting and also increase its range of characters. What the train gains in intensity it may be in danger of dissipating through monotony and Greene evades the dilemma with delightful effrontery. The first section of Part Three, 'Vienna,' opens with the previously unknown Josef Grünlich moving dangerously, and quite inexplicably, over an icy rooftop in driving snow. The physical excitement here is intense, although Greene claims to be weak at presenting action, and it is succeeded by macabre comedy as Grünlich slips into a middle-aged lady's bedroom:

She smiled and let out a long whistling breath. 'Oh, Anton.' He

jumped to his feet, and she dropped the towel and came towards
him, with the thin tread of a bird, in her black cotton stockings.
'One moment,' he said. 'One moment,' raising his hand
defensively, aghast at the antique lust he had aroused. (Part 3,
Ch. 1)

Grünlich's purpose becomes clear in the technically detailed
account of his attack on a safe but, because of his pride in never
being caught, he surrenders 'without a second thought one of
the easiest hauls of his career' on the unexpected return of the
railway superintendent, Herr Kolber. Grünlich shoots Kolber,
makes his escape and, confident of evading arrest, stops at a
nearby café for a cup of coffee. Only then does he discover a
trail of small change dropped from a hole in his trouser pocket!
Alarmed by this and the screams for help of Kolber's
housekeeper, he steals Mabel Warren's handbag and joins the
Orient Express, thus entering the main stream of the novel.

The whole episode lasts only some thirteen pages and its
functional precision in relation to the demands of the thriller is
rather like the workings of Grünlich's own mind: 'his brain
began to move like the little well-oiled wheels of a watch, one
thought fitting into another and setting a third in motion.'
(Part 3, Ch. 1). Although close reading suggests other levels at
work here, they coexist in perfect harmony with the
entertainment's excitement and with its relaxation of tension.
Nothing is imposed as a sop to the 'serious' reader because the
novel's levels of interest are unified in Greene's own
conception. These are, amongst others, a grotesque Freudian
and Catholic comedy in the phallic revolver which dangles on a
string between Grünlich's legs beneath his trousers. His
flirtation with Kolber's housekeeper, Anna, to gain access to
the safe, evades the consummation she so painfully desires and
Grünlich's weapon is raised to destroy life not create it. Again,
the sore rubbed on his leg by the gun has hints of the saint's
mortification of the flesh. Grünlich is, in fact, a parodic
double of the saint, a figure of total evil. (The similarities with
the films of the Catholic Hitchcock will be obvious to anyone
familiar with his work.) On the personal level, he is linked
with a more central character, Myatt, in a pattern of unease in
the face of human relationships. Grünlich falters momentarily
in asking Anna, '"Are you sure there's no one in the flat?" Her

face reddened as if he had made a crude advance. . . . His brain began to work again with precision; it was only personal relationships that confused him' (Part 3, Ch. 1). Myatt's possibility of salvation through Coral, an important theme in *Stamboul Train*, is ruined by a similar blankness: 'He was back in familiar territory, he was at home, no longer puzzled by the inconsistency of human behaviour.' (Part 3, Ch. 2). Grünlich's is infinitely the more extreme case, but he shares with Myatt, and most of the other characters, a walled-in egotism that contributes to the book's bleak view of human life.

Lastly, the novel's move into the contemporary world brings with it one of Greene's most lasting concerns, politics. Grünlich is not simply the first in his chilling gallery of killers; arising as he does out of the conditions of his time he has an unavoidably political dimension. As he sits stirring his coffee after Kolber's murder, he congratultes himself with the thought, 'Josef Grünlich, the man of destiny' (Part 3, Ch. 1). He believes that his destiny is never to be caught, which is literally true, but we can also see it as a joy in murder unlocked by his destruction of Kolber, his first venture into killing. That it won't be his last seems assured by his response to a close shave with Czinner who nearly catches him tampering with his luggage: 'If he'd tried to call the guard I'd have shot him in the stomach before he could shout a word. Josef laughed again happily, feeling his revolver rub gently against the sore on the inside of his knee: I'd have spilt his guts for him' (Part 3, Ch. 3). The horror of Grünlich's character is perfectly rounded out by the appalling sentimentality with which he greets Czinner's attempt at a song just before the doctor's seemingly inevitable execution; he begins to 'weep in a meaningless Teutonic way, thinking of orphans in the snow and princesses with hearts of ice.' (Part 4, Ch. 3). Destiny, violence, and emotionalism are all key elements in the Nazi mentality and their presence in a novel published the year before Hitler's accession to power seems like yet another example of that political 'clairvoyance' Greene has been so quick to deny. 'I prefer to call it common sense,' he tells his interviewer in *The Other Man* but if, as he remarks a few pages earlier, 'politics are in the air we breathe,'[14] it comes to the same thing. As with Percy Grimm of Faulkner's *Light in*

August, Grünlich is surely a proto-Nazi, an insight made more acceptable, perhaps, to those who dislike clairvoyance by Greene's long acquaintance with Germany which began as early as 1924 in the farcical episode of his journey, with Claud Cockburn, to the French occupied zone as a kind of spy for the German authorities. (It may be more than coincidence that in Essen he and Cockburn 'flirted with fear and began to plan a thriller rather in Buchan's manner.')[15]

Such a beginning, reinforced by Greene's well-documented interest in contemporary affairs, makes this view of Grünlich far from implausible. Whether consciously or not, Greene breathed the air of politics in a way that adds density and a lasting power to the gripping excitement of *Stamboul Train*. The point becomes irresistible when we remember the constantly reiterated motif of Myatt's Jewishness. Despite the security of his business base in London, for the novel's duration Myatt is literally a wandering Jew and Greene does all he can to accentuate his position 'as the centre of a hostile world' (Part 1, Ch. 1). The word 'Jew' echoes as an insult throughout the novel and reaches a climax during Myatt's attempt to rescue Coral, when he finds himself utterly alone with her guards: he becomes aware,

> with amazement and horror of the presence of danger; in the small hungry eyes shone hatred and a desire to kill; it was as if all the oppressions, the pogroms, the chains, and the envy and superstition which caused them, had been herded into a dark cup of the earth and now he stared down at them from the rim. (Part 4, Ch. 3)

The soil which nurtured the growth of Jewish persecution could hardly be more tangibly presented.

This investing of *Stamboul Train* with a dimension of serious interest is present also in the comic figure of Q.C. Savory, the Cockney novelist with sales of 100,000 who believes that integrity is compatible with popularity. The book's major element of light relief, his creation caused Greene a near disaster because of a threatened suit for libel by J.B. Priestley.[16] Part of the amusement generated by Savory stems from what now seems like a presciently up-to-date reflexiveness on the nature of the novel and the novelist. If it is possible in only a fourth book, and the first in which the writer truly finds his form, Greene appears to be playing with his own idea of himself as a writer by mocking a popular novelist within the context of what is itself a popular novel. A joke against himself must be intended when Savory, remembering to drop his aitches, remarks of the novelist, ' 'E's a spy.', highlighting one of Greene's most persistent views of his own function. Savory, it goes without saying, thinks little of '"modern literature . . . Joyce, Lawrence, all that?" "It will pass." . . . "You believe in Shakespeare, Chaucer, Charles Read, that sort of thing?" "They will live"' (Part 2, Ch. 1). This echoes Greene's deadpan insistence on the importance of writers of adventure stories in his own development rather than the sacred figures of modernist fiction. Even his central tenet of fictional techni-que, point-of-view, is parodied: Savory's latest novel, *Going Abroad*, is to be set in the East, but '"the great novelist . . . will view these distant lands through the eyes of a little London tobacconist."' (Part 3, Ch. 1). (Savory even has a trendy interest in film!) The fun of all this is not lessened by the paradox that Greene's own popular novel is rendered more serious by an evidently self-conscious awareness of the nature of the form within which he is working. Mabel Warren's ruthless avoidance of feeling in her pursuit of a story makes her an 'artist to examine critically, to watch, to listen; the tears were for paper.' Nearly fifty years later, in *The Other Man*, Greene says that the 'novelist's station is on the ambiguous borderline between the just and the unjust . . . and . . . he has to be unscrupulous.'[17] But there are differences here. Mabel pries journalistically into forms of suffering Greene evidently finds unendurable: 'a suicide, a murdered woman, a raped child' (Part 2, Ch. 1). This frontier is a dangerous one, but the nature of Greene's observations, and the use to which they are put, place him on the other side of it from Mabel. Similarly, popular novelists are of different kinds. Q.C. Savory and Graham Greene inhabit different worlds, although the ability of the one to toy with the other is a recognition of the hazards involved in even serious popularity. It is this recognition of danger built into the novel that makes *Stamboul Train* radically unlike Savory's *The Great Gay Round*.

Greene disagrees, rightly, with critics who find him a

'one-book man'[18] and there is no sense in which *Stamboul Train* is merely a blueprint for later work; it has too much lively individuality for that. On the other hand, it is interesting to note how many of Greene's later preoccupations are present here. Continuing the reflexiveness point, the book contains an amusing discussion on religion, politics and psychoanalysis between Mr Opie, Dr Czinner and Q.C. Savory—Greene will frequently return to this kind of fictionalised debate—in which the mockery directed at Opie and Savory arises out of an objectification of interests close to Greene's heart. Mr Opie is compiling a spiritual work which he aims to make of value to, say, cricketers on a sticky wicket because the 'Roman books are, what shall I say? too exclusively religious.' Dr Czinner's attempt to raise the question of confession starts Opie off on a harangue on its similarities with the analyst and his patient: 'The patient leaves the psycho-analyst with the power, as well as the intention of making a fresh start.' Although there is an element of fashionable chit-chat in Opie's reference to the 'Freudian censor' his comment on dreams as a form of confession touches a Greenian nerve. Whatever reservations he came to have about psychoanalysis after his own experience of it, Greene's interest in dreams remained a permanent acquisition despite the doubts he casts on Freudian interpretations through making fun of Opie. Evidence of this interest in *Stamboul Train* is clear from the revelatory dreams given to Coral and Myatt. Despite Opie's belief that they 'really have here the elements of a most interesting discussion' this comic exchange is terminated by Czinner's 'anger and disappointment' at its evident frivolity (Part 3, Ch. 3).

Dr Czinner, in fact, is the focus for a whole range of ideas and sympathies which will recur throughout Greene's career. If a note of peevishness creeps into Greene's comments on the critical response to *Brighton Rock* as a Catholic novel, this is understandable in terms of *Stamboul Train's* lightly touched-in religious concerns. The communist Czinner's position as a lapsed Catholic whose mind turns to memories of confession in the dark night of political disappointment seems obvious enough, at least with hindsight. His 'ashamed greed' for a 'belief which it had been his pride to subdue' (Part 3, Ch. 3) is linked to an absolutely central Greenian obsession, the search for peace, a peace only achieved by Czinner when he believes he faces imminent execution before the abortive escape engineered by Grünlich. From the novel's beginning, Czinner is seen as 'something weary and hunted' (Part 1, ch. 1); that is, seen with a sympathy Greene has always spared for his fictional enemies whether religious or political. The whisky priest's fanatical opponent in *The Power and the Glory* and the traitor-hero of *The Human Factor* are both, with Czinner, examples from different points in Greene's career of his central tenet that the novelist, whatever his own beliefs, is committed to a kind of fairness, love even, whose purpose is to enlarge, rather than diminish, the reader's sympathies. Greene is at pains to show, in fact, that Czinner's political beliefs are rooted in compassion and not ideology. Czinner first achieved a measure of international fame as the chief prosecution witness at the trial of a corrupt soldier-politician, General Kamnetz, for the rape of a child, a striking anticipation of the evils depicted in Visconti's film of the Nazi rise to power, *The Damned*. Czinner himself has risen from the suffering poor, becoming a doctor through his own, and his parents' sacrifice, only to realise that medical aid alone is insufficient to remedy the misery of an unjust society: 'He could do nothing for his own people; he could not recommend rest to the worn-out or prescribe insulin to the diabetic, because they had not the money to pay for either' (Part 3, Ch. 3). He is driven by 'great love and . . . great hate' rather than by mechanically abstract beliefs, emotions which take their origin from some of the more obvious contrasts of Greene's, and indeed our own, world:

> The world was chaotic; when the poor were starved and the rich were not happier for it; when the thief might be punished or rewarded with titles; when wheat was burned in Canada and coffee in Brazil, and the poor in his own country had no money for bread and froze to death in unheated rooms; the world was out of joint and he had done his best to set it right, but that was over. (Part 4, Ch. 3)

Despite Greene's insistence on the primacy of point-of-view, it is not hard to feel the weight of his own endorsement behind the passage. These are, after all, the commonplaces of political outrage in the 1930s and are, or should be, the commonplaces of our own time. Gloucester's echoing of Lear reminds us that the commonplace is not necessarily the cliché: 'So distribution should undo excess,/ And each man have enough.'

The inability to feel the right of each man to have enough is rooted in an absence of fellow-feeling and Greene's train journey provides a perfect metaphor for the paradox of human separation in close proximity to others. At this point, the entertainment's personal concerns mesh with the political, the most extended example being Myatt's relationship with Coral. Coral is common in every sense of the word and the familiarity of cheap attractivess enables Myatt to lay aside the burden of his Jewishness for an affair rooted in accessibility. Uncertainty enters his feeling for her when she becomes ill of a heart condition exacerbated by poverty, a situation that sets the stage for yet another of Greene's major concerns: 'helpless and sick . . . her body shaken by the speed of the train, she woke a painful pity' (Part 1, Ch. 2). Myatt puts self-interest aside when Coral disappears from the train because of a momentary, unwitting association with Dr Czinner and he makes a serious attempt to rescue her, only to recoil when he feels threatened by the mindless hatred of a Jew-baiting soldier. Becoming attracted to the beautiful, comfortably off Janet Pardoe, Myatt retreats into the safety of a known world, a defeat embodied in an interesting use of Greene's favourite stylistic device, the simile:

> He thought of Coral for a moment as a small alley, enticing a man's footsteps, but blind at the end with a windowless wall; there were others, and he though for a moment of Janet Pardoe, who were like streets lined with shops full of glitter and warmth, streets which led somewhere. (Part 4, Ch. 3)

The precision of his thoughts at this point does, in fact, rouse him to his last effort on Coral's behalf, but its failure is foreshadowed by his response to the two women. Significantly, his discovery of a racial link with Janet overcomes his earlier uncertainty in the face of her ease of manner: 'The knowledge that her mother had been a Jewess made him feel suddenly at home with her' (Part 5).

Sadness entwines the novel's political and personal worlds. Dr Czinner dies in secret agony, robbed of the speech at a public trial which might at least have been reported; his last, faint hope is to influence the simple soldier assigned to guard him. Myatt glimpses through Coral the possibility of a life open to change and development rather than the beaten track of 'settling down' with Janet. This theme's importance is clear from its appearance on the book's final pages. As Mr Stein, Janet's uncle, approaches him Myatt has 'a moment's grace' to summon to his 'assistance any thoughts likely to combat the smooth and settled future': 'He remembered Coral and the sudden strangeness of their meeting, when he had thought that all was as familiar as cigarette smoke, but her face eluded him, perhaps because the train at that moment had been almost in darkness' (Part 5). The poignancy of lost opportunity is an index of the seriousness of this brilliant entertainment. Greene wrote better than he knew or, at least, thought at the time, for what film, of the kind he was apparently aiming for, could have accommodated the moral and political pessimism of *Stamboul Train*?

SECTION C: *THE CONFIDENTIAL AGENT*

On the other hand, the toughest of Hollywood moguls would have been delighted with the conclusion, if no more, of *The Confidential Agent* (1939):

> A voice he knew said, 'That'll be Plymouth.'
> He didn't turn: he didn't know what to say. His heart had missed a beat like a young man's; he was afraid. He said, 'Mr Forbes . . .'
> 'Oh, Furt,' she said, 'Furt turned me down.' . . .
> He said, 'I'm an old man.'
> 'If I don't care,' she said, 'what does it matter what you are? Oh, I know you're faithful—but I've told you I shan't go on loving a dead man.' He took a quick look at her; her hair was lank with spray. She looked older than he had ever seen her yet—plain. (Part 4, Ch. 2)

Every detail reinforces the deadening familiarity of this 'happy ending': the heroine's invisible return, announced only by her voice, and the hero's reply without turning to her, belong to the conventions of the superior middlebrow film or novel. Not for them the luscious sunset, surging chords, two figures racing towards each other across a beach or struggling through an indifferent crowd. This is what Louis B. Mayer would have called art, fading not on a kiss, but 'You'll be dead very soon: you needn't tell me that, but *now* . . .'. Such comments may be harsh, but it is difficult not to feel an almost conscious abandonment of vision at this point, a disappointment that may explain an apparent lapse on the part of one of Greene's most perceptive critics, Miriam Allott: 'All of Greene's novels end sadly and violently'.[19] No novel should be judged by its ending alone, of course, but to say, with another critic, that *The Confidential Agent* 'would have been a good novel with the omission of the last page'[20] is a little too relaxed. The conditions of a book's composition are also irrelevant to aesthetic judgement, but it's hard not to see a link between weaknesses in the *The Confidential Agent* and the almost nightmare pressures that forced it into existence in only six weeks. 1938 saw Greene struggling with *The Power and the Glory* on his return from Mexico and worried for the future of his family by the evident onset of war. Fortified, if that's the word, by a daily dose of benzedrine, he produced 2000 words every morning (instead of his usual 500) of what he hoped would be a lucrative entertainment while continuing with *The Power and the Glory* in the afternoons. Not surprisingly, this amazing feat took its toll of his health and private life;[21] that it failed to produce a novel on the level of *Stamboul Train* or *The Ministry of Fear* is equally unsurprising.

But there remains much to enjoy and admire in *The Confidential Agent*. Greene was now well embarked as a professional writer—this was his ninth published novel—and a firm mastery of his craft is evident throughout. The level of writing, for example, is consistently high, from such detail as a dead bird on its back, 'with the claws rigid as grape stalks' (Part 2, Ch. 1) to the assurance of the novel's opening. Greene's skill as a craftsman is nowhere more evident than in his introductory pages; this is by no means one of the most unexpected or powerful, but it may stand as evidence of the high general level of his achievement:

The gulls swept over Dover. They sailed out like flakes of the fog, and tacked back towards the hidden town, while the siren mourned with them: other ships replied, a whole wake lifted up their voices—for whose death? The ship moved at half speed through the bitter autumn evening. It reminded D. of a hearse, rolling slowly and discreetly towards the 'garden of peace', the driver careful not to shake the coffin, as if the body minded a jolt or two. Hysterical women shrieked among the shrouds.

A vivid sense of foreboding is conveyed through this cunning deployment of key words: fog, hidden, mourned, wake, death, hearse, coffin, hysterical, and the punning shrouds. Rhythmically, the brief opening and closing statements (the latter reinforced by its alliteration of 'shrieked' and 'shrouds') contrast well with the complex sentences in between, the subtle movement of the second being particularly well handled. Our protagonist is neatly introduced by way of Greene's favourite stylistic device, the simile, with 'worry like a habit on his forehead.' And this gentle foreigner, a middle-aged scholar turned confidential agent by force of circumstances, finds himself in the maelstrom of one of Greene's most disliked groups, a gang of hearties; in this case, a 'rugger team' which 'scrummed boisterously for their glasses . . . "Offside." "Scrum," they all screamed together.' D. escapes from this uproar on to the deck, only to find it 'like a map marked with trenches, impossible positions, salients, deaths: bombing planes took flight from between his eyes, and in his brain the mountains shook with shell-bursts.' In short, he is in the process of entering a landscape which prefigures the moral, spiritual and economic devastation characteristic of the whole novel.

Verbal motifs convey the sense of D. falling into a trap, a powerful introduction to the novel's major theme, a theme developed with great interest and coherence. It is announced at the very beginning, in D.'s being 'haunted for a moment by the vision of an endless distrust' and echoes throughout the novel in inventively disturbing ways. In fact, its central paradox is, to use D.'s own words, that 'Nobody trusts a confidential agent' (Part 2, Ch. 3). Although D.'s left-wing materialism is conveyed with great sympathy, the government he represents (a fictional version of that of Republican Spain) is vitiated by a lack of trust at every level. Only the Second Secretary of its embassy is thought to be incorruptible and he is absent at a moment of desperate need for D. D. himself is suspect, and finds himself accountable to the murderously lesbian manageress of his hotel and K., the appallingly seedy language teacher whose job introduces the novel's major element of comic relief, the grotesque Entrenationo Language Centre. Greene is in fine Orwellian form here, savaging a motley crew of do-gooders including Dr Bellows, the inventor of this parody of what is itself a parody, Esperanto. Even here, 'in the centre of internationalism', where K. is fined a shilling if he is caught speaking English, 'there wasn't much trust': 'Once D. thought he heard Dr Bellows pass down the passage on rubber-soled shoes.' Rose, too, who belongs sufficiently to the world of humdrum reality to feel the threat of D.'s story of being shot at ('Don't you see that if things like that happened life would be quite different?') is enmeshed in falsity: 'You ought to know how it is—there's no trust anywhere' (Part 1, Ch. 2).

As so often in Greene, this miasma of treachery is counterpointed by that longed-for peace which forms the never-relinquished contrast to evil throughout his entire career. Given his view of the world, it is forced to take paradoxical forms. When D. contemplates the horrors of modern urban life, he reflects of London that it 'was technically known as a city at peace' (Part 2, Ch. 2), in contrast to his own devastated country. Again, when he is locked in a cell, after his final arrest, D. feels that he 'had not experienced such peace for a long time' (Part 3, Ch. 2). But, appropriately for a novel published in 1939, no real peace is to be found in either its present or its suggested future, unless we accept the apparently doomed brevity of his relationship with Rose. This explains a curious passage when D., on his journey to the Midlands, sees 'the porter, the general waiting-room, the ugly iron foot-bridge, the signalman holding his cup of tea, go backwards like peace' (Part 3, Ch. 1). Backwards because peace can only be found in the past, in D.'s life as a lecturer in Romance languages and his passion for the wife killed in error by his political opponents. As always in Greene, dreams are important: D. 'dreamed of lecture-rooms, his wife, sometimes of food and wine, very often of flowers' (Part 1, Ch. 1). Given the nature of the world created in *The Confidential Agent*, such delicate blooms are fated to wither. They certainly do nothing to weaken D.'s sense that there 'was no end to the circles in this hell.' This hellishness is memorably created, not just in the distrust which forms the book's major theme, but in the detail of a diseased civilisation, a 1930s waste land, which overwhelms D. in the face of the pathetic skivvy, Else:

> Fourteen was a dreadfully early age at which to know so much and be so powerless. If this was civilisation—the crowded prosperous streets, the women trooping in for coffee at Buzzard's, the lady-in-waiting at King Edward's court, and the sinking, drowning child—he preferred barbarity, the bombed streets and the food queues: a child there had nothing worse to look forward to than death. Well, it was for *her* kind that he was fighting: to prevent the return of such a civilization to his own country. (Part 1, Ch. 2)

We can add to this the sickening poverty of the miner's home which 'royalty' is prevented from entering ('It's as bare as a bone at Terry's. . . . It wouldn't have been nice for him' Part 3, Ch. 1) and the gimcrack holiday camp, a fictional idea Greene claims to have had 'long before Mr Butlin,'[22] presided over with ghastly bonhommie by Captain Currie. Like many, if not most, of Greene's protagonists, D. is fated to live out his life in a contemporary world that has become a vision of hell.

But if the novel's theme has coherence, so too does the book as a whole, at least as far as its relationship between theme and major character is concerned. That character and action are interchangeable, aspects of a central core of meaning, applies to the fit between D. and the novel's thematic preoccupations. At a superficial level, he belongs completely to his ravaged world, for wherever 'D. was, there was a war' (Part 1, Ch. 1) and, in an important strand of imagery, he carried his 'infection' with him everywhere, the most crushing example being Else's murder, the 'reward' for her fidelity to him. This is all the more painful because D.'s earlier life and character were clearly built on trust: the search for truth in his scholarly work and his passionate faithfulness to his wife, even after her death. Like Plato's perfectly just man, D. is drawn into deceit for the best of reasons. In an early discussion of matters of scholarship with his enemy, the aristocratic L., D. feels as if he is 'being tempted by a devil of admirable character and discrimination.' (Part 1, Ch. 1); in the process, an alternative to his own view of the world is created with real power:

> D. felt a little envious of him as he stood there in the yard among the cars—he looked established. Five hundred years of inbreeding had produced him, set him against an exact background, made him at home, and at the same time haunted—by the vices of ancestors and the tastes of the past. . . . But he recognised the man's charm: it was like being picked out at a party by a great man to be talked to.

L. is a ruthless connoisseur, a dilettante in the line of James's Gilbert Osmond, who gives the game away when he says lightly, '"These horrible things are bound to happen in war—to the things one loves. My collection and your wife"' (Part 1, Ch. 1). His inability to make even elementary moral discriminations is what leads D. to an avowal behind which it is easy to feel the weight of Greene's approval: 'You've got to choose some line of action and live by it. Otherwise nothing matters at all. You probably end with a gas-oven. I've chosen certain people who've had the lean portion for some centuries now' (Part 1, Ch. 2). In the fine understatement of the last sentence Greene surely embodies his own undeviating but unsentimental commitment to the underdog.

This fusion of theme and character lends the book an air of somewhat unexpected moral gravity, occasionally even the tone of a writer, George Eliot, distant from Greene in most respects. Else's ambition to escape the drudgery of her hotel work by becoming a prostitute's maid forces an agonised denial from D.: 'It was as if he had been given a glimpse of the guilt which clings to all of us without our knowing it. None of us knows how much innocence we have betrayed. He would be responsible.' And the contrast between D.'s present visit to London and memories of a happy past, a few pages later, creates a powerful sense of faithlessness: 'He felt like a young man who had given all his trust and found himself mocked, cuckolded, betrayed. Or who has himself in a minute of lust spoilt a whole life together' (Part 1, Ch. 2).

At a crucial point in the novel, D.'s attempt to shoot K.,
the narrative records his 'fear of other people's pain, their lives,
their individual despairs. He was damned like the creative
writer to sympathy' (Part 2, Ch. 2). Such a generalised link
between the novelist and his creation undoubtedly plays its
part in the deepening of D.'s character, stemming as it does
from the complexity of Greene's response to a real historical
situation. The Spanish Civil War, the novel's unspoken
background, presented him with a peculiarly painful dilemma. The anti-Catholic aspect of the Loyalist movement was
utterly repugnant to him, of course, but his left-wing
tendencies made Franco equally unacceptable. Greene found a
solution—'my sympathies were more engaged by the Catholic
struggle against Franco than with the competing sectarians in
Madrid'[23]—which satisfied both the religious and the political
sides of his nature. Greene's Mexican and Spanish experiences
provided emotional ballast to what he claims was his purely
intellectual conversion to Catholicism, but *The Confidential
Agent* is clear evidence that he thought, as well as felt, his way
through the personal significance of the Spanish Civil War. D.
is a full-scale extension of the creative response to character
embodied in Dr Czinner. Once again the 'enemy' is seen from
within with sympathy, with love, even, in D.'s case. An
element of caricature tinges the fanaticism of the priest-
hunting lieutenant in *The Power and the Glory*, but D. is
humanised through his doubts and uncertainties. ('After all,
there were aspects of economic materialism which, if he
searched his heart, he did not accept' (Part 1, Ch. 1). There is
nothing abstract in his love for the poor *en masse*, as we see
when his compassion is instantly aroused by a suffering
individual, Else. He is also allowed the dignity of belief,
although of a kind quite different from his creator's: 'If you
believed in God. . . . You could leave punishment, then, to
God. . . . But he hadn't that particular faith. Unless people
received their deserts, the world to him was chaos, he was
faced with despair' (Part 2, Ch. 1). His very lack of 'that
particular faith' implies a faith of his own which gives a secular
meaning to his life and so coherence to his character. Like
Arthur Rowe and Maurice Bendrix, D. has returned from the
'dead' in being buried in the rubble of an air-raid for hours, a

recurrent image of horror in the novel. But although he is born again into a hell of treachery and distrust, Greene never makes him totally despair of action.

With all this to enjoy, how should one find fault with *The Confidential Agent*? Not in a carping spirit certainly, but mainly because its weaknesses help to high-light the achievement of the later *The Ministry of Fear*. Not for the only time in Greene's career, the heroine is a weak link in the creative chain. Greene readily admits to this fault (no writer is more aware of his own limitations), perhaps the major barrier to his unquestioned status as an outstanding writer. The Rose of *The Confidential Agent*—the name will recur importantly in *Brighton Rock*—is a shadowy figure, without physical presence (she is, apparently, beautiful) and lacking in psychological or moral complexity. She herself explains her love for the much older D. as involved with rejection of her brutally domineering, capitalist father, thus drawing attention to the thinness of such popular Freudianism. At the opposite end of the social scale, although they share a working-class origin, is Else (why not Elsie, one wonders) a waif who seems to have come more from a possible reading of Dickens's *The Old Curiosity Shop*, in the shape of the Marchioness, than from the streets of contemporary London. Without the comic vitality of Dickens's imagination, however, Greene's skivvy becomes a figure of rather contrived pathos, plucky and faithful, but lacking the substantiality to render these qualities fully believable.

More serious is the book's structural weakness, a split between its novelistic and entertainment elements. The satisfying fusion of theme and character I have analysed makes *The Confidential Agent* highly successful as a novel; where Greene falters is in the embodying action needed to carry theme and character forward within its chosen genre. The setting up of the attempted shooting of D., for example, is highly unconvincing. It is frankly incredible that D., or anyone else, would allow himself to be drawn off into a side-street to spare the shame of even the most pseudo-genteel beggar. Anyone would feel threatened by such a palpably unnecessary move; all the more should the D. who is still, in the title of the novel's first part, 'The Hunted'. Even worse, because more central, is the last-moment removal of D.'s crucial identity papers by Lord Benditch's new butler, presumably as he is being helped off with his overcoat. The narrative serves only to heighten, rather than disguise, the scene's absurdity: 'D. put his hand to his breast pocket. They were gone. It was incredible' (Part 1, Ch. 3). That 'incredible' is fatal to even the hope of any suspension of disbelief, an embarrassedly murmured assent being the only possible response. Finally, the apparent reappearance of the murdered skivvy in the Midlands mining village lacks all of the plausibility, and thus shock, that such Greenian suprises can convey if handled properly:

> Then he tried No. 19, and the door came open at once before he expected it. He was off his guard. He looked up and there was Else. She said, 'Well, who do you want?' standing there like a ghost in the stone doorway, harried and undernourished and too young. He was shaken; he had to look closely before he saw the differences. (Part 3, Ch. 1)

It would be a mistake to suggest that these uncertainties represent a struggle, conscious or not, against the supposed limitations of the entertainment. The fact that his masterpiece in the genre, *The Ministry of Fear*, is yet to come should be enough to disprove that. Rather, they serve to illuminate the point that this form makes its own special demands on imagination and inventiveness. It is hardly surprising that Greene should have faltered a little with only one major success in the genre behind him; the idea that it would have been better at this stage for him to run to the safety of the novel proper is only open to those who are fundamentally out of sympathy with the popular side of Greene's talent. That his creative involvement with the entertainment was important to the author himself is revealed by some interesting remarks on his intentions in writing *The Confidential Agent*:

> The opening scene between two rival agents on the cross-channel steamer—I called them D and L because I did not wish to localise their conflict—was all I had in mind, and a certain vague ambition to create something legendary out of a contemporary thriller. . . . But what the legend was to be about in modern terms I had no idea.[24]

The transformation of reality into myth has been accomplished by varied art forms in the nineteenth and twentieth centuries. One line of development is represented by Dickens, Dostoevski, Kafka, Joyce and T.S. Eliot, writers whose urban experience is transformed into universal statements on the human condition. At the popular level, two kinds of film—the western and the thriller—have shared this capacity to turn reality into myths of good and evil. At this point, we can note a fusion of the high art and popular elements in Greene's artistic personality. The legendary ambition of *The Confidential Agent* subsides, rather lamely, into the Berne manuscript business with its identification of D., for Rose at any rate, as an Oliver rather than a Roland. Although this fits neatly into D.'s life as a lecturer in Romance languages, the device is faintly self-conscious in its use of the past to contrast with the present, in the manner of Eliot's *The Waste Land*. The thriller which is both legendary and contemporary is, surely, *The Ministry of Fear* where the ministry itself is transfigured by the intensity of Greene's vision from an institution concerned with espionage to a mythic recreation of aspects of twentieth-century life. The split between novel and entertainment is healed in the later work in such a way as to blend perfectly the excitement of the thriller with the insight of the novels; neither, in fact, is separable from the other.

SECTION D: *THE MINISTRY OF FEAR*

Some of Greene's less successful entertainments may represent a conscious changing down of gears from the novels proper, although this is largely true of works which belong, in any case, to the earlier part of his career. *The Ministry of Fear* (1943), however, fires on all cylinders with an intensity that makes a first reading shockingly powerful, while later consideration reveals a marvel of craftsmanship, a Chinese puzzle of extraordinary ingenuity which finally locks together to disclose meaning rather than mere cleverness—although this is the book which should finally convince the doubter of Greene's brilliance as a maker of fictions. *The Ministry of Fear* is inseparably a part of the seamless web of Greene's best work in the sense that it clearly engages with his deepest concerns in a way that is not true of his lesser entertainments. For example, it contains numerous echoes of Greene's life: he has never been afraid to make artistic use of his own experience. Indeed, that a writer's personal obsessions are his essential raw material is crucial to Greene's credo as a novelist. He remarks of Henry James that 'a sense of evil religious in its intensity' was the 'ruling fantasy that drove him to write'[25]; Greene's imaginative access to his own fantasies and obsessions—above all, in their source in childhood and youth—is central to much of his most powerful writing.

It is evident that a triangular relationship exists between Arthur Rowe's love for Anna when he still believes, through loss of memory, that he is Richard Digby, his memories of a youthful love, and Greene's experience, recorded with painful lucidity in *A Sort of Life*, of love for a family governess 'ten years or more older than myself.'[26] Because of his loss of memory, Rowe's 'experience was as new to him as adolescent love: like a boy he was drawn relentlessly towards inevitable suffering, loss and despair, and called it happiness' (Book 2, Ch. 6). And in one of the many poignant moments of nostalgia that pervade the novel, Arthur's present life as Digby is fused, through memory, with Greene's own experience: 'It was as if he were waiting again years ago . . . and the girl he loved was coming down the street, and the night was full of pain and beauty and despair because one knew one was too young for anything to come of this' (Book 2, Ch. 6). This link between personal life and art undoubtedly gives Greene's style an intensity that is sometimes lacking in his other work. But *The Ministry of Fear* fits into the body of Greene's best writing in ways more interesting than direct references to his own life. Perhaps the clearest sign of this is the novel's use of what I see as the master image, a door, and the key word, peace, of his entire output.

My first chapter has traced the sources of this image and word in Greene's inner life; the aim here is to show how they contribute to the power of this specific book. The image appears as childhood terrors are evoked in Rowe by the extinguishing of the lights at Mrs Bellairs's séance: 'In nightmares one knows the cupboard door will open: one knows that what will emerge is horrible: one doesn't know what it is.' This dissolves into 'the ominous door' from which it is impossible to escape in dreams, a predicament that leads to one of Greene's favourite insights into man as a social animal. Like the terror-stricken little gangster at the beginning of *Brighton Rock*, Rowe fails to protest at the menancing forces around him because 'sometimes it is more difficult to make a scene than to die' (Book 1, Ch. 4,1). It is, of course, Mr Cost who seems to die, apparently stabbed by Rowe, in a scheme to end his inquisitiveness. When this misfires, through his evasion of arrest, an attempt to blow him up lands Rowe in Dr Forester's sanitorium, suffering from amnesia. In this setting, Greene's use of the door image reaches a climax as Rowe steals secretly into the forbidden sick bay in a scene whose precision of detail is a sure sign of the writer's imaginative involvement:

> The next door brought him into the passage by Dr Forester's study. As he quietly closed each door behind him he felt as though he were cutting off his own retreat. His ribs seemed to vibrate to the beat-beat of his heart. Ahead of him was the green baize door he had never seen opened, and beyond that door lay the sick bay. He was back in his own childhood, breaking out of dormitory, daring more that he really wanted to dare, proving himself . . . .
> The door pulled easily open. It was only the cover for another door, to deaden sound and leave the doctor in his study undisturbed. But that door, too, had been left unlocked. As he passed into the passage beyond, the green baize swung to behind him with a long sigh. (Book 2, Ch.2,1)

The 'green baize door' is that of Greene's own childhood through which the 'school began just beyond my father's study.' The novel's emotional resonance at this point clearly relates to Greene's sense, at the age of thirteen, that in entering the upper school at Berkhamsted he had 'left civilisation behind and entered a savage country of strange customs and inexplicable cruelties: a country in which I was a foreigner and a suspect, quite literally a hunted creature, known to have dubious associates.'[27] The parallels with Rowe could hardly be plainer. Arthur is leaving behind the, in fact, false Eden of the sanitorium for a 'savage country', the eventual scene of the horrible killing of the innocent Stone, in which maturity will return with memory, bringing with it the knowledge to Richard Digby that he is Arthur Rowe, convicted of the mercy killing of his wife. Greene's memories of boyhood pain merge with the objectively created plight of the fictional character to evoke a dream-like horror in the apparently unending series of opening and closing doors, finishing with that accurate but also emotionally telling sigh, a seeming protest at Rowe's inevitable crossing of the threshold of self-knowledge and mature suffering.

Many ironies are apparent on a second reading of the novel; the opening, for example, of Book Two, 'The Happy Man':

> The sun came into the room like pale green underwater light. That was because the tree outside was just budding. The light washed over the white clean walls of the room, over the bed with its primrose yellow cover, over the big arm-chair and the couch, and the bookcase which was full of advanced reading. There were some early daffodils in a vase which had been bought in Sweden, and the only sounds were a fountain dripping somewhere in the cool out-of-doors and the gentle voice of the earnest young man with rimless glasses.

Although the word itself is not used, we are obviously in the presence of that 'peace' which is a key word in Greene's fictional vocabulary. Enjoying this delightful calm is a Richard Digby whom we only gradually discover to be Arthur Rowe, a man who believes that he has, through the mercy killing of his wife, destroyed his possibilities for peace for ever, just as Macbeth, through his crime, murders sleep. Despite being written between *The Power and the Glory* and *The Heart of the Matter*, the Catholic, indeed religious, aspects of *The Ministry of Fear* are extremely muted. A few images and similes make use of religious references and there is a hint that Rowe had been a Catholic—'his Church had taught him the value of penance' (Book 4, Ch.1,1)—but none of this is central. However, on the book's first page, Arthur's desperate desire for peace is rendered in a biblical quotation as he enters, once again, a false Eden, the fête which 'called him like innocence. . . . It all seemed perfect in the late summer Sunday afternoon. "My peace I give unto you. Not as the world knoweth peace"' (Book 1, Ch. 1,1). The religious echo adds an intensity to the pain, and ingenuity, with which the novel expresses Rowe's hopeless longing for a peace which he believes is forever unattainable because of his own actions. As Digby he has no memory of his wife's murder, but this peace is gradually weakened with the return of his consciousness and finally, irrevocably destroyed by a last, definitive act. The contrast between peace and the paranoic world of guilt and distrust which surrounds Rowe is embodied in an extended passage as he and the Special Branch man, Prentice, rush to the sanitorium as the novel nears its climax:

> A screech owl cried over the dark flat fields; their dimmed headlights just touched the near hedge and penetrated no farther into the wide region of night: it was like the coloured fringe along the unexplored spaces of a map. Over there among the unknown tribes a woman was giving birth, rats were nosing among sacks of meal, an old man was dying, two people were seeing each other for the first time by the light of a lamp; everything in that darkness was of such deep importance that their errand could not equal it—this violent superficial chase, this cardboard adventure hurtling at seventy miles an hour along the edge of the profound natural common experiences of men. Rowe felt a longing to get back into that world: into the world of homes and children and quiet love and the ordinary unspecified fears and anxieties the neighbour shared; he carried the thought of Anna like a concealed letter promising just that: the longing was like the first stirring of maturity when the rare experience suddenly ceases to be desirable. (Book 3, Ch. 2,2)

The imagery of exploration here is part of a wider pattern, as we shall see later; for the moment, however, we can register the intensity of his desire for the ordinary rendered so skilfully through Rowe's consciousness and see how the generalised Greenian concern with peace is brought into focus in this specific novel.

The book's setting performs this function and it's worth noting that *The Ministry of Fear* and *The End of the Affair*, two of Greene's best works, share the setting of the London Blitz of the second world war. The passage just quoted, with the earlier scenes in Forester's sanitorium, form an effective contrast with the hellish world of bombs and blackout which makes the London of the period a vision of nightmare. The realities of the time are brought vividly alive in Angus Calder's history, *The People's War*, and it's from within this context that he singles out *The Ministry of Fear* for particular praise: 'set in the Blitz, [it] is perhaps the most underrated of his metaphysical thrillers.'[28] Greene is himself a source for the social history of wartime London in the journal he kept as an air-raid warden, parts of which are reproduced in *Ways of Escape*. Direct experience helps Greene to make Rowe an organic part of the 'strange torn landscape where London shops were reduced to a stone ground-plan like those of Pompeii . . . he was part of this destruction as he was no longer part of the past' (Book 1, Ch. 3,1). The devastation of Rowe's personal life is mirrored in the wreckage of the city and his 'exile' from 'the old peaceful places' (Book 1, Ch. 3,2) gains in suffering from its association with those whose peace has been destroyed by war rather than by their own actions. Rowe acquires stature as a character through this identification with a tragedy wider than his own.

The sense of a context wider than the individual is enhanced by a thread of literary allusions woven throughout the novel. It may be entirely coincidental, but Greene's protagonist has an amazing likeness to another Arthur, the Arthur Clennam of Dickens's *Little Dorrit*. Rowe is first described as moving 'hesitantly like an intruder, or an exile who has returned home after many years and is unsure of his welcome.' (Book 1, Ch.1,1), a remarkable similarity to Clennam who comes back to London after a twenty-year exile in China in a very similar frame of mind. As Clennam's dreams are 'the uniform tendency' of his life because 'so much was wanting in it to think about, so much that might have been better directed and happier to speculate upon',[29] in Rowe too there 'remained the sense of innocence' because his 'dreams had never come true' (Book 1, Ch.1,1). Greene also uses imagery, common enough in itself, that is central to the structure of *Little Dorrit*. Arthur Rowe takes a perverse satisfaction in the destruction of London because this removes the associations of his past life 'like loosening the bars of a prison cell one by one' (Book 1, Ch.1,2). The image reaches a Clennam-like climax as Rowe wonders whether to trust Anna Hilfe and her brother (their surname means help in German, of course):

> Rowe watched them hesitatingly. But it is imposs'ble to go through life without trust: that is to be imprisoned in the worst cell of all, oneself. For more than a year now Rowe had been so imprisoned—there had been no change of cell, no exercise-yard, no unfamiliar warder to break the monotony of solitary confinement. A moment comes to a man when a prison-break must be made whatever the risk. Now cautiously he tried for freedom. (Book 1, Ch.3,2)

We know that Greene admires Dickens, but these similarities may be coincidental, although revealing for all that in the light they throw on Rowe's character. That Greene felt Conrad so strong an influence that he had to be rejected seems to remove the possibility of coincidence from an interesting series of parallels between *The Ministry of Fear* and *Heart of Darkness*. The guileless Johns and sinister Dr Forester are obviously not on the same level of complexity as Conrad's Harlequin and Kurtz, but the resemblances in the slavish, yet ultimately doubting, admiration of these underlings for their masters seem too strong to be accidental:

> Johns led the way. He filled with perfect tact a part which combined assistant, secretary and male nurse. He was not qualified, though the doctor occasionally let him loose on the simpler psyches. He had an enormous fund of hero-worship for the doctor, and Digby gathered that some incident in the doctor's past—it might have been the suicide of a patient, but Johns was studiously vague—enabled him to pose before himself as the champion of the great misunderstood. He said, 'The jealousies of medical people—you wouldn't believe it. The malice. The lies.' He would get quite pink on the subject of what he called the doctor's martyrdom. (Book 2, Ch. 1,1)

This echo leads into a pattern of language which bears directly on the novel's themes and which also relates to Rowe and Prentice's wild journey through the night. Lying in the wreckage of his bombed lodgings, Rowe feels as 'though he were in a strange country without any maps to help him' (Book 1, Ch. 1,3). The hint of Rowe as a Marlow bound on a voyage of exploration is developed in many interesting ways. In the attempt to regain his memory, Digby-Rowe recalls that he 'was very fond of books on African exploration . . . but there doesn't seem much opportunity for explorers nowadays' (Book 2, Ch. 1,1). This glimpse of childhood reading is part of Digby-Rowe's nostalgic entanglement with a peaceful past, but the image has just as much relevance to his present situation. On returning from his voyage to the forbidden sick bay, he 'felt as though he had explored a strange country and returned home to find it all a dream' (Book 2, Ch. 2, 2). During the partial recovery of his memory, Rowe tells Prentice at Scotland Yard that ' It's as if one had been sent on a journey with the wrong map' (Book 3, Ch. 1,2). The reference to Greene's book of West African exploration, *Journey Without Maps*, is obvious. And, in the novel's penultimate paragraph, Anna and Rowe sit 'on the edge of their ordeal, like two explorers who see at last from the summit of the range the enormous dangerous plain' (Book 4, Ch.1, 4). Arthur is caught up in journeying in several different ways. As Rowe, he travels constantly into a nostalgic past in an attempt to escape the guilt of murder. As Digby, he explores his fragmentary memories in the hope of becoming the ironic 'Whole Man' of the novel's last book. The paranoid complexities of the Ministry of Fear itself lead Arthur on a voyage of increasing confusion and duplicity. Finally, he and Anna face a life-long pilgrimage of distrust because of his failure to confess that, just before his suicide, her brother had revealed to him the last piece in the jigsaw of his memory, the murder of his wife.

The stages by which Rowe loses, then regains, self-knowledge are accomplished through a plot of dazzling ingenuity, filled with sinisterly comic surprises. Despite Greene's low estimate of the director's achievement, the Hitchcockian element in such moments forms the most striking analogy, rather than any purely literary comparison. When Rowe is on the run, desperate for money, he visits an old friend, estranged because of Arthur's crime, in the hope of cashing a cheque, only to make the hilariously delayed discovery that the friend's wife has just been killed by the Blitz and that the funeral is about to take place. The situation is clarified by his friend's mother:

We are proud of Doris. The whole post is doing her honour. We are going to lay her uniform—her clean uniform—on the coffin, and the clergyman is going to read about "Greater love hath no man"' . . . 'She was playing for England, Henry.' . . . She turned to Rowe and said, 'I think we ought to lay a hockey-stick beside the uniform, but Henry won't have it.' (Book 1, Ch. 6,3)

Echoes are detectable here of the 'funny and fantastic thriller'[30] Greene originally intended to write in emulation of Hammond Innes. A more darkly amusing moment occurs when the murderous Hilfe is rendered helpless by an old lady's making use of his hands to wind her wool. At their most serious level, however, the complexities of Greene's plot exist to embody that urban paranoia which I discussed in Section A. Another interesting link between the private and public emerges at this point. On his release from prison Rowe enters a 'secret world of assumed names, of knowing nobody, of avoiding faces, of men who leave a bar unobtrusively when other people enter' (Book 1, Ch. 3, 2). Because of his helplessly doom-laden entry to the fête—that it's his fate to do so is clear—Arthur's private paranoia turns rapidly into a world of 'they' and 'them' in which he is helpless to control his own future. The hotel in which one of his most disquieting moments occurs is a perfect paradigm of this terrifying universe, mechanical in its impersonality:

This was a modern building; the silence was admirable and disquieting. Instead of bells ringing, lights went off and on. One got the impression that all the time people were signalling news of great importance that couldn't wait. This silence—now that they were out of earshot of the whistle and the sigh—was like that of a stranded liner; the engines had stopped, and in the sinister silence you listened for the faint depressing sound of lapping water. (Book 1, Ch. 7,2)

We can see now how *The Ministry of Fear* differs from the thriller genre I examined in this chapter's first section. In the thriller, as defined by Palmer, a clear distinction is made between a circumscribed, criminal irritant which troubles the body politic only until it is removed by the hero. Greene's vision is infinitely more far-reaching; when, for example,

Rowe and Prentice leave London on their desperate journey to
Forester's sanitorium: 'Looking back, one could see only an
illuminated sky—bright lanes and blobs of light like city
squares, as though the inhabited world were up above and
down below only the dark unlighted heavens' (Book 3, Ch.
2,2). This image of a universe upside-down reinforces the
moral confusion in supposedly normal reality. In discussing
the British and German treatment of prisoners-of-war, Hilfe
asks Rowe, 'Do you think you are so different from us?' (Book
4, Ch. 3,1), a question that seems justified by several of the
novel's incidents. When the traitorous Mrs Bellairs protests,
'They don't hang women. Not in this war.' she receives the
reply, '"We may hang more people, ma'am," Mr Prentice said,
"than the papers tell you about"' (Book 3, Ch. 2,1). Again,
Prentice tells Rowe and the reluctant Mr Davis, who is roped
in to trap Cost, some war secrets only because 'well, we could
have you put quietly away for the duration if there was any
leakage' (Book 3, Ch. 1,3). The gullible Johns reveals a
possible source for this widespread infection of society:

> 'The Germans are wonderfully thorough. . . . They did that in
> their own country. Card-indexed all the so-called leaders,
> Socialites, diplomats, politicians, labour leaders, priests—and
> then presented the ultimatum. Everything forgiven and forgot-
> ten, or the Public Prosecutor. It wouldn't suprise me if they'd
> done the same thing over here. They formed, you know, a kind of
> Ministry of Fear—with the most efficient under-secretaries. It
> isn't only that they get a hold on certain people. It's the general
> atmosphere they spread, so that you can't depend on a soul.'
> (Book 2, Ch. 1,4)

It is this 'general atmosphere' of doubt and lies that the novel
generates so triumphantly, in the process creating a sense of
international paranoia quite beyond the limitations of the
conventional thriller.

That *The Ministry of Fear* is an entertainment-novel becomes
clear when we realise that its plot complications, paranoid
atmosphere and absurdist elements serve character and
meaning, supremely so in the trap that shuts tight on Rowe in
the book's final sentences. Greene himself sees the novel as
dealing with a theme he enlarged on in *The Heart of the Matter*,

'the disastrous effect on human beings of pity as distinct from compassion.'[31] And it is true that Arthur is the victim of a 'sense of pity which is more promiscuous than lust' (Book 1, Ch. 2,1). The most seedily unpromising subjects instantly become the recipients of this emotion in him. But the issue is complicated in various ways. It is pity for the horribly mistreated Stone that leads Arthur into action, prompted by the feeling that 'you couldn't let things stay as they were, with the innocent struggling in fear for breath and dying pointlessly' (Book 3, Ch. 3,3). (Stone's death clearly resembles a Nazi medical experiment or the gassing of Jews.) *The Ministry of Fear* is, however a fallen world, in which pity is powerless to avert the destruction of the blameless and in which the results of human action on the world of affairs is left in doubt. The last stage in the process of Arthur becoming 'a whole man' is his memory of the clergyman, Sinclair, at the sanitorium: 'Sinclair probably had a copy . . .' (Book 4, Ch.1,3); that is, of the precious microfilm on which the novel's whole plot has turned. The final stages of Arthur's recovery of memory are inflicted on him by Hilfe, a devil in one of his traditional guises as a gentleman—handsome, witty, debonair, and utterly careless of human life and feeling. As he hears, and so remembers, that he killed his wife, Rowe has his moment of revelation, before Hilfe's suicide, in the hellishly subterranean lavatory at Paddington Station: 'Pity is cruel. Pity destroys. Love isn't safe when pity's prowling around.' When, therefore, 'Hilfe's strained white face begged for his pity, Rowe turns from him to telephone the police about Sinclair' (Book 4, Ch.1,3).

The novel's brief final section draws its thematic and verbal concerns together with great revelatory power. Arthur had hoped that 'wherever Anna was there would be peace; coming up the stairs a second time he knew that there would never be peace again while they lived.' His decision not to tell Anna of her brother's filling the final gap in his memory means that, for her, he will remain in 'Digby's' innocent unawareness for the rest of their life together; it also means his enlistment in the Ministry of Fear:

To walk from Paddington to Battersea gives time for thought.

He knew what he had to do long before he began to climb the stairs. A phrase of John's came back to mind about a Ministry of Fear. He felt now that he had joined its permanent staff. But it wasn't the small Ministry to which Johns had referred, with limited aims like winning a war or changing a constitution. It was a Ministry as large as life to which all who loved belonged. If one loved one feared. That was something Digby had forgotten, full of hope among the flowers and *Tatlers*.

At this point the Ministry of Fear reaches its maximum degree of inclusiveness as a metaphor for the human condition, at least for those who, unlike Hilfe, love: love is the indispensable pass to this all-encompassing bureaucracy. Character, in its aspect of motivation, presents a problem here: why does Arthur decide to spare Anna the pain of his final self-knowledge? A close reading suggests that his 'enormous love . . . tenderness, the need to protect her at any cost' is prompted by compassion—a willed suffering with—rather than the instinctive outburst of a sentimental pity. And so, although 'like two explorers' about to enter a land in which they must guard forever their mutual knowledge from each other, it occurs to Rowe that by suffering in his love for Anna he may atone for the killing of his wife, Alice. The final fruit of this exercise of compassion is the merest hint of a highly qualified positive ending to *The Ministry of Fear*: 'It seemed to him that after all one could exaggerate the value of happiness . . .' (Book 4, Ch. 1,4).

NOTES

1. SL, p.151.
2. *Collected Essays* (Penguin, 1970), p.105.
3. Michael Draper, 'Christopher Caudwell's Illusions' in *The 1930s: A Challenge to Orthodoxy* ed. John Lucas (Sussex: The Harvester Press, 1978), p.91.
4. *Modern English Literature* (Oxford University Press, 1970), p.140. Jerry Palmer, *Thrillers: Genesis and Structure of a Popular Genre*
5. W.W. Robson, (London: Edward Arnold, 1978).
6. *Ibid.*, Pp.85–6.
7. Jack C. Ellis, *A History of Film* (New Jersey: Prentice-Hall, 1979), p.255.

8. Robson, *op. cit.*, p.140.
9. Palmer, *op. cit.*, pp.87 and 205.
10. P.J. Widdowson, 'The Saloon Bar Society: Patrick Hamilton's Fiction in the 1930s' in Lucas, *op. cit.*, p.120.
11. WE, p.59.
12. *Ibid.*, p.22.
13. SL, p.151.
14. OM, p.102.
15. SL, p.102.
16. *Ibid.*, pp.154–5.
17. OM, p.82.
18. *Ibid.*, p.22.
19. With Kenneth Allott, *The Art of Graham Greene* (New York: Russell and Russell, 1963), p.70.
20. Harvey Curtis Webster, 'The World of Graham Greene' in *Graham Greene: Some Critical Considerations* ed. Robert O. Evans (University of Kentucky Press, 1963), p.12.
21. WE, pp.68–9.
22. *Ibid.*, p.71.
23. *Ibid.*, p.59.
24. *Ibid.*, p.68.
25. *Collected Essays*, p.21.
26. SL, p.90.
27. *Ibid.*, pp.46 and 54.
28. Angus Calder, *The People's War: Britain 1939–45* (London: Jonathan Cape, 1969), p.514.
29. Charles Dickens, *Little Dorritt* Part the First, Ch. 3.
30. WE, p.74.
31. *Ibid.*, p.93.

CHAPTER THREE

Brighton Rock

This book's discussion of Greene's novels under such headings as politics, belief, and so on, is essentially a matter of practical convenience. It's a common enough critical strategy, although one that violates the unique individuality of any good work of art. In an ideal study of fiction, each novel would receive its own special attention alongside a more general discussion of groups of works in relation to themes and the writer's chronological development. The mere thought of such a critical enterprise reinforces one's gratitude that ours is not an ideal world. It would make intolerable demands on the reader's patience as well as insulting his intelligence in its assumption that he is quite unable to fill in critical gaps for himself. Commonsense has to prevail and with it the realisation that many literary careers *do* divide into periods of early, middle and late; into light and dark novels; moves from simplicity to complexity, and the reverse. Tact and discretion may make such distinctions acceptable, and even illuminating; the following attempt to make them with Greene does at least try to keep as closely as possible to a foundation of fact in chronological development. (The last category, 'The Later Greene', is if nothing else a recognition of the potential arbitrariness of such listings.) At the very least, it may help to justify *Brighton Rock's* possession of a chapter to itself.

Possible patterns in Greene's fiction:

1929 *The Man Within*
1930 *The Name of Action*   Romances.
1931 *Rumour at Nightfall*

1932	*Stamboul Train*	
1934	*It's a Battlefield*	Entertainments and early
1935	*England Made Me*	political novels.
1936	*A Gun for Sale*	
1938	*Brighton Rock*	
1939	*The Confidential Agent*	
1940	*The Power and the Glory*	Entertainments and
1943	*The Ministry of Fear*	Catholic novels.
1948	*The Heart of the Matter*	
1951	*The End of the Affair*	
1955	*The Quiet American*	
1958	*Our Man in Havana*	Politics
1966	*The Comedians*	
1961	*A Burnt-Out Case*	
1955	*Loser Takes All*	
1969	*Travels With My Aunt*	
1973	*The Honorary Consul*	
1978	*The Human Factor*	The Later Greene.
1980	*Dr Fischer of Geneva*	
1982	*Monsignor Quixote*	

Even without the trick of separating it by double spacing, *Brighton Rock* appears to occupy a special place in Greene's earlier career. The first three novels were clearly a dead end. Robert Graves, Mary Renault and others, have done something to rehabilitate the historical novel in the twentieth century, but one can only applaud Greene's insight and determination in forcing himself to write in a new manner after 1931. *Stamboul Train* is a complete success in its own terms, although it took Greene more than ten years to create his masterpiece in the genre, *The Ministry of Fear*. The three novels after *Stamboul Train* achieve their own measure of success, but it is hard to see any of them as the nourishing soil which would permit the kind of growth of which Greene was

obviously capable. Some ingredient was required to deepen
and intensify his vision, a discovery made in the very process of
writing *Brighton Rock*.

At a guess, such a view might be intensely irritating to the
author himself. What is undeniable is the haze of tetchiness
which surrounds his view of the book's reception. The source
of this bad temper is that, on its publication, he 'was
discovered to be—detestable term!—a Catholic writer', a view
that led to his well-known description of himself as a novelist
who happens to be a Catholic, rather than a Catholic novelist.
At the same time, Greene clearly has a particular fondness for
the book ('perhaps it is one of the best I ever wrote') and it
seems to have been created out of a special degree of
imaginative intensity: 'I have never again felt so much the
victim of my inventions.' Again, *Brighton Rock* opened a vein
of creative enquiry of great importance for the next stage of his
career. Greene had intended the novel to be 'a simple detective
story' (it began life as an entertainment), but although he
complains that it concerns a discussion of 'good-and-evil and
right-and-wrong' which is 'too obvious and open for a novel,'
he goes on to add that its meditation on 'the appalling
strangeness of the mercy of God' (Book 7, Ch. 11) is 'a mystery
that was to be the subject of three more of my novels.'[1]

It's not merely out of deference to its author, then, that one
hesitates to ascribe the novel's success to its open proclamation
of Catholicism. That would be to fall into the trap of ideology
and subject-matter, a danger neatly illustrated in an attempt
to evaluate the work of Henry Green within the context of
socialist novels of the 1930s:

> Let there be no misunderstanding. *Living* has a number of
> qualities not always to be found in Socialist novels: brevity of
> style, vernacular dialogue, power of observation. But what we are
> concerned with is whether it presents a truthful picture of factory
> life. . . . The answer is no [because it omits] the essential quality
> of factory life, the solidarity of workers in the action which they
> take.[2]

This is tantamount to saying that a good novel is not a good
novel because it lacks an extra-literary criterion imported into

the discussion of Green's book for purely ideological reasons. We might parody the passage in the words of a third-rate Catholic journal by saying that *Brighton Rock* has 'a number of qualities not always to be found in good novels: verbosity of style, artificial dialogue, confused observation. But since it presents a truthful picture of the Catholic faith it is a good novel after all.' If *Brighton Rock is* a fine book and an important work in Greene's development, even for a non-believer, this must be because it has strengths that belong specifically to the literary realm. Where better to look for this than in the quality of its writing? On the ground of strictly aesthetic criteria, *Brighton Rock* operates, in certain passages, on a level quite beyond Greene's earlier fiction.

For example, at the end of a discussion between the worried Spicer and Pinkie, in the latter's room, over the possibility of Rose having recognised the false Kolley Kibber, Spicer is dismissed with 'Turn out the light and get' and the chapter ends:

> The light went out and the moon went on like a lamp outside, slanting across the roofs, laying the shadow of clouds across the downs, illuminating the white empty stands of the racecourse above Whitehawk Bottom like the monoliths of Stonehenge, shining across the tide which drove up from Boulogne and washed against the piles of the Palace Pier. It lit up the washstand, the open door where the jerry stood, the brass balls at the bed end. (Book 1, Ch. 2)

We're already familiar with such vivid detail as the moon lighting 'the brass balls at the bed end' and Greene's use of the simile. The central example here ('the white empty stands of the racecourse . . . like the monoliths of Stonehenge') lacks the strain of forced comparison which is one of his besetting dangers, but it also has a special force which lifts this brief passage on to a plane new in Greene's writing. The moon, the sea and Stonehenge suddenly invest the sordid human reality with a sense of vastness, a shaft of eternity enters the novel with the unearthly beauty of the moonlight; for a moment the context is timeless, an effect achieved with total unpretentiousness and an absence of religious paraphernalia. An even more extraordinary scene—too long for quotation—occurs at the very end of Chapter Two of Book Six. After his wedding-night consummation Pinkie dreams of Kite, of death by drowning and, finally, of his parents' Saturday night sexual routine. He wakes in panic and, 'taken by a craving for air,' goes for a walk at the moment when 'the darkness . . . seemed to thin out across the vast expanse of a city.' We follow Pinkie's wanderings in prose of complete lucidity until their horrific climax:

> The lights were on in Montpellier Road. Nobody was about, and an empty milk bottle stood outside a gramophone shop; far down were the illuminated clock tower and the public lavatories. The air was fresh like country air. He could have imagined he had escaped. . . . In an alley between two shops, an old woman sat upon the ground; he could just see the rotting and discoloured face: it was like the sight of damnation. Then he heard the whisper, 'Blessed art thou among women,' saw the grey fingers fumbling at the beads. This was not one of the damned: he watched with horrified fascination: this was one of the saved.

The passage is both deeply mysterious and totally convincing. A hint as to its meaning is conveyed in Pinkie's feeling of freedom in air like that of the country. Clearly, then, Pinkie's walk is at least partly an image of the hope of release, but its meaning is complicated by the paradox of the hideous ugliness of 'the saved' where we feel ourselves on that plane of being where saintliness is validated by kissing the sores of lepers. Such scenes represent Greene at his most purely novelistic in that external detail is put to the service of inwardness of vision. The filmic Greene is in abeyance, for the relative externality of that medium could hardly chart the detailed, and yet other worldly, stages of Pinkie's inner journey.

Writing of this quality signals the maturing of talent into inspiration. We can only speculate about what led to this development, but the intensification of experience involved in Greene's frightful exploration of his own personal heart of darkness through the African adventure may well have played a part, as well as 'clumsy life again at her stupid work' forcing him to rethink—re-feel might be better—his religious belief in the face of the 'socialist persecution of religion in Mexico, and . . . General Franco's attack on Republican Spain' which 'inextricably involved religion in contemporary life.'[3] Whatever its sources, this heightened apprehension of sublunary life opened the way to various possibilities in Greene's writing. From the angle of belief, a subject I shall tackle in my next chapter, the latent Catholicism of the earlier novels could now be brought into the foreground. Greene himself makes the point that 'by 1937 the time was ripe for me to use Catholic characters' because it 'takes longer to familiarise oneself with a region of the mind than with a country.'[4] But it is surely also true that style itself has to be refined in certain ways if such intractable issues are to be confronted head-on. The vivid realism and rapid action of earlier Greene could hardly have accommodated the confrontation of heaven and hell which hovers so insistently over *Brighton Rock*.

Writing with a heightened intensity also allowed Greene to solve an aesthetic problem which relates to his honourable concern for social and political issues. As a novelist of the 1930s, Greene clearly felt impelled to draw sympathetic portraits of working-class people, an area in which he was hardly at his best. I shall argue later that *It's a Battlefield* especially is weakened by its unconvincing portrayal of working-class speech and behaviour. *Brighton Rock* is, in fact, the last novel in which lower-class characters occupy the centre of the stage. (In *The Confidential Agent* and later novels they are peripheral and Greene increasingly improves in his ability to sketch them in believable detail.) Pinkie, Rose, and the rest, are impressed on our imagination not because of some suddenly new-found ability to reproduce the cadences of Brighton slang, but because they inhabit the kind of novel where questions of realism are frequently inapplicable.

The issue is complex—this is part of the point of the book having a chapter to itself—because *Brighton Rock* is a transitional work. It began life as an entertainment and retains many of the elements of the 'detective story' Greene originally intended it to be, particularly in the satisfying pursuit of Pinkie by Ida Arnold. At this level, it required, and Greene was fully up to providing, many brilliant examples of precisely described and rapidly moving action. The novel's opening is justly famous, an extraordinarily successful evocation of

Brighton at a Whitsun holiday seen from within the
consciousness of the pathetic Hale and thus suffused with a
menace that stems from his knowledge that 'before he had
been in Brighton three hours . . . they meant to murder him'.
(Book 1, Ch. 1). Again, Chapter Two of Book Three is a
consummate little example of lessons learned from Greene's
masters in technique, James and Conrad, in point-of-view and
the time shift. Chapter One is devoted to the beginning of
Ida's investigation of Hale's murder and ends with a
characteristic mixture of her view and that of the omniscient
narrator:[5] "This is where I start from' . . . . He waited for me
here, Phil,' and she stared out over the red and green lights,
the heavy traffic of her battlefield, laying her plans,
marshalling her cannon fodder, while five yards away Spicer
stood too waiting for an enemy to appear' (Book 3, Ch. 1).
Chapter Two then begins 'Spicer was restless these days' and
moves back into a description of his uneasy wandering
'watching out for trouble,' in the course of which he meets
Crab who was once 'run . . . out' by Kite's gang and is now a
member of Colleoni's. He returns briefly to headquarters and,
when the telephone rings, indulges in a splendidly characteristic piece of free indirect speech, 'why should I do all the work
in this bloody gaff?' He eventually returns to the Parade and
the chapter ends at the point where we first discovered him,
taking 'up his stand between the turnstile of the pier and the
ladies' lavatory.' One last example within this mode is the
cinematically vivid description, the opening of Book Four, of
race day with the crowds surging 'like some natural and
irrational migration of insects up and down the front.' Some
critical stress has been laid on Greene's hostility to the world of
ordinary pleasures inseparable from Brighton as a holiday
resort, but the dehumanising simile of people as insects should
be set against the sympathy for mundane lives contained
within the narrative itself: 'The odds on Black Boy had
shortened, nothing could ever make life quite the same after
that rash bet of a fiver on Merry Monarch.' The extremes of
social contrast are revealed without any obstrusive commentary
by the juxtaposition of a relic of the first world war, 'a blind
band', with the hockey-playing schoolgirls of Roedean. And
the coincidences of melodrama are adroitly manipulated so

the words of Ida Arnold's song, sung on the knee of a man packed into 'a tiny rakish car', blew back 'along the dusty road to meet an ancient Morris' containing Pinkie on his murderous errand with Spicer.

These are riches indeed and the reader may experience a twinge of disappointment in the contrast between this splendid vitality and the sometimes flat inappropriateness of the language assigned to Pinkie and Rose. The problem is partly one of dialogue, but also of the handling of point-of-view as an entry to the characters' consciousness. Rose, for example, comes from the most degraded depths of the *lumpenproletariat*, a background conveyed with unforgettable horror in Pinkie's visit to her Nelson Place home. Despite this, Greene makes almost no attempt to reproduce the presumed inadequacies of her speech. He evades the difficulty partly by skilled craftsmanship. In a key exchange with Ida, for example, Rose does hardly any of the talking, although her brief responses are invested with great power. At a crucial point, also, Greene relies on narrative point-of-view:

> Precautions . . . Rose stood at the bed-end and pressed a hand against her body, as if under that pressure she could discover. . . . *That* had never entered her mind; and the thought of what she might have let herself in for came like a sense of glory. A child . . . and that child would have a child . . . it was like raising an army of friends for Pinkie. If They damned him and her, They'd had to deal with them, too. There was no end to what the two of them had done last night upon the bed; it was an eternal act. (Book 7, Ch. 1)

Greene is clearly having it both ways here, although in a perfectly acceptable way: the instincts belong to Rose, the language to the omiscient narrator. Pinkie presents more of a critical problem, perhaps, although we seem meant to assume that he has been educated to a higher level than Rose. Greene occasionally falls into downright infelicities with him, as in a passage where the newly married couple are wondering desperately where to spend the night: 'The crude quick ceremony was a claim on him. *She* didn't know the reason; she thought—God save the mark—he wanted her' (Book 6, Ch. 2). 'God save the mark' is utterly at odds with Pinkie's style,

in its curiously old-fashioned phrasing. And the unevenness of
Pinkie's dialogue is clear in such a fragment as "'You're
sensitive, that's what it is . . . like me." He said abruptly, "I
suppose you wouldn't recognise that newspaper man again? I
mean, he may still be about"' (Book 1, Ch. 2). But, again, the
fragmentariness may be deliberate, as though the craftsman in
Greene is unwilling to risk dangerously extended speeches for
Pinkie.

   Within the realistic world of, say, *It's a Battlefield* all this
might seem a serious limitation, but to assume this in *Brighton
Rock* is to confuse modes in an unhelpful way. Admittedly, the
novel may not be totally unified—Greene himself feels he
should have 'had the strength of mind to remove' its first fifty
pages and 'start the story again,'[6]—but the heightening of the
book's metaphysical aspect dissolves the problem I have been
discussing in an almost completely satisfactory manner. One
indispensable factor in this success is intensity, a point at
which we move to a level above craftsmanship, as in the 'dark
theology' between Pinkie and Rose in the wine cellar of Snow's
Restaurant:

> The lights came through a little barred window straight on to her
> white determined face: she was like a child who crosses her
> fingers and swears her private oath. She said gently, 'I don't care
> what you've done' as she might have denied interest in a broken
> window pane or a smutty word chalked on someone else's door.
> He was speechless; and some knowledge of the astuteness of her
> simplicity, the long experience of her sixteen years, the possible
> depths of her fidelity touched him like cheap music, as the light
> shifted from cheek-bone to cheek-bone and across the wall, as the
> gears ground outside. . . . The shadow of her sixteen-year-old
> face shifted in the moonlight on the wall. 'Right and wrong.
> That's what she talks about. I've heard her at the table. Right and
> wrong. As if she knew. . . . Oh, she won't burn. She couldn't
> burn if she tried . . . Molly Carthew burnt. She was lovely. She
> killed herself. Despair. That's mortal sin. It's unforgivable.
> Unless—what is it you said about the stirrup?'
> He told her unwillingly, 'The stirrup and the ground. That
> doesn't work.'
> 'What you did . . . did you confess it?'
> He said evasively, a dark stubborn figure resting his bandaged
> hand on the Australian hock, 'I haven't been to Mass for years.'

'I don't care . . . I'd rather burn with you than be like Her.'
(Book 4, Ch. 1)

The gears grinding outside and Pinkie's hand resting on the
bottle are enough to place the scene in a real world, but
transfiguration of reality is its key-note, the scorching away of
externals so that we feel ourselves in the presence of a naked
confrontation of souls. And, whatever its specific value to the
Catholic, the unbeliever is surely held fast by the human agony
of this exchange. At such moments, Greene is an Ancient
Mariner whose 'glittering eye' fixes us immovably to the spot:
we 'cannot choose but hear.'

This is the realm of a novel such as Hawthorne's *the Scarlet
Letter* where a certain attenuation of external richness is
unavoidable, desirable even, in order to heighten the spiritual
atmosphere. Intensity of such force moves character and action
on to a level where questions of realism become irrelevant, an
effect achieved in other ways also. Greene is a highly literary
writer—his work abounds in quotations and references from a
wide variety of sources—and *Brighton Rock* is particularly rich
in this area. Stylistic echoes of Henry James, references to
Hamlet and Marlowe's *Dr Faustus*, and memories of Greene's
earlier novels are commonplace, but a pattern of particular
interest centres on *Macbeth*, although this has been denied by
some critics. For Robert O. Evans, for example, 'the overtones
from *Macbeth* . . . are accidental.'[7] The objection seems hard
to sustain in the face of an extended instance (there are minor
ones throughout):

'If we don't do something quick it looks to me as if all Brighton'll
know we killed Fred. All England. The whole God-damned
world.' The boy went over to the basement window crunching on
the coke: a tiny asphalt yard with an old dustbin which hadn't
been used for weeks: a blocked grating, and a sour smell. He
said, 'It's no good stopping now. We got to go on. . . . Maybe
it's always that way—you start and then you go on going on.'
(Book 7, Ch. 2)

Blood may be a necessary ingredient in Greene's vision of the
world, but its presence in *Brighton Rock* surely reminds us of
Macbeth's

                              I am in blood
          Stepp'd in so far that, should I wade no more,
          Returning were as tedious as go o'er. (Act III, Sc.
          iv,136–8)

If the point is accepted it adds immeasurably, for the
non-believer at least, to the novel's range by giving it a
dimension of secular morality. *Macbeth* is surely the
profoundest study in English literature of the incremental
nature of evil, applicable as much to domestic life as it is to the
blood-soaked world of the play. Telling lies and committing
murder have in common a spiralling effect that draws their
perpetrators into what may appear an escalation from which
escape is impossible. Like Macbeth in his 'borrowed robes',
there is an element of black comedy in Pinkie's despairing
question, 'Christ! he thought, had he got to massacre the
world?' (Book 6, Ch. 2) which gives his dilemma an edge
painful even to those unsympathetic to the endlessly debated
theological niceties of his situation.

The next chapter of this book will directly confront the
problems of belief in relation to fiction. The purpose here has
been to reveal *Brighton Rock* as a watershed in Greene's earlier
career, a moment at which a combination of personal and
social circumstances deepened and intensified his vision and
with it the techniques through which vision is expressed,
above all language. As did Dickens in *The Pickwick Papers*,
Greene discovered a direction in the very act of creation, and
traces of first intentions are strongly evident in the novel. The
writer himself regrets this; it's hard to see why the reader
should do so. They add colour and vitality to the book, while
Ida's hunt for Hale's killers, a staple of detective fiction,
acquires the dimension of a more serious quest in an unforced
fashion. The confrontation of good and evil by right and
wrong may be a little badly stated, but it remains a topic of
perennial interest, one that Greene embodies with memorable
power in the antagonism between Ida and Pinkie/Rose. (Put
like that, the colour symbolism seems obvious. Although at
opposite poles of evil and good, Pinkie and Rose relate not as
black opposed to white, but with a link that symbolises the

intensity of their commitment to a chosen end.) My argument, then, is an attempt to reveal the power with which apparently identical actions are invested with, or stripped of, a dimension beyond the material, an experience to which readers of any belief, or none, should be capable of responding. An obvious example is Greene's treatment of sex, perhaps something of a bugbear to the 'healthy minded' general reader who may be surprised to learn that he 'would never regard the body as revolting.'[8] There seems plenty of evidence to the contrary in *Brighton Rock*, but a combination of vision and craftsmanship complicates the issue in a satisfying manner. Within the terms established for her character, the aftermath of Ida's fling with the amusingly evasive Phil Corkery is entirely convincing. Her earlier 'Bacchic and . . . bawdy mood' subsides:

> Fun . . . human nature . . . does no one any harm. . . . Regular as clockwork the old excuses came back into the alert, sad and dissatisfied brain—nothing ever matched the deep excitement of the regular desire. Men always failed you when it came to the act. She might just as well have been to the pictures. (Book 5, Ch. 6)

But if one is appalled by this good time, Pinkie's response to sex is even more repellent. For him, desire is like a sickness, a view at least partly conditioned by his childhood sight of his parents' regular Saturday night primal act. (This serves as a reminder that Greene the social critic is far from absent in *Brighton Rock*. Pinkie is not simply a metaphysical creation; what he is is at least partly conditioned by environment.) Greene shows great tact when the consummation with Rose finally arrives, the very absence of physical detail being important to his overall purpose; but the moment is not the nightmare Pinkie, and we, have been led to expect:

> He had an odd sense of triumph: he had graduated in the last human shame—it wasn't so difficult after all. He had exposed himself and nobody had laughed. He didn't need Mr Prewit or Spicer, only—a faint feeling of tenderness woke for his partner in the act. He put out a hand and pinched the lobe of her ear. The bell clanged in the empty hall. An enormous weight seemed to have lifted. He could face anyone now. (Book 6, Ch. 2)

It would be laughable to suggest that this 'faint feeling of tenderness' represents a breakthrough for Pinkie, but it is conclusive proof that he is not the monster suggested by some critics. And even his negative response to the experience endows it with a dimension lacking for 'big blossoming' Ida and poor Phil. What this is becomes clear at that moment when Ida puts the idea of a child into Rose's mind: 'There was no end to what the two of them had done last night upon the bed; it was an eternal act' (Book 7, Ch. 1). Other writers, Hardy and Lawrence for example, may seek this sense of eternity in ways very different from Greene, but its absence from either life or art reduces existence to a series of disconnected points on a graph.

My purpose in all this is not to secularise *Brighton Rock*, to pretend that its religious aspect is trivial. Rather, I am governed by a sense that the general reader is uninterested in theological disputation, the dancing of angels on a pin-point. Readers with such preoccupations will find plenty to sink their teeth into in *Brighton Rock*, but for others its religious dimension is perhaps best seen as a way of investing character and action with that more than purely personal dimension that we look for in all good fiction. One final example may help to suggest how Pinkie's life can be understood, within its religious perspective, in ordinary human terms, in his being a character in conflict with himself in quite a traditional manner. He may be committed to evil, but this commitment is never totally one-sided. Greene the novelist who happens to be a Catholic is strongly in evidence here; if he were a Catholic novelist, Pinkie's internal struggle would exist only in terms of religious repentance, but it also contains an element of moral complexity. A subtle motif bearing on this is the repetition of Pinkie's response to music, the first example occurring on Brighton pier: 'The orchestra began to play: he felt the music as a movement in his belly: the violins wailed in his guts' (Book 1, Ch. 2). We are left to assume that this 'grief in the guts' (Book 2, Ch. 1) is a visceral echo of the role played by music in Pinkie's Catholic upbringing, but it also hints at the faintest stirrings of humanity if only at a pre-conscious level. Through the boy's response to music Greene suggests that religious and moral promptings are inextricably a part of the blood, bones, the guts, of what it means to be human.

This relates to what I take to be a fundamental aspect of the conflict between Ida and Pinkie/Rose, highlighted by her answer to Rose's conviction that 'people change': 'Oh, no they don't. Look at me. I've never changed. It's like those sticks of rock: bite it all the way down, you'll still read Brighton. That's human nature' (Book 7, Ch. 1). Belief is too strong a word for Pinkie's sense of the possibility of change, but it is present somewhere in the depths of his being like the faint echo of music, an echo embodied in the novel's use of a poem which is quoted in full by Richard Johnstone in his *The Will to Believe*:

> 'My friend judge not me,
> Thou seest I judge not thee:
> Betwixt the stirrup and the ground,
> Mercy I asked, mercy I found.'

The residual nature of the possiblity for Pinkie is clear in one exchange between him and Rose:

> 'I don't take any stock in religion. Hell—it's just there. You don't need to think of it—not before you die.'
> 'You might die sudden.'
> He closed his eyes under the bright empty arch, and a memory floated up imperfectly into speech. 'You know what they say—"Between the stirrup and the ground, he something sought and something found."'
> 'Mercy.'
> 'That's right: Mercy'.
> 'It would be awful, though . . . if they didn't give you time. . . . That's what I always pray. That I won't die sudden. What do you pray?'
> 'I don't,' he said, but he was praying even while he spoke to someone or something: that he wouldn't need to carry on any further with her, get mixed up again with that drab dynamited plot of ground they both called home. (Book 3, Ch. 3)

The 'empty arch' of the sky is a sufficiently powerful reinforcement of the tenuous nature of the possibility, although its reality for Pinkie is clear when he hides, interestingly for later Greene, in 'a kind of potting shed' after he has been slashed on the race-course: 'Now, of course, was the time, while darkness drained into the bottom, for him to make his peace. Between the stirrup and the ground there wasn't time: you couldn't break in a moment the habit of thought: habit held you closely while you died.' A few pages later, the sense of an almost infinitely distant music is present again as he walks towards the room of the Spicer he thought had been killed in the same attack: 'for the second time he felt a faint nostalgia, as if for something he had lost or forgotten or rejected' (Book 4, Ch. 1). The human, as opposed to the metaphysical, aspect of these moments is inescapably clear as Pinkie plans Rose's murder in the fake suicide pact. He has a 'sense that somewhere, like a beggar outside a shuttered house, tenderness stirred' and, a few lines later, 'again he felt the prowling presence of pity.' These particles of human feeling drift up out of subterranean depths; they are prevented from surfacing, however, because Pinkie is 'bound in a habit of hate' (Book 7, Ch. 7). What Greene will later call the human factor—this time in its social dimension—again cannot be avoided. Pinkie's habit is at least partly conditioned by Nelson Place, unloving parents, the 'home', by the social as well as the spiritual horrors of the modern world as Greene sees them in *Brighton Rock*—for him, of course, they are ultimately the same thing.

But although I have been arguing strongly for the interest of the novel's sublunary aspects, the final emphasis must fall on the intensity with which everyday life is transfigured at key moments by the power of Greene's vision and language. As Pinkie drives towards what he believes will be Rose's murder, Greene rises to a passage which echoes, but completely outstrips, Myatt's rejection of Coral Musker in *Stamboul Train*:

It was quite true—he hadn't hated her; he hadn't even hated the act. There had been a kind of pleasure, a kind of pride, a kind of—something else. The car lurched back on to the main road; he turned the bonnet to Brighton. An enormous emotion beat on him; it was like something trying to get in; the pressure of gigantic wings against the glass. Dona nobis pacem. He withstood it, with all the bitter force of the school bench, the cement playground, the St Pancras waiting-rom, Dallow's and Judy's secret lust, and the cold unhappy moment on the pier. If the glass broke, if the beast—whatever it was—got in, God knows what it would do. He had a sense of huge havoc—the confession, the penance and the sacrament—and awful distraction, and he drove blind into the rain. (Book 7, Ch. 9)

The twin strands of my argument come together at this point. What is that 'kind of—something else' if not love and tenderness, emotions almost completely obscured behind the habit of hate engendered by Pinkie's hideous childhood and youth? But the visionary force of the language clearly stems from Greene's religious intensity. Those 'gigantic wings' must be for him the Holy Ghost, pressing against the glass of the car window 'trying to get in.' Yet, even at this terrific moment, the visionary and the mundane cohere through the association of these wings with the motif of gulls flying that is frequently present in the novel, most memorably when the haunted Spicer passes 'into shadow under the pier, and a cheap photographer with a box camera snapped him as the shadow fell and pressed a paper into his hand':

> Spicer didn't notice. The iron pillars stretched down across the wet dimmed shingle holding up above his head the motor-track, the shooting booths and peep machines, mechanical models, 'the Robot Man will tell your fortune'. A seagull flew straight towards him between the pillars like a scared bird caught in a cathedral, then swerved out into the sunlight from the dark iron nave. (Book 3, Ch. 2)

For the secular reader, those beating wings outside the little car may symbolise a human straining after moral change rather than the apocalyptic upheaval obviously central to the writer himself. What is without dispute is the power with which this moment, and many others in *Brighton Rock*, is actualised in that language of heightened intensity which has been a major concern of my discussion of this remarkable book.

NOTES

1. WE, pp.58, 62, 60.
2. M. Gustav Klaus, 'Socialist Fiction in the 1930s: Some Preliminary Observations' in Lucas, *op. cit.*, p.31.
3. WE, p.59.
4. *Ibid.*, p.58.
5. This technique is well discussed by Dominick P. Consolo, 'Graham Greene: Style and Stylistics in Five Novels' in Evans, *op. cit.*, p.71.
6. WE, p.60.
7. 'The Satanist Fallacy of *Brighton Rock*' in Evans, *op. cit.*, p.152.
8. Francis L. Kunkel, *The Labyrinthine Ways of Graham Greene*, (New York: Sheed and Ward, 1959), p.147.
9. Richard Johnstone, *The Will to Believe: Novelists of the Nineteen-thirties* (Oxford University Press, 1982), p.76.

CHAPTER FOUR

Fiction and Belief

SECTION A: PROBLEMS OF FICTION AND BELIEF

Greene's detestation of the label 'Catholic novelist' is only fully
understandable in the light of his view of English Catholicism.
His objection is partly aesthetic, of course: the category is so
limiting as almost to preclude the artistry without which the
novel degenerates into a mere pastime. But one suspects that
his real terror is of finding himself consigned to that world of
oddities he sees as inseparable from the English Catholic
tradition. Mauriac and Bernanos fuse fiction and belief with an
ease that stems from their place in a society, which, despite
French anti-clericalism, takes Catholicism seriously. Greene
clearly fears joining the company of Eric Gill, his essay on
whom forms a definitive picture of the outer limits of the
English Catholic world. Even the more central figure of
Ronald Knox, in his day a famous Catholic chaplain at Oxford,
is caught up in the 'meanness, jealousies, and misunderstand-
ings of the hierarchy' which seem an unavoidable part of
English Catholic life from at least the time of Newman
onward. Greene prefers the 'apostles of the darker, poorer,
more violent world—the priests I have encountered, on the
borders of a battlefield in Vietnam, in the region of the Mau
Mau or in the dying white world of the Congo.'[1] The villain of
the piece in all this for Greene is the class structure of English
society, for English Catholicism 'which should produce
revolutionaries produces only eccentrics (eccentricity thrives
on an unequal social system).'[2] The roots of this view must be
sought in history. To be an Englishman and a Catholic was,
after all, at one time to be a traitor, and the extremity of such a
situation leaves scars which are not quick to heal. The process

71

of assimilation itself was slow and not hastened by the fact that Catholicism was associated in the public mind with two groups outside the mainstream of national life: a relatively small number of aristocratic families and a relatively large number of poor Irish. Such a limited range of background might well prompt a frame of mind content to rest in the gratitude of being allowed to practise its faith in peace, rather than converting its fellow countrymen. And this sense of being at the margins could do nothing but increase the eccentricity which Greene rightly sees as fostered by social inequality.

It is entirely appropriate, then, that Greene's conversion should have been effected in Nottingham, one of his earliest experiences of a seediness he was to make his own. Whatever it may have been for the young Lawrence, for Greene the town was a perfect image of provincial limitations with its solitary tart, fish and chips and general air of wracking poverty. A young man—Greene was twenty-two—from the glittering world of public school and Balliol College, Oxford, must have realised that he risked stepping out of the centre of English social life into a backwater clearly at odds with his internationalist temperament. No single explanation can do justice to the complexity of Greene's life-long restlessness and need for travel, but one strand may be the sense that in embracing Catholicism he ran the risk of embracing the rigours of provincial dullness. This need to escape was also compounded by the fusion of his political and religious views. In Richard Johnstone's words, Greene's 'Catholicism prevented subscription to the left-wing orthodoxy of the period, but his socialist instincts place him outside conventional Catholicism.'[3]

Biography can, therefore, help to explain the comic outrage of Greene's response to being called a Catholic novelist, but the problems involved in fiction and belief demand more general discussion. Greene's own belief is another example of the ways in which he is set apart from the earlier generation of his great contemporaries in the twentieth-century novel. An abhorrence of belief as a muddier of the pure waters of fiction has been one of the central tenets of the modernist novel from James through Conrad, Joyce and Virginia Woolf. Lawrence may seem a large exception until we recognise that his doctrines are so completely his own that they have an almost entirely fictional status within the works themselves. Marxism and Catholicism are systems of belief whose objective existence in the social world presents serious difficulties for their use in works of the imagination. Lawrence's ideas, on the other hand, are worked out in the fiction itself and, despite his discursive writings, have no real life outside the novels as a widely held, systematic belief.

Joyce provides a particularly clear example of the modernist suspicion of commitment to ideas. *A Portrait of the Artist as a Young Man* is complex enough to be open to a series of readings, in one of which we see Stephen being progressively stripped of the delusions of belief until he is ready to perform his function as an artist. Nationalism and politics, religion and the family, even his country, all have to be abandoned before Stephen is ready to 'forge in the smithy of my soul the uncreated conscience of my race.'[4] Ultimately he is left with nothing but his aesthetic theory, as expounded to his friend Cranly, and his vocation as an artist. At the simplest level, Joyce's distrust of belief rests on its bias, the exclusion of that impartiality which he sees as crucial to the artist. Total commitment to any one belief may preclude the understanding of those who lie outside the system and so lead to an art which is unable to encompass the full complexity of experience. Virginia Woolf goes even further in thinking that belief prevents us from seeing what is there in front of us, not just in people but in things themselves.

In *The Will to Believe*, Richard Johnstone argues that the 1930s saw a shift from this purist conception of fiction towards a novel for which belief was of prime importance. Greene was joined in his Catholicism by Waugh, while Rex Warner and Edward Upward atempted to give Marxism a central role in their creative vision. As a group, these writers occupy a lower place in critical esteem than James, Contrad, Joyce and Lawrence. Even George Orwell, a major figure in English letters, is hardly a great novelist. Can it be argued, however, that this relative inferiority relates to a willingness to explore, or an obsession with, the relation of fiction to belief? Literary history has familiarised us with the phenomenon of the dominance of a form by a group of outstanding writers followed, in its turn, by a period of consolidation in which the achievements of the pioneers are assimilated rather than challenged. Talent not genius may be the hallmark of the novelists of the 1930s, but this isn't necessarily explained by an ideological shift in their conception of fiction.

How, then, can the problem be made part of the discussable realm of literary criticism? On a naive view, the success of purely didactic literature is outside this realm altogether. For Greene and Brecht, to take opposing examples, conversion could be seen as an ultimate criterion of value. Brecht clearly regarded engagement as a measurable aspect of his success as a dramatist even when, as in the case of *Mother Courage*, a 'deeply ingrained habit induces the audience in the theatre to pick out the more emotional aspects of the characters and ignore the rest.'[5] And, despite his disclaimers, it is hard to believe that Greene would be displeased by a correspondent's affirmation that a reading of, say, *The End of the Affair* had turned him towards the Catholic church. Many, if not all, writers hope to persuade at some level, and a complete unwillingness to entertain Joyce's doctrine of disengagement in *A Portrait* would imply artistic failure or a disqualifying lack of sympathy in the reader. The ideal reading self of the competent reader is open to a range of experience which implies a readiness to consider, if only imaginatively, views other than his own. Wayne Booth brings a helpful subtlety to such problems:

> The author creates . . . an image of himself and another image of his reader; he makes his reader, as he makes his second self, and the most successful reading is one in which the created selves, author and reader, can find complete agreement.

But persuasive as the concept of 'created selves' is, how often do we find ourselves in 'complete agreement' with a work of literature? Presumably this is an ideal norm for Booth and so, almost by definition, unattainable. In any case, some element, however small, of the tension of disagreement may be as valuable an aspect of our relationship to fiction as a possibly soporific identity of views. But even if Booth's position is granted in full, a severe difficulty remains. Time and again, the authorial beliefs Booth suggests that we share are highly generalised, as in the case of *King Lear*: 'Shakespeare requires us to believe that it is right to honour our fathers, and that it is wrong to kill off old men like Lear or grind out the eyes of old men like Gloucester.' The trouble is, of course, that there is no difficulty at all in acceding to such beliefs. As Booth himself says, 'Only a maniac, presumably, would side with Goneril and Regan against Lear.' (What, one wonders, would Booth make of the fact that an attempt was made to do this very thing in Peter Brook's production of the play!) And it is interesting to note Booth's unease with an author whose beliefs are more specific than a generalised humanitarianism; 'But it is impossible for me to conclude that incompatibility of beliefs is irrelevant to my judgement of Lawrence.'[6]

The problem Greene sets us is clearly of another order of difficulty and centres on the systematic nature of the beliefs involved in his conversion to Roman Catholicism. Booth's criterion of 'complete agreement' is simply irrelevant at this point and for several reasons. The concept of the author's second self turns on a distinction between the real man who fallibly goes about the business of everyday life and the writer who transcends his limitations to create an ideal self in the act of writing. Some key examples of this phenomenon in the English novel are George Eliot and Henry James; that is, writers whose personal lives are marked by an absence of dogmatic belief and who, perhaps of necessity, formulate the moral criteria by which their fictional worlds are to be judged in the very act of creation itself. Even in the case of one of Booth's favourite examples from the past, Henry Fielding, we are more aware of a genial humanity than of the formal beliefs which, as an eighteenth-century man, he undoubtedly held. The case of the Catholic, and Marxist, writer is entirely different. (I link them, as central examples of a system of belief, for the reason suggested by Richard Johnstone: 'Communism and Catholicism were increasingly singled out in the thirties as the alternative cures for the sickness of a generation.'[7]) For the dogmatist, I use the word in its neutrally descriptive sense, the creation of an ideal second self in the act of writing would surely be a dangerous enterprise. However fallible in his personal life, his ideal self already exists within his system of belief. A human being is not going to be a better Catholic or Marxist by writing novels, but by living his beliefs. The committed writer therefore faces a peculiar difficulty: to embody his beliefs in a fiction which will be acceptable to the uncommitted reader and, at the same time, not to falsify what may be a highly detailed system of belief.

The problems for the reader are equally complex. It is frankly incredible to expect complete agreement between an uncommitted reader and a work of fiction to which a detailed system of belief is central. Booth's ideally open-minded and competent reader may legitimately be expected to give alien ideas a sympathetic hearing. If the work concerned is both subtle and powerful it may compel a degree of vicarious involvement in which an unfamiliar vision of the world is experienced in some, if not all, of its pain, joy and intellectual complexity. This is as much, surely, of a 'conversion' as the committed writer can hope for and even this victory will be won only by works of true artistry. The stress falls on artistry because beliefs must be subsumed in character, plot and language with peculiar subtlety if the novel, in this case, is not to seem propagandist. Hectoring narrative commentary or a merely allegorical arrangement of the book's elements are bound to appear weaknesses for a writer such as Greene who has, quite properly, courted popularity throughout his career. The sadness—he admirably avoids bitterness—of Greene's account of his ten years in the wilderness from the early success of *The Man Within* to *The Power and the Glory* emphasises the dilemma of the professional writer for whom some degree of popular acclaim is a welcome necessity. In these circumstances Greene's fictional exploration of his faith is an act of courage, a point one feels he would dismiss impatiently, however. Like any real writer, Greene's subjects chose him, a truth to which he constantly recurs in the autobiographical writing. Nonetheless, the success of his entertainments might have tempted a lesser man into the safety of work which avoided the risk of offending co-religionists and unbelievers alike.

These preliminary observations have attempted to set up a context for the discussion of the novels themselves, but no claim is made for their theoretical sophistication. In the end we seem stuck with the platitude that novels are novels; that the criteria for judging them are not radically dissimilar despite differences of genre. Different categories do exist, of course: realism, naturalism, symbolism are not mere counters in an intellectual game. But neither are they rigid divisions. Overlapping ensures that most novels belong only by tendency to one or the other. Nonetheless, these, as well as the more modern categories—science fiction, thrillers, the detective story—demand some change of emphasis in critical discussion. But if we sympathise with Greene's rage at being labelled a Catholic novelist, we must avoid the related trap of placing even some of his work in one of the dreariest corners of the bookshelf as Catholic novels. They belong in a legitimate and definable category, the novel of belief, which poses severe problems of understanding and judgement. But since they are novels, these problems can be resolved by the techniques and methods common to literary criticism.

SECTION B: *THE POWER AND THE GLORY*

Ten years after *The Man Within* Greene achieved his first complete success with a novel of high seriousness in *The Power and the Glory* (1940). Within its own terms, it's hard to see how the book could be improved in any major way. Some critics have objected to the handing on of the priestly line which involves the 'conversion' of the boy, Luis, at the very end of the book, but if this is a blemish it is a very minor one. It is possible that aspects of the novel's achievement may be explained negatively; the lack of any need for a central woman character enables Greene to sidestep what is for him a major difficulty. But in all essential respects the success is positive: the creation of the sights and smells of an alien landscape; the physical hardships of fever, blinding heat, hunger and thirst; two memorable central characters in the priest and the lieutenant; and the working out of opposing beliefs through behaviour, response and action: that is, without the somewhat obtrusively stated conflict in *Brighton Rock's* right-wrong, good-evil dichotomy. Greene himself claims that *The Power* is 'the only novel I have written to a thesis.'[8] One can only assume, if this is so, that the strength of his imaginative involvement dissolved his schematic intention into a novel which has all the resonance of lived experience rather than mechanical contrivance.

This depth of involvement may throw some light on the vexed question of Greene's use of exotic settings, undoubtedly a factor in his wide general popularity. Greene went to Mexico in 1937 for a specific purpose, to investigate government persecution of the Roman Catholic church; his travel book, *The Lawless Roads*, had been commissioned by a publisher, but he 'had no idea . . . that a novel . . . would emerge from my experiences.'[9] When the novel did come to be written—it arose initially out of Greene's memory of an actual whisky priest mentioned by one of the many people he met in Mexico—it clearly bore a relation to his inner life at the opposite pole from that of the writer who travels simply to acquire background material. The writer in search of copy observes an exotic setting from the outside; his detail, however vivid, remains finally decorative. One senses, on the other hand, that the ordeals endured by Greene on his Mexican, and African, trip were all-consuming at the time. And so he earns the reward of his lived experience, however painful, in that his emotions recollected in tranquillity bear the authority of an end rather than a means, something gone through in the service of life itself, not primarily as the raw material of art.

One final biographical detail is relevant in validating the imaginative depths from which *The Power and Glory* emerged, the truly appalling mental conditions in which it was written. I have described already the benzedrine-powered genesis of *The Confidential Agent* in the mornings of a six-week period during which *The Power* was 'ground on slowly with . . . in the afternoons,' proceeding 'towards its end at the same leaden pace.'[10] Making every allowance for the biographical fallacy, it remains true that only a work with an unshakeable hold on its imagination could have been created in such a nightmare context; that a book of the quality of *The Power and the Glory* emerged is little short of miraculous.

Where, then, to begin the analysis of this remarkable novel? The atmospheric trivialities of Greeneland, and the finely weighed pros and cons of the state of the priest's soul seem equally unappetising. And, with his usual critical intelligence, Greene suggests that characterisation itself would not make the most profitable of starting points. There is undoubtedly a critical dilemma here. Greene has given us a host of fascinating characters but one's gratitude, however justified, is no warrant for elevating them to the level of Anna Karenina, the Pip of Dickens's *Great Expectations*, the Raskolnikov of *Crime and Punishment*, figures who repay, demand even, pages of explication. Greene himself would be the last man to claim such complexity for his creations; the priest and the lieutenant will require discussion at some point, but it would be critically naive to over-complicate them, especially as Greene himself makes no claims for their development as characters:

> *The Power and the Glory* was more like a seventeenth-century play in which the actors symbolize a virtue or a vice, pride, pity, etc. The priest and the lieutenant remained themselves to the end; the priest, for all his recollection of periods in his life when he was different, never changed.[11]

Perhaps the single most memorable feature of *The Power*—taking a hint from my discussion of *Brighton Rock*—and its largest advance over Greene's earlier work, is the description of the priest's night in a crowded cell in Chapter Three of Part Two, a passage which might reasonably be claimed as the best extended piece of writing in his entire career. Quotation at length is clearly impossible, while selective quotation ruins the cumulative power of the whole episode, but a reminder of its quality is crucial to my argument. We enter this hell with a paragraph of total authority at the end of the preceding chapter: 'The sergeant unlocked a small grated door and let out with his boot at something straddled across the entrance. He said, "They are all good fellows, all good fellows here," kicking his way in. A heavy smell lay on the air and somebody in the absolute darkness wept.' The sense of physical palpability is only increased by Greene's uncanny ability to suggest the impenetrability of total blackness (something like Milton's 'darkness visible'): the stink of the bucket filled with piss; the utterly pervasive sound (unmistakeable to those who have experienced it) of mosquitoes 'like a small machine, an electric belt set at a certain tempo;' the 'finished cry of protest and abandonment and pleasure' of sexual contact; the agonising pressure of bodies cramped without possibility of movement. Out of this solid foundation of sensory detail arises a host of echoes and resonances. The cell is at once an image of 'the world: overcrowded with lust and crime and unhappy love, it stank to heaven;' a home for the Christ-like acceptance of the lowest depths of human degradation; and a circle in a Dantesque vision of hell. Richness of this order can only be grasped fully through engagement with the entire passage; a single quotation may, however, hint at the power of Greene's artistry:

> The old man seemed to be uneasily asleep; his head lay sideways against the priest's shoulder, and he muttered angrily. God knows, it had never been easy to move in this place, but the difficulty seemed to increase as the night wore on and limbs stiffened. He couldn't twitch his shoulder now without waking the old man to another night of suffering. Well, he thought, it was my kind who robbed him: it's only fair to be made a little uncomfortable. . . . He sat silent and rigid against the damp wall, with his dead feet under his haunches. The mosquitoes droned on; it was no good defending yourself by striking at the air: they pervaded the whole place like an element. Somebody as well as the old man had fallen asleep and was snoring, a curious note of satisfaction, as though he had eaten and drunk well at a good dinner and was now taking a snooze. . . . The priest tried to calculate the hour: how much time had passed since he had met the beggar in the plaza? It was probably not long after midnight: there would be hours more of this.

But, and by now we will hardly be surprised by the paradox, this is also a place of 'peace': 'Again he was touched by an extraordinary affection. He was just one criminal among a herd of criminals. . . . he had a sense of companionship which he had never experienced in the old days when pious people came kissing his black cotton glove.' One is reminded of the doctor, of a seediness to arouse Greene's envy, who delivers Dickens's Little Dorrit in a cell whose 'walls and ceiling were blackened with flies': '"We have got to the bottom, we can't fall, and what have we found, Peace. That's the word for it. Peace."'[12] The priest, too, can fall no further; he believes that his ceaseless wanderings will be ended by certain discovery (the 'ten years' hunt was over at last'), and at the very bottom of this heap of degraded humanity there exists the possibility of love: he is 'moved by an irrational affection for the inhabitants of this prison.'

It is entirely appropriate that just before dawn the priest dreams, and this characteristically Greenian recourse to the mysterious double life which parallels reality puts the final seal on what I want to call again, following *Brighton Rock*, the scene's visionary power, although in this, the later, work Greene achieves something like a Dostoevskian intensity. A memorable sentence from *The Lawless Roads* is relevant at this point: 'One felt one was drawing near to the centre of something—if it was only of darkness and abandonment.'[13] This relates to an interesting complaint that Greene makes in *The Other Man*, when looking back on his entire career; what he calls 'the general refusal to grasp the importance of fantasy in my books. . . . The intrusion of dreams and fantasy into my other books has been overlooked in the same way.'[14] Failure to discuss the dream element in Greene is certainly an extraordinary critical omission, as I tried to make clear in my opening chapter. Fantasy is perhaps a more debatable area and I would like to suggest an alternative to the author's choice of word. As in Coleridge's fancy-imagination distinction, fantasy has slightly dubious overtones of escapism and whimsy. Perhaps my use of visionary may help to correct the imbalance of an excessively realist view of Greene as the traveller who journeys only to depict the journalistic surface of the contemporary world. My point is simply that Greene has the imaginative insight to use reality in the service of his developing and changing conceptions of human life, life in the widest sense that encompasses religion at one end of the scale and politics at the other.

For all its realistic detail, which can be checked against *The Lawless Roads*, the Mexico of *The Power and the Glory* is essentially 'a state of mind', a moral battleground for issues more perennial in their interest than the persecution of the Roman Catholic church which first led Greene to the country. This imaginatively created world solves, once again, problems at the level of craftsmanship. We have already seen an

uneasiness in Greene's use of working-class dialogue; tone and
level are easier to handle for the poor of this country of the
mind. Dangers remain, of course: one thinks of the hideously
stilted dialogue thought appropriate for 'natives' by Hollywood (Red Indians, for example) or indeed the cadences
perpetrated in the great John Ford's unfortunately arty film
version of the novel. Greene's achievement, apparently artless,
is of a neutrally dignified tone throughout, a decorum which
forbids irrelevantly realistic questions about Spanish and
allows the novel's allegorical aspects to arise without strain.
The many point-by-point similarities between the novel and
The Lawless Roads might seem to weaken this point unless one
notices a particular emphasis in Greene's comments on the
book in *Ways of Escape*: 'Of invented characters how very few
seem to remain apart from the two protagonists, the priest and
the Lieutenant of Police.'[15] Few perhaps and yet how totally at
the heart of the novel these invented characters are. Imagination, then, is the generating force for all that is most
important in the book, however securely this is embedded in a
surface that has been lived through rather than simply
observed. That this is especially true for the lieutenant helps to
clarify the novel's theme and structure. Although the germ of
the idea for the whisky priest came from direct experience,
Greene claims not to have seen any of the 'idealism or integrity
of the Lieutenant . . . among the police and *pistoleros* I had
actually encountered—I had to invent him as a counter to the
failed priest: the idealistic police officer who stifled life from
the best possible motives: the drunken priest who continued to
pass life on'.[16] The necessity, as Greene saw it, for such
invention makes a neat distinction between life and art.
Greene may have felt that these positive qualities were in short
supply in the Mexico he experienced, a judgement which
hardly admits of testing by objective historical evidence; as a
record of his sense of the country, *The Lawless Roads* is nothing
if not honest in its admission of hatred: 'I loathed Mexico.'[17]
But the artistic fairness which for Greene is the linch-pin of
creative integrity, to the extent of subverting his own most
deeply held views, makes such one-sidedness inappropriate to
the level of truth demanded, however paradoxically, by
fiction.

This commitment to truth-telling as opposed to ideology operates on the Catholic side of the novel's basic conflict as much as in the portrait of the lieutenant whose fanaticism fails to prevent the priest calling him at one point 'with astonishment . . . "a good man"' (Part 2, Ch. 3). Greene is constantly at pains to depict the dreary pieties of respectable Catholicism. Like Joyce's paralysed Dubliners who 'whisper of innocent transgressions in the latticed ear of a priest,'[19] the whisky priest's past is filled with plump good living, the unctuousness of Guild suppers, card tricks for children, harmless jokes to tickle old ladies, all the emptiness of 'the old days when pious people came kissing his black cotton glove' (Part 2, Ch. 3). However, Greene avoids the sentimentality inherent in the book's conflict by showing that even a beleaguered present is not free of such platitudes. The priest may be pared to the spiritual bone by his eight years without the support of conventional custom and ritual, but the little motif of pietistic reading by a drearily orthodox mother to her children is a reminder of the dangers liable to overtake any institution untroubled by self-doubt. It also reveals Greene in the perhaps unfamiliar role of a brilliant parodist, creating the kind of cheerless fun envisaged in George Orwell's vision of a socialist children's literature:

> No, young Juan was a true young Mexican boy, and if he was more thoughful than his fellows, he was also always the first when any play-acting was afoot. One year his class acted a little play before the bishop, based on the persecution of the early Christians, and no one was more amused than Juan when he was chosen to play the part of Nero. And what comic spirit he put into his acting—this child, whose young manhood was to be cut short by a ruler far worse than Nero. His class-mate, who later became Father Miguel Cerra, S.J., writes: 'None of us who were there will ever forget that day . . .'. (Part 1, Ch. 2)

Greene calls himself a committed writer—in the best sense of the word he obviously is—but commitment may have obscured for some his 'negative capability', his convincing ability to enter modes of consciousness radically unlike his own. The novel's inbuilt criticism of pietism, for example, is powerfully reinforced by the revulsion it causes in the lieutenant:

> Something you could have almost called horror moved him when he looked at the white muslin dresses—he remembered the smell of incense in the churches of his boyhood, the candles and the laciness and the self-esteem, the immense demands made from the altar steps by men who didn't know the meaning of sacrifice. The old peasants knelt there before the holy images with their arms held out in the attitude of the cross: tired by the long day's labour in the plantations they squeezed out a further mortification. And the priest came round with the collecting-bag taking their centavos, abusing them for their small comforting sins, and sacrificing nothing at all in return—except a little sexual indulgence. (Part 1, Ch. 2)

A craftsmanlike as well as a thematic purpose is at work here also. By the time he came to write *The Power and the Glory*, Greene had fully absorbed the lessons of the early entertainments; at one level the novel's basic structure is that of the pursuit. Before the book begins, the priest has been wandering, not aimlessly, but with the sole purpose of keeping alive his priestly function. With supreme cunning, Greene saves his deepest fall from grace, in the technical sense at least, the act of lonely and drunken lust with Maria, for the past; sympathy would have been too hard to maintain, even for the unorthodox perhaps, if it had occurred in the novel's present. Once into this present, the priest's 'realistic' meanderings are sharpened into art by one of Greene's favourite devices, the hunt, a pursuer and pursued whose relationship is essentially metaphysical while losing none of the excitement of the chase itself. Used without tact this form can degenerate into a remorseless linearity, but Greene diversifies his narrative with a memorable little group of figures, amusing and horrifying (at their perhaps characteristic best, both) who add richness to the novel's texture and, simultaneously, contribute to its theme. The horribly named dentist, Mr Tench, is a profoundly Greenian creation whose future life was decided at the moment of finding 'a discarded cast' in his dentist father's wastepaper basket:

It had been his favourite toy: they tried to tempt him with Meccano, but fate had struck. There is always one moment in childhood when the door opens and lets the future in. The hot wet river-port and the vultures lay in the wastepaper basket and he picked them out. (Part 1, Ch. 1)

His utterly fruitless existence is a truly memorable image of spiritual nullity, a life stripped to bedrock, like the priest's, but in Tench's case revealing nothing. Padre José also seems fixed forever in a hell where 'a quick furtive look at the sky where the constellations wheeled' (Part 3, Ch. 4) is the only link with his former vocation, hauled off continuously by his gigantic wife to amorous encounters we are thankfully left only to guess at. The Lahrs appear to offer something altogether more positive, although a note of unease is struck immediately by the use of one of Greene's favourite little words: 'the whole scene was *like* peace' (Part 3, Ch. 1). The brother and sister are genuinely likeable, with their physical angularity and almost monastic austerity (Mr Lahr is a childless widower; his sister has never married). But Greene continually builds tiny qualifications into the picture: Mr Lahr's face is 'shrewd' as well as 'idealistic' and can wear a 'look of innocent craft'; their 'ordinary German-American homestead . . . was in its way, an admirable mode of life.' Living with them engenders in the priest 'a mixture of tenderness and dependence' and as he resumes a life like that 'before the persecution' he 'could feel the old life hardening round him like a habit, a stony cast which held his head high and dictated the way he walked, and even formed his words' (Part 3, Ch. 1). This whole episode is beautiful in its way (as Greene might remark) and, again, craftsmanship is at work in it. The Lahrs' life forms an oasis in the midst of what might otherwise seem excessively unrelieved gloom, a lightening before the return of darkness and pain—and ultimate hope, of course. Thematically, however, they fuse with some of the novel's deepest concerns. They help to focus various senses of one of Greene's key words, peace; the peace represented by their well-regulated respectability (Miss Lahr's horror of even 'knowing', never mind living, the contents of the *Police News*) contrasts with, and defines, the truest peace ever experienced by Greene's protagonist, the hellish night of pain, stench, sex, and yet love, in the prison cell. Again, their celibate goodness links with the lieutenant's idealism (his room is 'as comfortles as . . . a monastic cell' Part 1, Ch. 2); yet the kindness of the one and the fanaticism of the other masks an inability to love while the whisky priest, laden with sin and human weakness, is unable not to love, even his yellow-fanged Judas.

The novel's linear structure of pursuit is, then, deflected by these functional digressions, but its form, and so meaning, is enriched even further by a pattern of mirroring which operates throughout. A series of contrasts is set up between figures who are similar and yet different, in such a way as to render the book's spiritual universe highly complex, the very reverse of ideologically one-sided. The priest and the policeman are one obvious example. Both desire with total dedication what they consider happiness for mankind. The painfulness of the latter's dilemma and the sympathetic inwardness with which Greene presents 'his little dapper figure of hate carrying his secret of love' deserves quotation; a particularly moving moment is his attempt to establish communication with a group of children by showing them his revolver:

> He stood with his hand on his holster and watched the brown intent patient eyes: it was for these he was fighting. He would eliminate from their childhood everything which had made him miserable, all that was poor, superstitious, and corrupt. They deserved nothing less than the truth—a vacant universe and a cooling world, the right to be happy in any way they chose. He was quite prepared to make a massacre for their sakes—first the Church and then the foreigner and then the politician—even his own chief would one day have to go. He wanted to begin the world again with them, in a desert. (Part 1, Ch. 4)

The priest's centrality allows, perhaps demands, another contrasting similarity, with the significantly named American gangster, James Calver. Their photographs side by side on the wall of the police station make the point forcibly enough: 'he was responsible for the American as well: the two faces . . . were hanging together . . .as if they were brothers in a family portrait gallery. You didn't put temptation in a brother's way' (Part 2, Ch. 4). The priest's love and sense of brotherhood is obvious; less obvious is their moral polarity. With every last fault remembered, goodness is still the only word for Greene's whisky priest; total evil finds its embodiment not in his disgustingly pathetic betrayer, but in the ruthless killer who makes a child his shield in his final shoot-out with the police. And yet—and here Greene agrees with Baudelaire and Eliot—there is a kind of perverse virtue in his total commitment to evil. Nothing could be more powerfully laconic than his response to the attempt to save his soul, 'Beat it, father.' Like the priest himself, in his half-breed betrayer's whining complaint, he can 'do nothing in moderation' (Part 3, Ch. 2).

The last example of this mirror pattern is that of the two little girls, Coral Fellows and the priests's own illegitimate child. Neither is a child in any real sense: Coral's hopelessly inadequate parents have forced a premature adulthood on her while the latter is predetermined in her apparently almost self-conscious sexual awareness. The contrast between them is clearly expressed in one of the priest's memories:

> He could see her very clearly . . . the neat accurately moulded face with the two pinched pigtails. He remembered her readiness to swear eternal enmity against anyone who hurt him, and he remembered his own child enticing him by the rubbish-dump. (Part 2, Ch. 4)

Both, however, are Godless (Coral explains, 'You see, I don't believe in God. I lost my faith when I was ten.' Part 1, Ch. 3) and yet our last sight of her hints at what may turn out to be a fundamental difference between the two children. Experiencing her first menstruation, Coral examines the hiding place to which she had helped the priest:

> Then the torch lit the back wall: low down near the ground somebody had scrawled in chalk—she came closer: a lot of little crosses leant in the circle of light. He must have lain down among the bananas and tried to relieve his fear by writing something, and this was all he could think of. The child stood in her woman's pain and looked at them: a horrible novelty enclosed her whole morning: it was as if today everything were memorable. (Part 1, Ch. 4)

Perhaps there is just a hint in this scene of an influence that the priest himself will remain unaware of, in this life at least.

I pointed earlier to the novel's structure of an elemental pursuit; the simple outlines of this are obvious. But, as well as being the hunted, the whisky priest is also a hunter in quest of what is presumably life's most important object, its meaning. For him this can be found only within not just a religious, but a Catholic, context. Once again we can see a fruitful connection between this novel and *Brighton Rock*. Greene doesn't repeat himself in a mechanical fashion as a writer, but with that transitional novel he entered a stage when his inner life became dominated for some years by the mystery of the 'appalling strangeness of the mercy of God.' The word mystery itself, and its associations, echo throughout *The Power and Glory*. They are implicit in José's memory of 'what made him worthy of damnation:' that is, 'the gift he had been given which nobody could take away . . . what made him worthy of damnation—the power he still had of turning the wafer into the flesh and blood of God' (Part 1, Ch. 2). An aspect of the priest's being stripped to bedrock is that 'after a time the mystery became too great, a damned man putting God into the mouths of men'. The priest may feel himself to be damned, but nothing can prevent him giving communion, neither fear of the police nor fear of himself. Fundamental to our sympathy for him is the fact that 'in his innocence he had felt no love for anyone; now in his corruption he had learnt . . .' (Greene leaves us to fill in the dots for ourselves.) The acquiring of grace through evil while losing it through venial sins is 'another mystery' (Part 2, Ch. 3). And at the climax of one of those discussions between the priest and the policeman which never degenerate into a mere undramatic exchange of ideas, the former affirms with passionate intensity, 'I don't know a thing about the mercy of God' (Part 3, Ch. 3). But his insistence that if ever a man has been damned then he will be too provokes a reverse reaction from us. It is Greene's triumph to create a character who, while he may break every rule of Catholic dogma and some of secular morality also, is revealed to us from the inside as overflowing with a loving concern for mankind. If the rules take precedence over that, so much the worse for the rules is surely Greene's implication.

The priest's tragedy, at the novel's climax, is to feel his own total unworthiness but is this not, even for the dogmatist, a sign of grace? At the last, fear of damnation and of physical pain (he insists always on his cowardice) fades into 'only an immense disappointment because he had to go to God empty-handed with nothing done at all.' But if intention and desire are a kind of doing, we know this to be untrue although he isn't, of course, at the end the 'only one thing that counted . . . a saint' (Part 3, Ch. 4). In the last analysis, his fate is created by his own willed insistence on performing his duty, seeing Calver being the last example. It seems hard to expect any man, even a priest, to achieve more.

SECTION C: *THE HEART OF THE MATTER*

The six years separating *The Heart of the Matter* from *The Power and the Glory* (1948) reveal even greater advances in artistry than we have seen already, but certain underlying preoccupations remain. The mystery of God's mercy is a continuing theme, but one brought to a focus through an issue suggested in the earlier book. Looking with shock at his child, the priest is 'aware of an immense load of responsibility . . . indistinguishable from love.' The fusion of love and responsibility are central also to the dilemma of Major Scobie, a point worth making not to perpetuate the *canard* that Greene is a one-book man, but to bring out how intensely his inner life was dominated by certain issues over a long period. An attempt will be made to explain this intensity shortly; for the moment, it may be of interest to examine Greene's view of critical responses to his novel.

A sinking of the heart is engendered by opening *A Sort of Life* and *Ways of Escape* to see what Greene thinks of his own work: his critical discernment is such that one fears redundancy for the professionally trained reader. Over *The Heart of the Matter*, however, disagreement is unavoidable. For Greene, the novel has been more popular with the public and critics 'than with the author', although he admits that 'perhaps what I really dislike in the book is the memory of personal anguish.' Such a verdict is ultimately only of interest in relation to the author's life; as such it can hardly be disputed. What is open to objection is his acceptance of the fact that 'his critics have complained . . . that "I laid it on too thick."'[19] The 'it' in question is Greene's use of local colour and this novel is as good a book as any in which to tackle this question head on.

The problem relates as much to sociology as to literary cricism. Since its inception, the novel has performed a wide range of functions other than the pursuit of high art. Apart from simply passing the time or entertaining on a higher level, the novel has been a way of reflecting back to a society an image of itself at work and play, an exploration of unknown or disreputable levels of an otherwise known world and, of relevance to Greene, a purveyor of information about other times, places and cultures. One factor, then, in Greene's popularity in the immediate post-war period may have been the glimpse of exotic parts of the world afforded to general readers whose mental picture of Africa, the Far East, and so on, probably came mainly from the printed word. If this is so, it could have seemed a limitation to the critic trained to concentrate on what one must ultimately agree are the novel's central functions: insight into people and the exploration of language as a medium for communicating a vision of social as well as personal life. A generation increasingly moulded by colour in the cinema and above all by the travel documentary beloved of television obviously gains its picture of the world in ways different from those of earlier periods. At this point, sociology merges with literary criticism because the transition just sketched would, if accurate, have been disastrous to the reputation of a writer who simply travelled the world in order to paint its surface in highly coloured descriptive prose. In Greene's case, however, the change is all to his advantage in helping one to grasp that exotic landscape could hardly be more lightly sketched than in *The Heart of the Matter*. Wilson's trip to the local brothel; the touching Ali and comic Yusef; the famous pink sunsets which, suddenly and momentarily, touch a sordid world into beauty—these are parts of an artistically justified setting, not the externalised extravagances of scene-painting.

It would, of course, be absurd to say that the book might just as well have been set in South London as West Africa. The colonial setting's importance is clear at a moment when Scobie swerves his car to 'avoid a dead pye-dog':

> Why, he wondered . . . do I love this place so much? Is it because here human nature hasn't had time to disguise itself? Nobody here could ever talk about a Heaven on earth. Heaven remained rigidly in its proper place on the other side of death, and on this side flourished the injustices, the cruelties, the meanness that elsewhere people so cleverly hushed up. Here you could love human beings nearly as God loved them, knowing the worst: you didn't love a pose, a pretty dress, a sentiment artfully assumed. (Part 1, Ch. 1,5)

This stripping of life to the bone is quite feasibly the response of a colonial official during the time (the 1940s) and in the place (Sierra Leone, the source of the novel's fictional colony) when Greene was absorbing his later impressions of West Africa after the exploration recorded in *Journey Without Maps*. If chance had taken him to, say, Nigeria he could hardly have failed to register a cultural richness and diversity which would have complicated his vision of Africa and perhaps made the novel as we have it now impossible. As it was, Sierra Leone provided a perfect image of human nature unmediated by the layers of spiritual, material and cultural complexity to be found in many parts of the continent. Also, expatriates in any alienating environment frequently find a diminution in that sense of the self which is more than purely personal, springing as it does from a cultural inheritance in its natural setting. The club, golf, and sundowners may then form the frailest of links with a home which can only be recreated in its externals in a foreign land.

What all this means is that just as the Mexico of *The Lawless Roads* is a 'state of mind,' so the context of *The Heart of the Matter* is essentially an inner landscape, one created with formidable intensity. The genesis of any work of art is never really explicable, but the circumstances of Greene's life at the time seem partly to elucidate the novel's depth of feeling as well as some of its general concerns. The lapse of time between it and his previous novel made Greene feel that his 'writing had become rusty with disuse and misuse'[20] and this appears to have given a renewed energy to thoughts on the nature of his craft, similar perhaps to those involved in the painful shift from *Rumour at Nightfall* to *Stamboul Train*. The section of *Ways of Escape* concerned with *The Heart of the Matter* certainly contains several brilliantly interesting discussions of purely technical problems, above all Greene's perennial concern, point-of-view; especially striking are his comments on the reinsertion into a later edition of the novel of the scene between Wilson and Louise on their evening walk at the beginning of Book One, Chapter Two, Part Two. I shall try to show later how the scene materially affects our sense of Mrs Scobie's character; for the moment, though, my stress is on the force with which Greene bore down on such problems.

The gap in time between novels is not, however, enough to explain the book's claustrophic intensity, its feeling of inhabiting a limited number of minds, with Scobie as the dominating centre, of course. The answer lies, one would guess, in the fusion of these technical difficulties with problems in Greene's personal life. He writes of how 'the booby-traps I had heedlessly planted in my private life were blowing up in turn. I had always thought that war would bring death as a solution in one form or another, in the blitz, in a submarined ship, in Africa with a dose of black-water fever, but here I was alive, the carrier of unhappiness to people I loved.' The crucial link between life and art is provided by his admission that he was 'even contemplating . . . suicide when I was interrupted in that game by . . . a telegram . . . from someone whom I had made suffer and who now felt anxious about my safety.'[21] T.S. Eliot's distinction between the man who suffers and the artist who creates has enjoyed a long vogue in twentieth-century criticism, but it is impossible to feel its usefulness here. By his own admission Greene was enduring anguish both as man and novelist; the reward (for the reader, at least) is the sustained power of *The Heart of the Matter*. For the writer, the book involved the by now familiar conflict between novel and entertainment, only finally resolved when he plumped for Scobie rather than Wilson as the book's centre, but for the reader of the completed and revised novel these difficulties have been dissolved by artistry. Everything rings true—language, character, structure, theme—with a confidence that assures us of the total absence of base metal.

A final disagreement with the author may take us more deeply into the heart of the matter itself. Having unravelled some of the book's supposed weaknesses, Greene speculates that perhaps Scobie 'should have been a subject for a cruel comedy rather than for tragedy . . .' but a line or two earlier he remarks that suicide was 'Scobie's inevitable end'[22] and it's here that my own initial emphasis would fall. The stuff of tragedy is inseparable from the clenching inevitability of Scobie's downfall. Out of circumstance, and his own character, life springs its trap on him, as he recognises on his return from the Fellowes's dinner-party, where he pretended to a merely casual acquaintance with Helen Rolt, and finds Yusef asleep 'stretched in a chair' with a sense of being at home that gives Scobie the feeling that 'life was closing in on him.'[23] The trap's mechanism, though not its marvellous emotional and psychological complexity, is revealed at what should have been the climax of Scobie's personal and professional life, his delayed promotion to the Commissionership of Police:

> The Commissioner said, 'Come in, Scobie. I've got good news for you . . . Baker is not coming here. They need him in Palestine. They've decided after all to let the right man succeed me.' Scobie sat down on the window-ledge and watched his hand tremble on his knee. He thought: so all this need not have happened. If Louise had stayed I should never have loved Helen, I would never have been blackmailed by Yusef, never have committed that act of despair. I would have been myself still. . . . But, of course, he told himself, it's only because I have done these things that success comes. I am of the devil's party. He looks after his own in this world. I shall go now from damned success to damned success, he thought with disgust. (p.228)

This wonderful sense of the roads taken, and not taken, in human life poses an acute critical problem given the novel's richness of insight and structure; for, although the book centres itself so firmly within Scobie's consciousness, with few ventures outside, this in no way lessens its delicate complexity. A complete disentangling of the factors that lead Scobie to his apparently despairing death would involve a dreary re-hash of the entire book in one's own words.

Perhaps one major example may serve to reveal something of Greene's skills working at full stretch in the novel. What leads the middle-aged Scobie and the pathetically youthful widow, Helen Rolt, into their affair? The easy answer would be that 'responsibility . . . indistinguishable from love' mentioned in *The Power and the Glory*. But one must beware of making mere catchwords of Greene's use of such key terms as 'peace,' 'pity,' and 'responsibility.' At their best, they acquire a sense of redefinition from their incremental use, a re-examination by Greene of some of the commonplaces of religion and morality. The roots of Scobie's love for Helen, for example, lie at the very heart of his character and of one of the key experiences of his life. Probably the first stage in Scobie's disintegration is his failure to report the Portuguese sea-captain's secreting of a letter in a lavatory cistern, an offence which Scobie as a policeman should transmit instantly to the proper authority, thereby severely weakening the captain's chances of continuing his career. The seeds of Scobie's downfall occur in a little exchange of dialogue:

> 'A man is ruined because he writes to his daughter.'
> 'Daughter?' (p.50)

Up to this point there has been merely a passing reference to a photograph of an 'only child who had died at school in England three years ago—a little pious nine-year-old girl's face in the white muslin of her first communion.' (p.22) The shattering anguish of the incident for Scobie is only revealed much later when he tells the now beloved Helen of something he 'had never mentioned . . . before to anyone, not even to Louise,' the fact that in an attempt to ease the blow his wife had sent two telegrams which arrived out of order, the first telling of his daughter's death, the second that she was seriously ill. (A similar confusion, on his father's death, occurred in Greene's own life.) The episode's horror is compounded by the hideous comedy of a mistake which transmutes Louise's 'darling' into 'diving' (one thinks of Forster's 'God si love' from *A Passage to India*). But this direct knowledge of Scobie's suffering is prepared for by a web of references to children which transforms it from direct statement to an acknowledgement of pain which we have by then grasped intuitively for ourselves. Dicky Pemberton's suicide (the echo of Louise's nickname for Scobie, Ticki, is unmistakable) is a beautifully worked out episode which helps to prepare us for Scobie's ultimate fate, but the novel's amazingly controlled pattern of cross-references links it also to the matter in hand when Scobie registers surprise that the picture rail from which Pemberton hanged himself didn't collapse: 'He can weigh very little, he thought, and he remembered a child's bones, light and brittle as a bird's.' (p.88) This moving commonplace of the parent's memory of a dead child helps us to understand Scobie's agony when he is forced to relive his own child's death through that of the girl rescued after forty days at sea. By a 'trick of the light' her mosquito net becomes momentarily the 'white communion veil' of his daughter's photograph and Scobie is made to realise that 'after all one never really missed a thing.' He had always been grateful for avoiding his own child's death in England, but now finds that he has to endure the 'small scraping voice' calling him 'Father', the 'breast . . . struggling for breath.' In a moment central to works as widely spaced throughout Greene's career as *The Power and the Glory*, *The End of the Affair*, and *The Potting Shed*, Scobie prays God to 'take away my peace for ever, but give her peace.' The thought of the child's certain death had already provoked Scobie to question God's mercy: 'that the child should have been allowed to survive the forty days and nights in the open boat—that was the mystery, to reconcile that with the love of God.' (pp.120–1) However, his ordeal is still not over, although Greene lightens the tone somewhat in the scene where Scobie transforms *A Bishop among the Bantus* into suitable, Rider Haggard-like reading material for a sick boy, another survivor of the torpedoed ship on which Helen's husband of a few months has died.

Scobie describes the tale of 'Arthur Bishop' in the best Greenian manner, as 'a kind of detective story . . . because he's a secret agent of the British Government' but, on turning the page, he is 'temporarily put out by a portrait of the bishop in whites with a clerical collar and a topee, standing before a wicket and blocking a ball a Bantu has just bowled him.' The boy's plea to him to start reading is unexpectedly reinforced: '"Yes, begin it," said a low voice from the other bed, so low that he would have discounted it as an illusion if he hadn't looked up and seen her watching him, the eyes large as a child's in the starved face.' (p.129) Foreshadowing has already prepared us for Helen's future importance to Scobie by means of a detail that reinforces the link between his love for her and the loss of his child: 'Scobie always remembered how she was carried into his life on a stretcher grasping a stamp-album with her eyes fast shut.' (p.121) and Greene reminds us of it immediately before they fall in love: 'When she turned and the light fell on her face she looked ugly, with the temporary ugliness of a child.' (p.159) This discussion is not designed to show that the nineteen-year-old Helen is a daughter-substitute for the middle-aged Scobie; that would be paperback Freudianism with a vengeance. What I hope to have revealed is the extraordinary delicacy with which Greene unlocks the deepest recesses of Scobie's inner life, turning him, in the process, into one of the memorable characters of mid-twentieth-century fiction. Light is also thrown, I think, on the paradox of the novel's intense concentration on Scobie's consciousness combined with its sense of richness, a fusion that stems from the fullness with which we come to know the ramifications of his personality and character. His fundamentally unwilling betrayal into love is only made possible by the way in which the totally convincing detail of the fate Greene creates for him taps the deepest levels of his being. That Scobie loves against, as well as with, the grain is revealed by another motif, his profound desire for peace which in his case takes the form of a special kind of loneliness. We are familiar by now with the importance of dreams in Greene's art; a striking example occurs as Scobie rattles along in the police van to investigate Pemberton's suicide:

> When he slept he went smoothly back into a dream of perfect happiness and freedom. He was walking through a wide cool meadow with Ali at his heels: there was nobody else anywhere in his dream, and Ali never spoke. Birds went by far overhead, and once when he sat down the grass was parted by a small green snake which passed on to his hand and up his arm without fear,

and before it slid down into the grass again touched his cheek with a cold, friendly, remote tongue. (p.83)

This astonishingly beautiful passage is surely the Eden of an unhappy, middle-aged man. The Ali of so many contented expeditions of the past is a comfortingly silent presence and the stress on a kind of distant coolness reminds one of the lunar longings of Mr Sammler in Bellow's *Mr Sammler's Planet* where the moon stands in utter contrast to the opulent sexuality and materialism of modern New York. The motif is continued, with visionary intensity, when Scobie sets out to visit a newcomer to the local Nissen huts who turns out to be Helen Rolt: 'It seemed to Scobie later that this was the ultimate border he had reached in happiness: being in darkness, alone, with the rain falling, without love or pity.' (p.135) Scobie also feels 'an extraordinary happiness' when he leaves Helen, but this 'he would not remember as happiness as he would remember setting out in the darkness, alone.' (p.140)

That such a man should love, and love convincingly, is a tribute to the level of artistry Greene had reached by the time he came to write *The Heart of the Matter*. The novel's total grasp of the complexities of human relations and, above all, of the mysteries of personal motivation is embodied in a pattern of motifs and key words so delicate that they invest the book with the feeling of life itself rather than mechanical contrivance. Two tiny examples are the broken rosary which is mentioned only twice, separated by a distance of more than 150 pages, and the comic yet moving involvement of Yusef with Othello, although this also opens out a much larger pattern. Just as Othello himself both loves and doubts Desdemona, so Yusef is embroiled in a simultaneous urge to self-advantage and longing for Scobie's friendship; as he so forlornly maintains, 'And formerly I was your friend':

'You very nearly were,' Scobie reluctantly admitted.
'I am the base Indian.'
'The base Indian?'
'Who threw away a pearl,' Yusef sadly said. 'That was in the play by Shakespeare the Ordnance Corps gave in the Memorial Hall. I have always remembered it.' (p.200)

And, sure enough, the pearl turns up, in the shape of the diamond he sends Scobie in gratitude for his enforced co-operation. Yusef, his 'fat hand upon his sincere and shallow heart' is a wonderful creation; perhaps above all in the advice he offers Scobie on the 'woman trouble' he has had in his life: 'Now it is better because I have learned the way. The way is not to care a damn, Major Scobie.' (p.241)

He is only one of a small range of characters, expertly touched in, who give the novel a hint of range and density, preventing it from collapsing into a Scobie-dominated solipsism. The ineffable Harris, for example, is a splendid comic character with his cockroach hunts and loyalty to the unhappiness of his dreadful public school. Again, it's impossible to accept Greene's verdict on Wilson as a character 'who obstinately refused to come alive.'[24] His face—'pink and healthy, plump and hopeless' (p.63) – is a perfect index of his uselessness in tying on cummerbunds, his secret love of appalling poetry, his lack of any 'capacity for friendship or for equality' (p.75), especially with women, a limitation which leads him to either the brothel or a falsely idealised love for Louise Scobie. Louise herself steps forward with a sufficient sense of independent life in the passage Greene reinserted into later editions of the novel, telling Wilson brusquely, 'For God's sake . . . don't be humble.' (p.75) Her loving hatred of Scobie makes her 'someone of human stature with her own sense of responsibility' (p.96) rather than simply an object for her husband's pitying concern. Helen Rolt, too, is effective especially as the relationship begins to break down for her under the pressure of its secrecy and in her moving attempt to give up Scobie for his own good so that he will have 'peace.' Their failure to part also illustrates Greene's complete control in this novel of those sometimes troublesome similes: 'As they kissed he was aware of pain under his mouth like the beating of a bird's heart.'(p.251)

But Scobie himself is, finally, our centre of attention and Helen's disbelief—Catholicism is 'all hooey to me' (p.211)— performs an important function in situating our response to his character. While I don't intend to add to all those wearisome arguments about salvation and damnation generated by Scobie's behaviour, I also find it impossible to accept Greene's view of Scobie's 'almost monstrous pride.'[24] There is an over-reaching element in him, of course: like a tragic version of Jane Austen's Emma, he believes he can understand people completely and arrange their happiness for them. There is something truly outrageous in that, although he accepts that he shares responsibilities with 'all human beings,' it 'sometimes seemed to him that he was the only one who recognised his responsibility.' (p.122) But it is the pain of Scobie's attempt to be responsible, rendered by Greene in all its complex detail, which strikes me as central. In the process of unravelling the threads of Scobie's dilemma Greene does something like justice to one of the profoundest difficulties of human life. As with Yusef and Othello, and with a hint of the latter's suffering, Scobie desires with complete urgency two things which are incompatible. Helen, performing her function of non-believer, says, 'If there's one thing I hate it's your Catholicism. . . . It's so bogus. If you really believed you wouldn't be here':

> 'But I do believe and I am here.' He said with bewilderment, 'I can't explain it, but there it is. My eyes are open. I know what I'm doing.' (p.232)

It's a tribute to Greene that in attempting to explain this paradox we can turn to another of Shakespeare's plays, *Macbeth*, which I have already suggested is helpful in elucidating *Brighton Rock*.

In that novel it was possible to see Pinkie's killings as analagous to those of Macbeth; here the link is with the untruths that have to be told by a man 'unaccustomed to lies.' (p.53) As Scobie plunges ever more deeply into his problems, he feels himself, in characteristically Greenian language, to be entering 'the territory of lies without a passport for return' (p.199) which results in the sensation of his 'whole personality' crumbling 'with the slow disintegration of lies.' (p.209) This is yet another of those motifs of patterned repetition which Greene weaves so skilfully throughout the novel. Towards the end of his ordeal Scobie begins to sink into a morass of moral and spiritual difficulties: 'There were so many lies nowadays he couldn't keep track of the small, the unimportant ones.'

(p.231) The connection with *Macbeth*—I'm not suggesting a direct influence, merely a comparison which is all to Greene's credit—lies in the spectacle of a man who desperately desires to be good but who, through character and circumstance, finds himself enmeshed in evil. In the wonderfully achieved scene between Scobie and Yusef towards the end of the book, Scobie finds himself remembering 'the long trek beside the border: innumerable lunches in the forest shade, with Ali cooking in an old sardine-tin . . . Ali always at hand.' (p.245) This occurs just before the terrible cry which signals Ali's murder, a throat-cutting for which Scobie is ultimately responsible. The heart of the matter I am considering at this point is crystallised in Father Rank's statement in the confessional and Scobie's response:

> 'You can't desire the end without desiring the means.'
> Ah, but one can, he thought, one can: one can desire the peace of victory without desiring the ravaged towns. (p.221)

Macbeth desires to be king of Scotland, and a good man, but the only way he can achieve the first ambition is by murder. Scobie desires the eternal life of Catholic salvation, but cannot bear to inflict pain on two human beings and his way of dealing with the second dilemma renders the first unachievable.

There is clearly an element of moral and spiritual confusion in these difficulties; some would even say absurdity. On discovering Ali's corpse, Scobie wishes he could weep, which is rather like Macbeth's surprise at his inability to say amen at the sight of Duncan's body. The simple response to these problems is to say that it's their own fault if they can't weep or pray; the distinction of works of art is to reveal the hopeless inadequacy of such a response. Macbeth's desire for kingship, urged on by his wife, has a palpable reality which makes the other reality, eternal damnation, a cloud no bigger than a man's hand. Scobie can see, feel and hear the suffering of Louise and Helen; in his internal dialogue with God he points out that he 'can't observe your suffering. I can only imagine it.' (p.258) So he opts for the present having rather than the future hope. This comparison with *Macbeth* musn't be pressed too far, of course. Macbeth's present having—illegitimate kingship—is unambiguously evil and achieved through murder. As I suggested in this chapter's first section, Macbeth's actions lie outside any specific system of belief and so command general moral condemnation. Scobie's behaviour, on the other hand, may threaten a split in the ranks of readers between believers and non-believers—the fog of wearisome dispute again threatens to descend.

Perhaps a way of keeping the ranks unified is by stressing, once more, the novel's power as a work of art. Given the premisses of Scobie's character and belief, there is undoubtedly an element of 'monstrous pride' in his 'God can wait, he thought: how can one love God at the expense of one of his creatures?' (p. 187) The possibilities here for self-deception and having it both ways are clear. The artistic justification for such a problem is that we should be made to feel that it isn't an easy option for Scobie, that opting for it carried him to the outer limits of human suffering. And this is surely precisely what we do feel in the quite tremendous scene of his deliberate acceptance of Christ's body and blood in a state of mortal sin, guided by Louise's 'kindly firm detective hand' and feeling 'like a spy in a foreign land' as he kneels to become 'aware of the pale papery taste of an eternal sentence on the tongue.' (p. 225)

However strange in its detail to some, the nature of the experience voluntarily undergone here is capable of arousing both pity and terror. And in Scobie's moment of extinction— one of the more powerful death scenes in fiction—Greene rises to a level of writing which answers to the problems he has set himself. A tiny motif of turmoil in the weather reaches its climax at this point ('"A storm," he said aloud, "there's going to be a storm." '). As Scobie tries to get to his feet to close the windows, the beloved Ali is remembered and, as in *Brighton Rock*, there's a sense of someone outside trying to get in, a someone 'appealing for help, someone in need of him. And automatically at the call of need, at the cry of a victim, Scobie strung himself to act.' It is too late for action now, but just before he falls Scobie says aloud, 'Dear God, I love . . .'. (p. 265) Here the angels begin to become agitated on the point of their pin. Is Scobie saved in the split second as his body crashes to the ground or must the act of self-destruction stand as a final damnation? Who can say? My stress would fall on the nature of a man who dies with the word 'love' on his lips. Whatever moral errors and spiritual sins Scobie has committed stemmed from love, a love on which Greene has expended all his skill so as to make us feel it at the level of experience not statement.

In loving God's creatures to such an extent, doesn't Scobie justify Father Rank's final judgement: 'I think, from what I saw of him, that he really loved God?' Whether this is true or not, we cannot doubt that, like Louise, we don't 'know a thing about God's mercy.' (p.272) What we do know is truth to life, the ability to unravel human motive, the power to communicate suffering, when we meet them in the pages of a novel as we so unmistakeably do in *The Heart of the Matter*.

SECTION D: *THE END OF THE AFFAIR*

Greene's use of apparently miraculous occurrences in *The End of the Affair* (1951) has, inevitably, involved the novel in controversy and so this section might usefully begin with a bald claim. In my judgement it is a book of such power as almost to annihilate problems of belief. Its fusion of technical brilliance and passionate feeling give it a very special place in twentieth-century fiction as a love story of extraordinary intensity. Echoes of Barbara Cartland might seem to consign such a category to the lowest pit of damnation. However important sexual love has become as a topic in the modern novel, in the greatest works it is often only part of a wider vision of personal and social life. The concentration of *Lady Chatterley's Lover* on its couple has appeared to many a limiting, risible even, feature of the book, although I remain unrepentantly a defender of its tenderness and beauty. A more relevant comparison with Greene's novel is Faulkner's *The Wild Palms* which exhibits a similar combination of technical virtuosity with the joys and sufferings of passionate love. The structure of Faulkner's book might almost be said to be wilful in its apparently total separation of the two strands, 'Wild Palms' and 'Old Man', which make up its plot, especially when compared with the more functional brilliance of Greene's form. But the cry of anguish for the human condition both books emit belongs to the same universe of pain. This comparison is intended to map out the territory of Greene's achievement rather than suggest a direct influence. If that territory contains difficult problems of belief for the uncommitted reader, it also conveys triumphantly the ambition of its novelist-hero, Maurice, nourished by seeing with Sarah the mediocre film version of one of his books: 'I had wanted to convey the sense of passion' (Book 1, Ch. 7). That sense, and the means used to achieve it, are what remind one irresistibly of *Wuthering Heights*, a novel of whose amorality Greene might well disapprove. One small detail reinforces this affinity, the episode when Maurice discovers Sarah's childhood books:

> I couldn't work that evening. I lay on the floor with the books and tried to trace at least a few features in the blank spaces of Sarah's life. There are times when a lover longs to be also a father and a brother: he is jealous of the years he hasn't shared. *The Golliwog at the North Pole* was probably the earliest of Sarah's books because it had been scrawled all over, this way and that, meaninglessly, destructively, with coloured chalks. In one of the Beatrix Potters her name had been spelt in pencil, one big capital letter arranged wrongly so that what appeared was SAЯAH. In *The Children of the New Forest* she had written very tidily and minutely 'Sarah Bertram Her Book. Please ask permission to borrow. And if you steal it will be to your sorrow.' They were the marks of every child who has ever lived: traces as anonymous as the claw marks of birds that one sees in winter. When I closed the book they were covered at once by the drift of time. (Book 5, Ch. 6)

The poignant beauty of the simile which modulates exquisitely into the final metaphor is a guarantee of Greene's depth of feeling at this point; the relevant moment in *Wuthering Heights*, the scrawled repetition of Catherine Earnshaw's name, is more central to the book, but both share the pain of childish things past. A stronger link is in the novel's complex manipulation of point-of-view. Emily Brontë has seven narrators to Greene's two, but their purpose is remarkably similar. At one moment, Catherine tells Nellie that she wants to 'give you a feeling of how I feel'[25] and that attempt to communicate the impalpable is thematically crucial. It is a precondition of the novel's success that we should be made to feel powerfully, and that cannot be achieved by authorial statement alone. Hence, Emily Brontë's barrage of narrative devices which convey feeling from a multiplicity of sources. If we can be made to accept the force of the characters' emotions, then we may be willing to accept the strangeness of their behaviour—Catherine's profound, but non-sexual, love for Heathcliff, for example. Perhaps most unnerving is the episode when Heathcliff apparently looks at something in front of the wall which Nellie initially thinks he is staring at; such a moment is acceptable only within the narrative framework the writer so brilliantly deploys.

Greene, too, uses the paraphernalia of a diary, letters, and dual viewpoints to convey how his characters feel, their 'sense of passion.' Also, in view of the ultimate direction of his novel, it is crucial that we should surrender to this sense of passion as the indispensably human foundation of what is to come. Not that this is a mere question of craftsmanship, the cunning sleight of hand which prepares for metaphysical nonsense (to the unbeliever) by giving the reader the solace of humanity. In my view, Greene welds human love and the love of God into an indissoluble unity which renders acceptance of one part of the book and rejection of the other an absurdity. Human love, though, is conveyed with an intensity which makes nonsense of claims that Greene rejects the body; in the erotic power of Maurice and Sarah's second love-making, for example:

> There was never any question in those days of who wanted whom—we were together in desire. Henry had his tray, sitting up against two pillows in his green woollen dressing-gown, and in the room below, on the hardwood floor, with a single cushion for support and the door ajar, we made love. When the moment came, I had to put my hand gently over her mouth to deaden that strange sad angry cry of abandonment, for fear Henry should hear it overhead . . . I crouched on the floor beside her and watched and watched, as though I might never see this again—the brown indeterminate-coloured hair like a pool of liquor on the parquet, the sweat on her forehead, the heavy breathing as thought she had

run a race and now like a young athlete lay in the exhaustion of victory. (Book 2, Ch. 1)

One keynote of their relationship is struck in Maurice's 'watched and watched, as though I might never see this again,' a longing which might seem to support an argument for the neurotic obsessiveness and jealousy of this 'sinful' affair. The area is controversial, but of one thing we can be sure, that Maurice is alive in the fullest sense at such moments in his passionate apprehension of beauty and the human, perhaps all too human, desire to arrest time; later he says to Henry, 'I wanted love to go on and on, never to get less' (Book 2, Ch. 4). I have said already that Greene is in the line of Baudelaire and Eliot in loathing above all the hollow man, and Maurice is nothing if not rounded, in his hate as well as his love. This sense of life is present in the intimacy of his knowledge of Sarah's body: 'I had spent everything I had, and was lying back with my head on her stomach and her taste—as thin and elusive as water—in my mouth' (Book 2, Ch. 5). And, regardless of dogma, it is impossible to be unmoved by his unbeliever's response to Father Crompton: 'Our hairs are all numbered, you say, but I can feel her hair on the back of my hand: I can remember the fine dust of hair at the base of her spine as she lay face down on my bed. We remember our dead too, in our way' (Book 5, Ch. 3). The artistic validity of such moments is endorsed by the precision of their imagined detail: that 'fine dust of hair,' for example, or 'the sparkle of frost between the fronds of hair on the hard ground' (Book 2, Ch. 2) during another act of love. A special triumph of Greene's technique is to show us, through Sarah's stolen diary, that she equalled Maurice in the abandon of her love for him:

> Sometimes I get so tired of trying to convince him that I love him and shall love him for ever. I know he is afraid of that desert which would be around him if our love were to end, but he can't realise that I feel exactly the same. What he says aloud, I say to myself silently and write it here. (Book 3, Ch. 2)

The power of Sarah's love for Maurice is thus movingly conveyed in a way which creates the ache of lives lived in parallel after separation, as in the moment when she follows him to a pub they used to frequent:

> I stood at the door and watched him go up to the bar. If he turns round and sees me, I told God, I'll go in, but he didn't turn round. I began to walk home, but I couldn't keep him out of my mind. For nearly two years we had been strangers. I hadn't known what he was doing at any particular hour of the day, but now he was a stranger no longer because I knew as in the old days where he was. He would have one more beer and then he would go back to the familiar room to write. The habits of his day were still the same and I loved them as one loves an old coat. I felt protected by his habits. I never want strangeness. (Book 3, Ch. 7)

Passionate intensity of feeling is, then, a hallmark of *The End of the Affair*, combined with formal brilliance, a fusion of apparent opposites which testifies to the novel's imaginative power. Emotion and intelligence are present here in equal measure. One victory gained by Greene's first-person narrative is the total ease of its conversational flow. The book opens with an intimate immediacy—again, like Lockwood's diary at the beginning of *Wuthering Heights*—which is maintained throughout:

> A story has no beginning or end; arbitrarily one chooses that moment of experience from which to look back or from which to look ahead. I say 'one chooses' with the inaccurate pride of a professional writer who—when he has been seriously noted at all—has been praised for his technical ability, but do I in fact of my own will *choose* that black wet January night on the Common, in 1946, the sight of Henry Miles slanting across the wide river of rain, or did these images choose me? It is convenient, it is correct according to the rules of my craft to begin just there, but if I had believed then in a God, I could also have believed in a hand, plucking at my elbow, a suggestion, 'Speak to him: he hasn't seen you yet.' (Book 1, Ch. 1)

Greene's narrative choice makes for negative as well as positive successes, of the kind I have previously referred to; that is, it enables him to avoid certain weaknesses in his own writing. I have already drawn attention to Greene's sometimes unhappy reliance on simile; even as late as *The Power and the Glory* he can write of a child eaten into by the sun: 'The gold bangle on the bony wrist was like a padlock on a canvas door which a fist could break' (Part 1, Ch. 3). Apart from the clash of 'wrist' and 'fist', the whole comparison is strained and unnatural. It's hard to make out the similarity between a bangle and a padlock; harder still the connection between a 'bony wrist' and a 'canvas door.' First-person narrative reduces this kind of thing dramatically if only because of the demands of realism: even writers, presumably, don't talk habitually in similes.

More seriously, first-person narrative eases a difficulty which bears directly on problems of literature and belief: Greene's penchant for narrative generalisation. *The Power and the Glory* again provides an example:

> Now they were both tired and the mule simply sat down. The priest scrambled off and began to laugh. He was feeling happy. It is one of the strange discoveries a man can make that life, however you lead it, contains moments of exhilaration; there are always comparisons which can be made with worse times: even in danger and misery the pendulum swings. (Part 2, Ch. 1)

Two questions arise here, one specific, one general. Clearly, this is not one of Greene's more profound utterances—there's always somebody worse off than yourself. Even the attempt to shelter behind point-of-view is hardly helpful. If these are the character's thoughts, rather than the narrator's, a man suffering as the priest suffers might be expected to come up with something a bit more interesting than this. The general question concerns the status of literary generalisation as a technique. Its supreme exponent in the English novel is probably George Eliot and even she cannot always claim the assent which seems necessary if the work is not to be disrupted by rancorous disagreement, rather than the creative dissent to which I referred earlier. The difficulty for the novel of belief is clear. Generalisations on matters of dogma are liable to provoke a disabling failure of communication between author and reader. And they may also tempt the writer into an ultimately delusive ease of statement instead of the attempt to embody his beliefs in dialogue, character and action. Once again, the problems are eased, if not completely solved, by

Greene's technique in *The End of the Affair*. The point-of-view difficulty simply dissolves. Any generalisations are Bendrix's, or Sarah's in her diary, and so can be viewed unambiguously as a revelation of character. There remains the odd touch of uncertainty in the writing—it's hard not to smile at the banality of Maurice's 'How twisted we humans are, and yet they say a God made us' (Book 1, Ch. 1)—but the creative tension of maintaining a consistent point of view lends a bracing clarity to Greene's style, as when Maurice remarks that he is 'back in the territory of trust' after reading Sarah's diary (Book 4, Ch. 1).

Greene is thus justified in congratulating himself on his novel's strengths as he does in *Ways of Escape*: 'There is much in the book I like—it seems to me more simple and clearly written than its predecessors and ingeniously constructed to avoid the tedium of the time sequence.'[26] If anything, though, these claims are too modest. Simplicity and clarity are the vehicles of a burning intensity of feeling, of hate and jealousy as well as love. And the brilliance of the novel's structure is an artistic embodiment of the difficulties of belief and not simply a craftsman's care for his readers' pleasure and interest. Sarah's diary and the letters scattered throughout the book ease one of the dilemmas of first-person narrative by giving the novel a density which may be absent when we see the world through only one pair of eyes. Sarah's claim that Maurice 'who thinks he hates . . . loves, loves all the time' (Book 3, Ch. 3) must be set against Maurice's opening statement that 'this is a record of hate far more than love' (Book 1, Ch. 1). A complex and truthful person, which Maurice is forced to be in his profession of writer, is more likely to present an unflattering portrait of the self than otherwise. To herself, for example, Sarah is a 'bitch and a fake' (Book 3, Ch. 3). And in the context of Bendrix's obsessional, almost Othello-like jealousy, it is salutary to take into account an unmentioned act of bravery on his part: 'I thought of a new scar on his shoulder that wouldn't have been there if once he hadn't tried to protect another man's body from a falling wall. He didn't tell me why he was in hospital those three days: Henry told me. That scar was part of his character as much as his jealousy' (Book 3, Ch. 5). This density is, however, more than a matter of seeing characters from different angles. To extend a point from a moment ago, it contributes to the sense of lives going on separately but in parallel, even when Greene is describing moments the characters share together. *The End of the Affair* generates an extraordinary poignancy and aesthetic pleasure from its playing off of the same scene from different perspectives, an extended example being the lunch Sarah and Maurice share after two years' separation. It is only possible to experience the full force of this effect in the flow of reading, but two brief quotations suggest something of its power. Sarah and Maurice are returning to the restaurant where they first dined together and which became 'theirs' as a result:

As you go up Maiden Lane on the left-hand side there is a doorway and a grating that we passed without a word to each other. After the first dinner, when I had questioned her about Henry's habits and she had warmed to my interest, I had kissed her there rather fumblingly on the way to the tube. I don't know why I did it, unless perhaps that image in the mirror had come into my mind, for I had no intention of making love to her: I had no particular intention even of looking her up again. She was too beautiful to excite me with the idea of accessibility. (Book 1, Ch. 5)

Fifty pages later, we encounter Sarah's version:

Had I broken that old promise lunching with Maurice? A year ago I would have thought so, but I don't think so now. I was very literal in those days because I was afraid, because I didn't know what it was all about, because I had no trust in love. We lunched at Rules and I was happy just being with him. Only for a little I was unhappy; saying good-bye above the grating I thought he was going to kiss me again, and I longed for it, and then a fit of coughing took me and the moment passed. I knew, as he walked away, he was thinking all kinds of untrue things and he was hurt by them, and I was hurt because he was hurt. (Book 3, Ch. 7)

The force of this technique lies chiefly, I think, in the peculiar intensity with which we assimilate the characters' experience. When we read of Sarah's longing to be kissed, our prior access to the situation removes the necessity for circumstantial detail.

The very flatness of her statement evokes our pity because we already know what has happened, although we now know even more in taking the full measure of her suffering. Greene achieves this effect with consummate ease despite the difficulty of bringing it off in the novel, where the writer runs the risk of his repetitions being merely mechanical. Greene may have learned something from Ford's *The Good Soldier* here, but it's worth noting that the technique can be achieved with great flexibility in the cinema. An outstanding example is Kurosawa's *Rashomon* which had its European première in the same year, 1951, as Greene published his novel.

Parallelism of this kind reinforces the reality of a world outside Maurice's head thus preventing the novel from degenerating into a monotonous and, for Greene, an ultimately unChristian subjectivism. This real world consists of a beautifully contrasted little group of characters who contribute to the novel's variety in a thematically functional manner: the literary reviewer, Waterbury, and his girlfriend; Sarah's mother, with her absurd mishearing of 'the Great Auk' for 'the Great All' (Book 5, Ch. 4); the disfigured rationalist, Smythe, and his sister; and the almost Dickensian pathos and humour of Parkis, the private detective, and his little boy. These characters form part of a setting which itself plays a key role in establishing the atmospheric context of Sarah and Maurice's relationship. Their love moves from the period of the so-called phoney war of 1939 through the violence of the London blitz—their sexual relationship ends as the result of a bomb attack—into the uneasy post-war years, a historical setting which allows Greene a fresh exploitation of his key word, peace. He acknowledges, in a fine passage, the difficulty of conveying happiness as compared to the 'sense of unhappiness:'

> But happiness annihilates us: we lose our identity. The words of human love have been used by the saints to describe their vision of God, and so, I suppose, we might use the terms of prayer, meditation, contemplation to explain the intensity of the love we feel for a woman. We too surrender memory, intellect, intelligence, and we too experience the deprivation, the *noche oscura*, and sometimes as a reward a kind of peace. The act of love itself has been described as the little death, and lovers sometimes

experience too the little peace. It is odd to find myself writing these phrases as though I loved what in fact I hate. . . . And yet there *was* this peace . . . (Book 2, Ch. 1)

The ironies of an actual peace and war as a metaphor for the violent alterations of feeling in this love relationship are clear enough, as in the sadness of Maurice's explanation of Sarah's dislike of his latest book, made at their reunion lunch: '"It was a struggle to write at all just then—Peace coming . . ." And I might just as well have said peace going.' (Book 1, Ch. 5)

The final test of the novel's complex artistry is, however, its relationship to belief. If artistry and belief are separable at this point, the novel falls apart in chaos, its ending an incredible mish-mash of miraculous events. What follows is an attempt to show that, even for the uncommitted reader, Greene succeeds in some of the appalling tasks he sets himself by refusing to violate the novel's form through crude manipulation of events. For a start, one can feel grateful that Greene didn't tamper with its length. In *Ways of Escape*, he explains that he lost interest in the book when only 'a philosophical theme was left behind' and that it should have been 'at least as long after her [Sarah's] death as before,' that coincidences were meant to continue over the years, battering Maurice into 'a reluctant doubt of his own atheism.'[27] Like the happy accident of Renoir's magical *Partie de Campagne*, whose filming was interrupted by the second world war, *The End of the Affair* has its own perfect economy of length. Greene's lack of interest is, in my view, the unconscious recognition that artistry had done its work and that only the spectre of didacticism remained. The novel has an artistic pattern which is, simultaneously, a pattern of belief, but this patterning is more often than not achieved with subtle unobtrusiveness. One of its truly painful little episodes is Maurice's badgering of Henry, Sarah's husband, after a horrible lunch at his horrible club. Maurice hands over a report of the detective agency's trailing of Sarah which Henry puts 'straight into the fire and rammed . . . home with the poker. I couldn't help thinking the gesture had dignity.' Outside, a tearful Henry has suddenly realised that Sarah and Bendrix were lovers and asks, '"Why didn't she leave me?" Had I got to instruct him about the character of his own wife? The poison was beginning to work in me again', a poison which finally oozes out in unforgivable cruelty:

> 'You pimped for me and you pimped for them, and now you are pimping for the latest one. The eternal pimp. Why don't you get angry, Henry?'
> 'I never knew.'
> 'You pimped with your ignorance. You pimped by never learning how to make love to her, so she had to look elsewhere. You pimped by giving opportunities . . . You pimped by being a bore and a fool, so now somebody who isn't a bore and a fool is playing about with her in Cedar Road.' (Book 2, Ch. 4)

Novels aren't written to facilitate critical discussion and so the formal brilliance of Greene's time shifting at this point makes ordered discussion difficult. The chapter ends with the only possible justification for Maurice's savagery, his passionate cry that he 'wanted love to go on and on, never to get less' which evokes Henry's quiet, 'It's not in human nature. One has to be satisfied . . . .'. This provokes Maurice's memory of 'the end of the whole "affair"' which follows in the next chapter, perhaps the most brilliant of all. But it is only much later, in Sarah's diary, that Maurice can see the full effects of his 'poison.' After following him to the pub, Sarah had decided that she must return to him, even at the expense of breaking her vow to God. She packs, writes a letter to Henry and is about to leave when Henry returns from his lunch with Bendrix. She discovers him crying and the sight of his misery ('If you don't see misery you don't believe in it' Book 4, Ch. 7) ends her resolution to live with Maurice. In terms of belief, we can interpret this as a punishment for Maurice's evil, but Greene's use of first-person narration ensures that it is conveyed without comment, while the distance between these contiguous events, through time-shifting, removes any hint of didacticism.

The heart of Greene's problem, as I see it, and a triumph of his artistry occurs in Chapter Two of Book Five which marks the 'end of the whole "affair"'. The central event, Maurice's supposed death, is structured within a beautifully cadenced opening and close. The chapter begins with a reference to the meeting with Sarah, after the absence of two years, which prompts their lunch date:

> She had said to me—they were nearly the last words I heard from her before she came dripping into the hall from her assignation— 'You needn't be so scared. Love doesn't end. Just because we don't see each other . . .'. She had already made her decision, though I didn't know it till next day, when the telephone presented nothing but the silent open mouth of somebody found dead. She said, 'My dear, my dear. People go on loving God, don't they, all their lives without seeing Him?'

It ends, '"You needn't be so scared," she said, "love doesn't end . . ."' and nearly two years pass before that meeting in the hall and, 'You?' After the explosion, Sarah comes downstairs and sees Maurice lying under the front door. Her response is 'I knew for certain you were dead' and the result is her prayer to 'anything that might exist' because 'When you are hopeless enough . . . you can pray for miracles. They happen, don't they, to the poor, and I was poor.'

One can only admire the courage of a writer attempting this kind of thing in the middle of the twentieth century. But Greene also has the artistry to make belief acceptable and the key to this seems to me to lie in the profoundly interesting passage which recounts Maurice's response to the explosion:

> As I ran down the stairs I heard the next robot coming over, and then the sudden waiting silence when the engine cut out. We hadn't yet had time to learn that that was the moment of risk, to get out of the line of glass, to lie flat. I never heard the explosion, and I woke after five seconds or five minutes in a changed world. I thought I was still on my feet and I was puzzled by the darkness: somebody seemed to be pressing a cold fist into my cheek and my mouth was salty with blood. My mind for a few minutes was clear of everything except a sense of tiredness as though I had been on a long journey. I had no memory at all of Sarah and I was completely free from anxiety, jealousy, insecurity, hate: my mind was a blank sheet on which somebody had just been on the point of writing a message of happiness. I felt sure that when my memory came back, the writing would continue and that I should be happy. (Book 2, Ch. 5)

Maurice's world is changed literally and, for a moment, metaphorically so that he is reborn into a sphere without 'jealousy, insecurity, hate,' a world with a potential for happiness that doesn't include sexual desire for Sarah. I felt it important at an earlier stage to stress the positive elements in Maurice and Sarah's sexuality because Greene himself celebrates them. But at this moment of extremity, created with a powerful economy of language, the reader is forced, whatever his personal views, to experience imaginatively with Maurice an alternative plane of being which embodies a positive escape from the entanglements of the physical. It is on the foundation of this artistically created belief in another mode of existence that the novel's later developments—securely to my mind—rest.

Greene is insistent that the 'miracles' which follow Sarah's conversion are all open to a 'completely natural explanation.'[28] To this end, he changed Smythe's affliction from a strawberry mark to spots in a later edition of the novel. These occurrences are open-ended and the reader is at liberty to make up his own mind on the matter. What I have attempted to show is that the novel is artistically unified and that questions of belief are not divisive of this unity. My final point is a return to Greene's respect for the real world. Whatever the poison of jealousy and hate in Maurice, his capacity to arouse the deepest levels of Sarah's potential for human love is inextricably bound up with her eventual love of God, as in the letter from her he receives after her death:

> 'I've caught belief like a disease. I've falled into belief like I fell in love. I've never loved before as I love you, and I've never believed in anything before as I believe now. I'm sure. I've never been sure before about anything. When you came in at the door with the blood on your face, I became sure. Once and for all. Even though I didn't know it at the time . . . I used to think I was sure about myself and what was right and wrong, and you taught me not be sure. You took away all my lies and self-deceptions like they clear a road of rubble for somebody to come along it, somebody of importance, and now he's come, but you cleared the way yourself. When you write you try to be exact and you taught me to want the truth, and you told me when I wasn't telling the truth. Do you really think that, you'd say, or do you only think

you think it? So you see it's all your fault, Maurice, it's all your fault. (Book 5, Ch. 1)

Belief could hardly pay a more moving tribute to the substantiality of the human world.

NOTES

1. 'Three Priests 1. The Oxford Chaplain,' *Collected Essays*, p.283.
2. 'Eric Gill,' *Ibid.*, p.262.
3. Johnstone, *op. cit.*, p.13.
4. James Joyce, *A Portrait of the Artist as a Young Man* (London: Jonathan Cape, illus. edn. 1956). p.257.
5. Martin Esslin, *Brecht: A Choice of Evils* (London: Eyre and Spottiswoode, 1959), p.204.
6. Wayne Booth, *The Rhetoric of Fiction* (Chicago University Press, 1961), pp.138, 141, 142, 139.
7. Johnstone, *op. cit.*, p.3.
8. WE, p.66.
9. *Ibid.*, p.64.
10. *Ibid.*, p.69.
11. OM, p.136.
12. *Little Dorrit*, Book the First, Ch. 6.
13. *The Lawless Roads*, p.114.
14. OM, p.143.
15. WE, p.65.
16. *Ibid.*, p.66.
17. *The Lawless Roads*, p.184.
18. Joyce, *op. cit.*, p.225.
19. WE, pp.92–3.
20. *Ibid.*, p.89.
21. *Ibid.*, p.92–3.
22. *Ibid.*, p.94.
23. Since the novel's division into books, parts, chapters and sections would make for clumsy referencing, page numbers following quotations refer to the Penguin edition (1971). This quotation is from p.196.
24. WE, p.94.
25. Emily Brontë, *Wuthering Heights*, Ch. 9.
26. WE, p.107.
27. *Ibid.*
28. *Ibid.*

CHAPTER FIVE

Fiction and Politics

SECTION A: *IT'S A BATTLEFIELD* AND *ENGLAND MADE ME*

It's a Battlefield (1934) and *England Made Me* (1935) reveal a
conflict inherent in discussing the output of a writer who is
both prolific and long-lived. Certain works may have an
interest, in relation to society or to the writer's development,
to some extent independent of critical judgement. These
novels are subjected legitimately to a merely descriptive
analysis by D.E.S. Maxwell in *Poets of the Thirties* and by
Richard Johnstone in *The Will to Believe*,[1]; legitimate because
Maxwell's centre of interest isn't fiction and Johnstone is
pursuing a thesis which doesn't stand or fall on the artistic
quality of the works he discusses. Coming so neatly in the
middle of the pre-war decade, both novels are clearly
important for anyone attempting to understand the literary
culture of the 1930s and they also mark a decisive change of
direction in Greene's career. After the success of his first
published novel, Greene plunged disastrously with *The Name
of Action* and *Rumour at Nightfall*. Although the first is set in
the 1920s, in Trier, both continue the vein of romantic
adventure characteristic of his first book; indeed, *Rumour at
Nightfall*'s setting of nineteenth-century Spain gives it an even
richer romantic colouring than *The Man Within*. Posterity, and
the contemporary reader, seem well served by their author's
steadfast refusal to have them reprinted. When Greene woke
to what he calls the 'worthlessness of all the work I had done
till then,'[2] it was to the contemporary world of unromantic
anxiety and deceit that he turned for the first of his
'entertainments', *Stamboul Train*. *It's a Battlefield* and *England*

116

Made Me continue this ruthless self-criticism, a remarkable change of direction for a young writer at the beginning of his career, by being located in the modern world, although without the support of the popular, thriller aspect of the earlier work.

These novels are important, then, for their place in Greene's career as a whole, but they also demand consideration as elements of a literature of the 1930s which is increasingly being seen to have significant differences from the preceding period of literary modernism. With his usual insight, Greene points to a major underlying cause of these differences:

> I think of those years between 1933 and 1937 as the middle years for my generation, clouded by the Depression in England . . . and by the rise of Hitler. It was impossible in those days not to be committed, and it is hard to recall the details of one private life as the enormous battlefield was prepared around us.[3]

Just as the Hungry Forties of the nineteenth century demanded the condition-of-England novel from the sensitively aware writer, so the events of the 1930s seem to have demanded some engagement with politics, in the widest sense, from those capable of giving a moment's consideration to events outside a purely private life. Despite Greene's disclaimer that the title of *It's a Battlefield* was intended to be 'ironic' rather than 'political',[4] there is every reason to regard it as a condition-of-England novel for its own time; *England Made Me* also belongs to this category despite its wider international setting.

Greene's later view of both novels is concerned to stress their private dimension. For him, the main theme of the first is 'the injustice of men's justice' while Krogh, the international industrialist of the second, is 'there only for the story:' the story, that is, of Kate and Anthony.[5] But while injustice is, at one point, given a universal dimension as inseparable from basic human processes ('it was as much a part of the body as age and inevitable disease', Ch. 2) it clearly has specific and local meanings: 'the laws were made by property owners in defence of property.' (Ch. 4) Dealing effectively with the theme of incest in a context of left-wing political sympathies and international intrigue is a tall order; the personal and the social are in danger of jarring disconcertingly. But if these novels have limitations, they also have a reach that exceeds their grasp of a private concentration on personal life.

The fictionalised debate on justice in *It's a Battlefield* turns on the conviction for murder of Jim Drover whose 'gentle obtuseness' (Ch. 1) doesn't prevent him from the defensive killing of a policeman who seems about to attack his wife at a political meeting that gets out of hand. His possible execution becomes a matter entirely of politics: whether his pardon would appear a sign of weakness to the 'Reds' or, alternatively, his death a cause of aggravation. In either case, 'it would cost the country fifty million. . . . More taxes and we lose the next election. What happens then? . . . No peerage for the Minister . . . . And no under-secretaryship for me.' (Ch. 1) The disarming frankness of the Minister's private secretary masks a ruthless juggling with human life which is reflected in Drover's respectably established brother, Conrad, when he thinks of shooting someone:

> But I've seen through that; you can't shame me any longer with a word like murderer; I know what a murderer is—Jim is a murderer. The law has told me that, impressed it on me through three long days, counsel have made expensive speeches on the point; six shopkeepers, three Civil Servants, two doctors, and a well-known co-respondent have discussed it together and come to that conclusion—Jim is a murderer, a murderer is Jim. Why shouldn't I be a murderer myself? (Ch. 3)

The sense of justice being manipulated from above links to the novel's pervasive sympathy for working-class people which it is impossible not to feel has the weight of authorial approval despite being filtered through the consciousness of individual characters. The Assistant Commissioner muses over 'the beauty of the young tinted faces' of girls passing in the street:

> Their owners handed over pennies for packets of fried chips, they stood in queues for the cheapest seats at the cinemas, and through the dust and dark and degradation they giggled and chattered like birds. They were poor, they were overworked, they had no

future, but they knew the right tilt of a béret, the correct shade of lipstick. . . . They are admirable, he thought. (Ch. 1)

Greene attempts to extend these responses into a structure that will justify his sympathy intellectually by giving it a foundation in analysis. Chapters One and Two, for example, equate the prison which houses Drover with the match factory which employs his sister-in-law, Kay Rimmer. Both contain three blocks (A, B and C) between which prisoners/workers are moved for good behaviour/improved skill: "'Of course if there's any complaint against them, they get shifted down. It's just like a school," the warder said. . . . In the courtyard the manager pointed. . . . "Everyone in Block C is a skilled employee. . . . Any serious mistake and they are moved back to Block B."' (Ch. 1) A lack of subtlety is evident here; more effective, partly because of its greater vividness of language, is a passage concerning influence and the old-boy network, which creates a 'world humming and vibrating with the pulling of wires.' (Ch. 2) And it is hard to disagree with Lady Caroline's description of the state of England:

> Do you believe in the way the country is organized? Do you believe that wages should run from thirty shillings a week to fifteen thousand a year, that a manual labourer should be paid less than a man who works with his brains? They are both indispensable, they both work the same hours, they are both dog-tired at the end of their day. Do you think I've the right to leave two hundred thousand pounds to anyone I like? (Ch. 5)

The novel's left-wing sympathies are, then, obvious, but its treatment of politics is complicated both by Greene's hostility to communism and by a degree of uncertainty in his artistic presentation of working-class characters. The attitude towards working people displayed in *It's a Battlefield* was commonplace among intellectuals of the 1930s, although nonetheless deeply felt for that. But while, for many, these sympathies led directly to an intellectual conviction that only Marxism could heal a Europe torn by the Depression and incipient war, such a solution was debarred to Greene by his religious convictions. Indeed it is hard to disagree with Richard Johnstone at this point: 'To write a novel at such a time pointing out the inadequacies of Communism as a belief was for a man of Greene's outlook a particularly courageous step.'[6] Greene's lack of belief in a purely material solution to England's, and Europe's, problems is no doubt one of the factors that led him towards the novel's horrifying conclusion. Drover is condemned to the living death of a life sentence by the 'mercy' shown him by the authorities while his wife, Millie, is robbed of Conrad Drover's love through his senseless extinction. The suffering involved in Conrad's death is evoked in language of great power, as his life ends on a note of total isolation:

> He never knew that he screamed in spite of his broken jaw; but with curious irrelevance, out of darkness, after they had left him and his pulses had ceased beating and he was dead, consciousness returned for a fraction of a second, as if his brain had been a hopelessly shattered mirror, of which one piece caught a passing light. He saw and his brain recorded the sight: twelve men lying uneasily in the public ward with wireless headpieces clamped across their ears, and a nurse reading under a lamp, and nobody beside his bed. (Ch. 5)

But if the impressiveness of the novel's final pages is rooted in Greene's disbelief in the goodness of a purely earthly order, this disbelief also leads him into a major artistic weakness in the creation of Mr Surrogate, the Communist Party intellectual from the upper classes. At this point, descriptive analysis must give way to a more rigorous weighing of actual achievement. Like some other critics, Francis L. Kunkel gives an adequate enough account of the confusions in Mr Surrogate's personality, but fails to ask some elementary questions about his aesthetic presentation.[7] The name itself, meaning substitute, could alert us to certain confusions in *It's a Battlefield*. Such allegorical naming of a single character in what is, on the whole, a realistically presented novel highlights some of the difficulties felt by the novelists of the 1930s in attempting to combine the fruits of modernism with a more socially oriented fiction. In several of his early books Greene attempts some 'experimental' writing. Here it takes the form of the montage in Chapter Three where a series of short paragraphs shifts us back and forth between a group of different characters and settings. Greene passes his own critical judgement on this kind of thing in its disappearance from his later work. Mr Surrogate is, in fact, a kind of Pecksniff wandering in a world which cannot accommodate him artistically. The uneasiness of tone that results is illustrated by the section in which he is seen preparing for a C.P. meeting. At one point, he discovers a mouse in his bookcase:

> "Poor little mouse." He thought of the great Russian novelist comforted in the Siberian prison by the nightly visitation of a mouse. "I too. The prison of this world," and his eyes filled with tears, withdrawing from *The Capital Levy* to gaze through the window at the lamps and the plane trees. He went to the sideboard and found a little bit of cheese.

It goes without saying that, as he leaves, this bourgeois revolutionary orders his servant to 'set a mousetrap by the bookcase.' (Ch. 2) Such broad strokes, reminiscent of Aldous Huxley's earlier satirical novels, are simply not Greene's forte. His attitude to character is too fundamentally serious for this kind of mockery and it is significant that the book's other characters, whatever their weaknesses, are treated quite differently.

At the C.P. meeting, which to Greene himself now 'lacks authenticity,' we are told that Mr Surrogate believes 'with complete sincerity that he would one day get into touch with the worker.' (Ch. 2) One can only feel that this is something Greene himself has failed to do artistically, whatever may have been the case in life, since the novel's working-class characters are frankly unbelievable. Perhaps the clearest example is Jim Drover's sister-in-law, Kay Rimmer. As a London factory girl she, presumably, occupies the lowest rung of the book's social ladder, a fact which makes her interior viewpoint and dialogue totally unconvincing. After a long day making matches, Kay debates whether to return home to comfort her sister or to go the C.P. meeting in the hope of some sexual excitement:

> Milly never liked Jim taking me to the meetings. Milly loved him. Milly was jealous. A cold wind swept the pavement,

bearing a scrap of silver paper from a chocolate box across the lamplight. Milly loved him. Kay Rimmer hugged herself for warmth and thought of love, her orange lips parted, her sister's misery fighting in her face with excitement, expectation, the touch of a man in darkness. . . . There was ferocity even in her tread, light and quick, like an animal pacing the cave-mouth in protection of its young. Milly loves him. But she flashed to the help of her happiness breathing with weak trust in the darkness. . . . They'll reprieve him. He isn't a murderer. (Ch. 2)

As with so many artists of the time—film-makers and composers as much as writers—no amount of good intentions can create the authentic rhythms of working-class conscious- ness. Greene's uneasiness is startlingly revealed in the incoherence of this writing. The simile comparing Kay with maternal protectiveness is inappropriate to a girl for whom a baby would be the result of having been 'caught'. And 'she flashed to the help of her happiness' is almost meaningless in its infelicity. In short, Kay is more like one of Waugh's bright young things than a London proletarian, as a paragraph of dialogue with Conrad reveals:

'Where've you been?'
'Enjoying myself,' she said . . . 'I'd better be off.' She was remembering the factory, the rattle of the boxes and the clangour of the machines.
'To-morrow's Sunday.'
'So it is. To-morrow,' she caressed the word and watched him with malicious amusement . . . .
'Why don't you go to bed?'
'Do you grudge a girl a little fun?'
'What do you mean?'
'You'd do it yourself if you could. . . . It makes a girl tired all the same, but thank God for men' (Ch. 3)

All of this is in striking contrast to Greene's sureness of touch in handling the idioms of a slightly seedy middle-class slang in *England Made Me*. An Orwellian note is struck early on in Anthony's possessing 'the shallow cheer of an advertise- ment' (Book 1, Ch. 1), a note continued in a stream of phrases which reflect his resemblance to a 'second-hand car which has been painted and polished to deceive' (Book 1, Ch. 1); 'thirty bob to the good' (Book 2, Ch. 2); "'I've been on my uppers before'" (Book 2, Ch. 3); "'Yours truly on the upgrade.'" (Book 3, Ch. 2) The other object, and user, of this saloon-bar lingo is the horribly convincing Minty who, before entering the General Post Office, 'parked his cigarette in a spot where a beggar was unlikely to find it' (Book 3, Ch. 1) and who goes to sleep, 'his body stretched doggo in the attitude of death' (Book 3, Ch. 5). This is Greene in the security of known territory, deploying its inhabitants' ghastly attempts at cheeriness with consummate ease. But he is after bigger fish than the dead-pan accuracy of dialogue and free indirect speech of this aspect of the book, a condition-of-England novel perhaps deeper than *It's a Battlefield* with its bias towards the surface of society. One sign of *England Made Me*'s ambitiousness and, ultimately, its partial failure lies in its division into three major segments which lack the integration of complete unity. For Greene himself the personal story of the unrecognised incestuous love of Kate and Anthony is the heart of the book. This is surrounded by the world of international high finance and through Minty, as a reinforcing figure to Anthony, Greene introduces the theme implied in the novel's title.

Greene is, of course, a marvellous inventor of titles, and a fascinating ambiguity haunts this one. Who is this surprisingly personal 'me'? Minty is an obvious candidate: 'Anthony looked back and England was again outside, keeping a watch on him . . . one bloodshot eye on each side of a tender branching iron plant' (Book 3, Ch. 2). But when we notice that Kate and Anthony's father was a 'little bit of England' (Book 2, Ch. 4) the hunt becomes satisfyingly wide-ranging. What Greene is attempting, in fact, is nothing less than an examination of the roots of Englishness below the surface of manners, although he conveys these deftly enough at the moment when the parents of Anthony's temporary girl-friend are introducing themselves:

'Ah,' the man said. He hesitated: 'We come from Coventry.' He was one of those men who are scrupulously fair in sharing information. He screwed his eyes up at her as if he were watching the movement of a delicate laboratory balance: another milligram was needed. 'Our name's Davidge.' His wife, a little behind him, nodded approval: the balance was correct. She sighed with relief at the delicate adjustment; she was able now to think of other things, to correct the set of her gown in the large mirror on the back wall, to tuck away a stray grey hair, to smooth her gloves, to hint with delicacy that they would soon be gone. (Book 1, Ch. 3)

The moral constipation of such an attitude to personal relationships is also amusingly present in the appalling letter Minty receives from his aunt after a silence of years. But deeper, and darker, currents run beneath this surface. Greene clearly wishes to suggest links between their background and Anthony's charming fecklessness, Kate's colder efficiency, and a capacity for love that finds expression only in their unacknowledged feelings for one another. Simultaneously, the fact that middle-class Englishness is a spent force is related to Krogh's internationalism: he "'doesn't think in frontiers'" but belongs to a world in which "'nationality's finished'" (Book 4, Ch. 3).

The separate items of this triangular relationship—incest, bourgeois England, international capitalism—are handled skilfully, but it remains doubtful whether Greene fuses them into a whole. Minty himself is a brilliant little creation with his cold coffee, fags sticking to his yellow lips and his habit of referring to himself in the third person. ('This is the way that Minty goes, Minty goes, Minty goes' Book 3, Ch. 1). And we understand perfectly how such a ghastly creature could have emerged from such a ghastly background. His 'passionless coition' with Harrow, an intercourse 'that leaves everything to regret, nothing to love, everything to hate' (Book 3, Ch. 3) is the paradigm of a life where human commitment is dodged in favour of an allegiance to forms, shows, institutions. Greene even casts a cold eye on religious belief in Minty's adherence to a faith without charity. But the attempt to develop a similar equation for the dark complexities of Kate and Anthony's emotions is a more difficult matter. As a given, the nature of their mutual involvement is an adequate metaphor for an England turned in on itself in a self-regard that is set for disaster. But in succumbing to the pressure of explanation, Greene becomes embroiled in rather unconvincing socio-psychological analysis, as in Kate's chapter of interior monologue, which begins with some reflections on her father:

> But these were his maxims. Do not show your feelings. Do not
> love immoderately. Be chaste, prudent, pay your debts. Don't
> buy on credit. 'Devoted' was too strong. On Mother's grave
> 'affectionate husband', he did not grudge five letters in the good
> cause of accuracy . . . Anthony learning (the beating in the
> nursery, the tears before boarding school) to keep a stiff upper
> lip, Anthony learning (the beating in the study when he brought
> home the smutty book with the pretty pictures) that you must
> honour other men's sisters. Anthony learning to love with
> moderation. Anthony in Aden, Anthony in Shanghai, Anthony
> farther away from me than he had ever been. (Book 2, Ch. 4)

In failing to get behind, or beyond, Kate's feelings for
Anthony, we are left with a relationship that harks back to the
earlier romantic fiction and so seems rather out of place in the
chromium and plate-glass world of Krogh's.

But, again taken in itself, this world is created with real
power, from its surface of the firm's costly avant-garde
headquarters (a 'cube of glass and steel' Book 2, Ch. 1) to its
underlying economic structure (the 'intricate network of
subsidiary companies . . . knitted together by his personal
credit.' Book 2, Ch. 1) However, here Greene is working in a
vein so richly mined by others that comparisons become
inevitable. It is hard to avoid the sensation that we have
encountered the Krogh 'who so obstinately . . . refused to
come alive'[9] in the person of the Merdle of Dickens's *Little
Dorrit*. His 'weariness and anxiety' combined with his
preoccupation with 'Money, figures, shares, morning till
night' (Book 2, Ch. 2); the wide range of those who invest in
him, from the English Minister to Lois's parents—all of this is
authentically Dickensian. Of course, these themes and
interests are carried forward into the modern world, but hardly
mark an advance on the profundity of their treatment in *Little
Dorrit*.

Dickens's novel may simply be a standard by which to judge
the fictional treatment of high finance, rather than a direct
influence on *England Made Me*. But there seems no question of
the literary indebtedness of *It's a Battlefield*. In *Ways of Escape*,
Greene suggests antecedents for some of the novel's characters

almost in the spirit of justifying his move from romance and antiquarianism to the world of living experience. Lady Caroline (Lady Ottoline Morrell), Mr Surrogate (John Middleton Murry), the Assistant Commissioner (an uncle) are admitted to, as it were, but without any hint that literature itself might have assisted in the transition. Nothing would be more natural, however, than for a young writer seeking a radical break in his apparently downward progress to turn to established masters for guidance. This seems unmistakeably true of the connections between *It's a Battlefield* and Conrad's *The Secret Agent*. Most obviously, they share a character in common, an Assistant Commissioner. Both are fish out of water and for similar reasons. Conrad's policeman's 'career had begun in a tropical colony' but, having married, he had turned to work in London where 'he felt himself dependent on too many subordinates and too many masters.'[10] Greene's, too, began work in 'Eastern forests' (Ch. 1) and feels himself badgered by superiors while he, in turn, badgers those below him. In the direct line of Dickens's Ferdinand Barnacle who tells Arthur Clennam 'You have no idea how many people want to be left alone,'[11] Conrad has his Toodles who guards his government Minister from exhausting encounters in the midst of his attempt to get a fishing industry bill through Parliament. Just as an 'inferior henchman' of 'that brute Cheeseman was up boring mercilessly a very thin House with some shamelessly cooked statistics' (Ch. 10) so Greene's Minister, who is embroiled in licensing, is being made to 'fight every inch of the way . . . . And he's never at his best when he misses his cup of tea.' (Ch. 1) If Conrad can borrow from Dickens, there's no reason in principle why Greene shouldn't borrow from Conrad, except that in this case the dependence seems a shade heavy. As well as Lady Ottoline Morrell, the other model for Greene's Lady Caroline is surely Conrad's 'lady patroness of Michaelis' (Ch. 6) and these borrowings also extend to some of Conrad's most important themes. Like Conrad's Assistant Commissioner, Greene's sees himself as a defender of civilisation, at least in its external forms:

It was something to realise that the defence of this city was in his hands; it was easy to imagine for a moment that its enemies were all outside, that evil did not naturally belong to this peace, this ease and contentment, that the death at Streatham was a successful foray from the country; but always he had only to turn and the yellow flag would be there, dangling in his rear. The war which he fought was a civil war; his enemies were not only the brutal and the depraved, but the very men he pitied, the men he wanted to help; if he had done his duty the unemployed man would have been arrested for begging. The buildings seemed to him then to lose a little of their dignity; the peace of Sunday in Pall Mall was like the peace which follows a massacre, a war of elimination; poverty here had been successfully contested, driven back on the one side towards Notting Hill, on the other towards Vauxhall. (Ch. 4)

And he makes sense of his life through the central dictum of the value of work of the Marlow of *Heart of Darkness*: 'The more one was alone, the more one clung to one's job, the only thing it was certainly right to do, the only human value valid for every change of government, and for every change of heart.' (Ch. 2) The sense of life's complexity in Greene's Assistant Commissioner is so great indeed, that he finds it 'impossible for a man to found his life on any higher motive than doing his job.' (Ch. 2)

These novels are, then, brave forays into a serious fiction which attempts to fuse personal and social concerns through themes with a strongly political bias, rather than total artistic successes. *It's a Battlefield*'s originality is sapped by an excessive dependence on, rather than the influence of, Conrad's *The Secret Agent* and its presentation of working-class life lacks conviction. *England Made me* is almost too rich in its deployment of three areas of interest which are insufficiently integrated. It is instructive to note that it was in Greene's next novel, the 'entertainment' *A Gun for Sale* (1936), that he achieved, if only in passing, a richer sense of the politics of ordinary living than we can find in the two preceding works. The threat of fascism is a constant in left-wing political thinking in the 1930s and incipient fascism is hinted at in *It's a Battlefield*, in an inside view of the improbable Jules Briton:

Jules thought . . . of the talk to which he was going. Men would

be making speeches to a late hour, reconstructing England in
theory, abolishing poverty on paper. He felt sullen and
dissatisfied as he turned the corner by the policeman and met the
man's amused glance. He wanted something he could follow with
passion, but Communism was talk and never action, and
patriotism puzzled him; he was not English and France meant
nothing but holy statues and Napoleon III, prostitutes and stolen
cigarettes. He wanted someone to say to him, 'Do this, Do that.
Go there.' He wanted to be saved from the counter and the tea
urn, the 'Weights' and the heartless flippancy of the café. (Ch. 2)

This insight remains unresolved, however, either in action or
in terms of the characters' development. But the medical
students' 'rag' which forms part of the exciting machinery of *A
Gun for Sale* is also used unobtrusively to create a sense of
disorder and violence by being presented through the
consciousness of those taking part:

> They were all having the hell of a time at the hospital. It was the
> biggest rag they'd had since the day of the street collection when
> they'd kidnapped old Piker and ran him to the edge of the Weevil and
> threatened to duck him if he didn't pay a ransom. Good old
> Fergusson, good old Buddy, was organizing it all . . . only five
> years ago there had been a scandal and an inquiry because a
> woman had died on the day of a rag. The surgeon attending her
> had been kidnapped and carried all over town dressed as Guy
> Fawkes. Luckily she wasn't a paying patient, and, though her
> husband had been hysterical at the inquest, the coroner had
> decided that one must make allowance for Youth. (Ch. 7,1)

The rag, is, in fact, a civil defence exercise, the students' part
in which is led by the oafish Buddy Fergusson, but it rapidly
takes on a quality of fascist street violence:

> Buddy was having the hell of a time. Everyone was scampering to
> obey his orders. He was the leader. They'd duck or pelt anyone he
> told them to. He had an enormous sense of power; it more than
> atoned for unsatisfactory examination results, for surgeons'
> sarcasms. . . . Like a great beast which is in need of exercise,
> which has fed on too much hay, Buddy Fergusson was aware of
> his body. He felt his biceps; he strained for action. . . . While
> they surged round him he imagined himself a leader of men. (Ch.
> 7,1)

One aim of the exercise is the practice of gas-mask drill, a purpose which allows Greene to invest the whole scene with a note of surrealist horror: 'They ran down the empty Tanneries, half a dozen masked monstrosities in white coats smutted with soot.' (Ch.7,1) The Hitchcockian climax of this strand of the novel's plot arrives when the hired killer, Raven, disappears into the mask he has taken from Buddy to wreak vengeance on those who had betrayed him. At this point we return firmly to the world of the thriller; indeed, many readers may never have left it, but Greene's ability to endow some passages of the novel with a level of political insight adds a richness that in no way impedes the forward drive of its action or the complications of its entertaining plot. This integration of politics, in the widest sense, with action will be a hallmark of Greene's later political fiction.

SECTION B: *THE QUIET AMERICAN*

One senses a note of pride in *The Other Man* when Greene says to his interviewer of *It's a Battlefield*, 'I do attack the government head on.'[12] Political currents run in his work from an early stage; it is fascinating that they should resurface at the point in his career marked by *The Quiet American* (1955). The years from 1938 to 1951 were a period of intense creative activity. After the comparatively minor shift of *Stamboul Train*, Greene moved direction radically with *Brighton Rock*, brought the entertainment to its highest level in *The Ministry of Fear* and crowned this stage of his achievement with three novels—*The Power and the Glory*, *The Heart of the Matter* and *The End of the Affair*—of remarkable intensity. It seems reasonable to suggest that something had been worked through during these years. For some, of course, they are the Catholic novels *par excellence*; put more generally, and taking the group as a whole, we might see them as metaphysical examinations of certain basic problems of the moral and spiritual life not bounded by a commitment to dogma. Despite the richness, sometimes exoticism, of their settings these works are distinguished by an inwardness, a preoccupation with the inner life embodied not infrequently with visionary power. The exhaustion of a creative vein, if not of the writer himself, could well be involved in such an effort, the end of a line which may have prompted a turning to more public themes for inspiration.

Written just after *The Quiet American*, although in the same year (1955), the little entertainment *Loser Takes All* is relevant here. Greene was clearly in search of relaxation, in life as well as art: the book was written, as well as set, in a luxury hotel in Monte Carlo. But a serious purpose is detectable also. In attempting to write 'an amusing, agreeably sentimental *novella*—something which neither my friends nor my enemies would expect' Greene hoped to explode his reputation, a facet of a professional writer's life which can be 'like a death mask. I wanted to smash the mask.'[13] My suggestion is that the attempt began, perhaps unconsciously, rather earlier, with *The Quiet American*; again, we can turn to biography for confirmation. For Greene, the 1950s were 'a period of great unrest . . . I was in that mood for escape which comes, I suppose, to most men in middle life' especially, one might add, after some years of intense creative effort. From this time on, Greene began his series of world-wide adventures, financed usually by journalism, which took him to some highly dangerous places in the attempt to 'regain the sense of insecurity which I had enjoyed in the three blitzes on London.' The source of *The Quiet American*, as far as setting is concerned at least, is to be found in the four winters, 1951–55, Greene spent in Vietnam covering the French colonial war for *The Sunday Times* and *Le Figaro*. Clairvoyance, or luck, were again on his side, for the experience enabled him to chart the point at which disaster for the French and greater involvement by the Americans fused in the drift towards the horrors of the American war in Vietnam.

In purely political terms, Greene has every reason to congratulate himself on his prescience in *The Quiet American*. A very recent, and authoratative, historical study has shown how close America came to a nuclear intervention in Indochina in 1954.[15] And the novel's detailed background material seems amply to justify the political aptness of Pyle's role in the book, although in a dedicatory disclaimer Greene says, 'This is a story and not a piece of history.' In *The Other Man* Greene admits that he 'would go to almost any length to put my feeble twig in the spokes of American foreign policy,'[16] a wheel that appears to be turning with ever greater rapidity if current events in Central America are anything to go by. In short, although Greene adopts a highly partisan position on such matters, evidence from outside *The Quiet American* can be brought to bear to reveal his grasp of at least some of the intricacies of international power politics. Indeed, one of the truly honorable aspects of Greene's career is this continuing thread of concern for the political and social, not just spiritual, plight of the world he inhabits, from the condition-of-England subject matter of the earlier books to the internationalist phase we can see beginning with *The Quiet American*.

However, as Greene himself says, what we are dealing with here is a 'story' and the criteria of artistic success are rather more exacting than whether or not Greene got things right about Indochina in the early 1950s—although I personally don't regard his ability to do so as negligible. And so perhaps I should say immediately that *The Quiet American* seems to me one of Greene's failures, a tired novel whose lack of life is revealed by its willingness to fall back on devices already successfully exploited in the immediately preceding work. For example, there is an extraordinary flatness in its dialogue, as this little exchange on the desolation of the town of Phat Diem shows:

> Little shops had already been set up below. I said, 'It's like an enormous fair, isn't it, but without one smiling face.' The priest said, 'They were terribly cold last night. We have to keep the monastery gates shut or they would swamp us.'
> 'You all keep warm in here?' I asked.
> 'Not very warm. And we would not have room for a tenth of them.' He went on, 'I know what you are thinking. But it is essential for some of us to keep well. We have the only hospital in Phat Diem, and our only nurses are these nuns.' (Part 1, Ch. 4,1)'

Such flabby writing is part of a general banality—Fowler's twice repeated, 'I hate war' merely prompts the thought that most of us do—which afflicts the book at almost every level. Scobie's eventual promotion in *The Heart of the Matter*, a revelation which provokes real pain, is reduced here to the double twist in the plot of Fowler's being allowed to stay on in

Indochina, combined with his wife's 'unexpected' agreement to instigate divorce proceedings so that Fowler can marry Phuong. Surprise is an important element in Greene's narrative technique, but these examples have the mechanical patness of the ending of a short story by O. Henry.

Characterisation is also far below the level of the preceding group of novels, the feeblest example being Phuong herself, the girl shared by Fowler and Pyle. Her foreignness, especially the difficulty of communicating with her in English, is possibly an attempt to disguise the weakness in her presentation, but the result is frankly appalling, an excursion into the world of Suzie Wong:

> 'Kiss me, Phuong.' She had no coquetry. She did at once what I asked and she went on with the story of the film. Just so she would have made love if I had asked her to, straight away, peeling off her trousers without question, and afterwards have taken up the thread of Mde Bompierre's story and the postmaster's predicament. (Part 2, Ch. 3,1)

A similar element of caricature pervades the creation of Pyle (his name, for Fowler, 'has got associations'), but without any sign that we are within a world of 'cruel comedy'[17] which would aesthetically justify such treatment. He may come to see the local people as 'childlike' (Part 4, Ch. 2,1), but Greene fails to make the connection that this is precisely how he himself presents Phuong. Again, even Pyle is not such a fool that we can accept his plaintive 'After all you are my best friend' (Part 2, Ch. 1,1) to Fowler as even faintly acceptable; nothing in the character, or in his relationship with Fowler, is sufficiently embodied to make such a claim anything but unbelieveable. Pyle is, of course, meant to be a simple, in the worst sense, personality, but simple characters can be presented in a complex manner; Pyle remains cardboard throughout. Fowler himself, in Greene's view, is the fruit of 'the two year's practice I had had in the use of the first person' in *The End of the Affair*. For once, Greene's acute estimate of his work has deserted him: he believes, incredibly, that *The Quiet American* is 'technically at least, perhaps a more successful book.'[18] But where artistry is shaped by intensity of feeling in the earlier work, in the latter it descends to the level of mere contrivance. Similarly, Bendrix's fear of losing Sarah and his quarrel with God are evoked in emotions of longing and violence presented in a host of memorable details. Fowler is clearly a doubting Thomas (his first name), but these doubts—about political commitment, his relationship with Phuong, of 'that Somebody in whom I didn't believe' (Part 2, Ch. 2,1) are a pale shadow of Bendrix's agonised convulsions of thought and feeling.

I've already suggested that the disappointments of *The Quiet American* may be the result of creative tiredness following a period of outstanding achievement. Another possibility is raised by the exchange provoked by Pyle's question to Fowler about his 'deepest sexual experience':

> I knew the answer to that. 'Lying in bed early one morning and watching a woman in a red dressing-gown brush her hair.'
> 'Joe said it was being in bed with a Chink and a negress at the same time.'
> 'I'd have thought that one up too when I was twenty.'
> 'Joe's fifty.'
> 'I wonder what mental age they gave him in the war.' (Part 2, Ch. 2,3)

It is almost painful to draw attention to such crudity; it is, fortunately, a rare phenomenon in Greene. The reader will need no reminding, or will have guessed, that Joe is an American. At one point Fowler talks to Pyle of 'European duplicity' (Part 2, Ch. 3,3) which suggests that the ghost of Henry James is hovering somewhere in the background, but Greene's attempt at an European-American conflict is a betrayal of the master he so reveres. For the delicate complexities of, say, *The Europeans*, Greene offers the most banal kind of America-baiting, although he tries to excuse it by a technical sleight-of-hand, Fowler's admission that he 'began—almost unconsciously—to run down everything that was American' (Part 3, Ch. 2,2) out of the self-hatred generated by his part in Pyle's death. Such special pleading seems to me, however, an aspect of that mechanical contrivance to which I've already referred. The novel is so permeated by attacks on American food, education, social habits, and the rest, that one can only believe that they stem from that 'revulsion' of Greene himself to which he confesses in *The Other Man*. He tries to shift the balance by creating some sympathy for Pyle's innocence in contrast to Fowler's cynicism through making Fowler refer to 'all I *thought* I hated in America' (Part 4, Ch. 2,3, my italics) and in attempting to evoke pity for the oafish Granger's sorrow over his son's illness. But the damage has been done by this stage in the book; the bitter taste of personal animosity is what remains in the mouth.

If *The Quiet American* is in some sense a political novel, this prejudice amounts to a failure in politics as well as in artistry. His early travel book on Mexico, *The Lawless Roads*, and parts of *The Other Man* and *Ways of Escape* reveal Greene's capacity to make thought-out criticisms of America. The earlier book has trenchant things to say about the spiritual blankness of a materialist society while the later ones show an acute grasp of America's imperialist role in international politics in the middle of the twentieth century, and at least some of these objections get into the novel itself. But the final impression left by *The Quiet American* is of an intelligent and creative mind subsiding into antagonism as a substitute for a reasoned and also an imaginatively worked out response to a political reality. This double weakness relates to what is probably the book's deepest source of failure, its use of 'more direct *reportage* . . . than in any other novel I have written.'[19] *The Quiet American*, unlike *The Power and the Glory* and *The Heart of the Matter*, makes use of Greene's personal experiences, rather than arising out of them. One sign of this is its descent into local colour, in the exotic detail of Phuong's preparation of Fowler's opium pipes, for example, and the travelogue-like descriptions of 'the gold of rice fields under a flat late sun.' (Part 1, Ch. 2,1) Comparison of the novel with the relevant sections of *Ways of Escape* shows how strongly fiction had to rely on reality in this case, but it also permits another, fascinating, point to emerge: the superiority of these sections, in their own style, to the novel itself. One feels that in *The Quiet American reportage* became a substitute for imagination, that Greene simply lacked the creative energy to work his way through to a new kind of novel and that this overall failure is mirrored in the weaknesses of detail to which I've already referred.

This novel might well have suggested that Greene's career had ground to a halt in the attempt to change direction, but the quality of the non-fictional writing contemporary with it, in *Ways of Escape*, is a clear indication of what we now know, that this career was far from over. Three examples will make the point: at one end of the scale, the little anecdote of how Greene and a friend tease 'Monsieur Dupont,' a policeman from the Sûreté, by getting him tipsy and luring him into a Chinese massage parlour; at the other, the 'doom-laden twenty-four hours . . . spent in Dien Bien Phu in January, 1954'; in between, is the richly textured detail of Greene's pleasurable obsession with opium.

The Dien Bien Phu episode is a masterly evocation, in only a few pages, of the tensions gripping those involved in the hopelessness of a modern colonial war, all summed up in one splendidly observed moment:

> One scene of evil augury comes back to my mind. We were drinking Colonel de Castries' excellent wine at lunch in the mess, and the colonel, who had the nervy histrionic features of an old-time actor, overheard the commandant of his artillery discussing with another officer the evacuation of the French post of Na-San during the last campaigning season. De Castries struck his fist on the table and cried out with a kind of Shakespearian hysteria, 'Be silent. I will not have Na-San mentioned in this mess. Na-San was a defensive post. This is an offensive one.' There was an uneasy silence until de Castries' second-in-command asked me whether I had seen Claudel's *Christophe Columbe* as I passed through Paris. (The officer who had mentioned Na-San was to shoot himself during the siege.)[20]

The keenness of Greene's eye for significant detail, in relation to tactical considerations on both sides, is revealed by his reference to the 'heavy fog, curiously not mentioned by either General Navarre or M. Laniel' (the soldier and the politician who engaged in a 'battle of words' through their respective books on the war): it 'filled the cup among the hills every night around ten, and it did not lift again before eleven in the morning. . . . During that period parachute supplies were impossible and it was equally impossible for planes from Hanoi to spot the enemy's guns.' In short, the French position could not be defended, but neither was there any need for their enemy, General Giap, to attack as he did:

> So the battle had to be fought with the maximum of human suffering and loss. M. Mendès-France, who had succeeded M. Laniel, needed his excuse for surrendering the north of Vietnam just as General Giap needed his spectacular victory by frontal assault before the forum of the Powers to commit Britain and America to a division of the country.[21]

If this is journalism, it is journalism of a very high order, shaped by a detailed grasp of historical and political realities.

In complete contrast is the wit and gaiety of Greene's journal record of his love-affair with opium. He adored the *ambiance* of what I suppose the puritan would have to call the opium den:

> The hard couch, the leather pillow like a brick—these stand for a certain austerity, the athleticism of pleasure, while the small lamp glowing on the face of the pipe-maker, as he kneads his little ball of brown gum over the flame until it bubbles and alters shape like a dream, the dimmed lights, the little chaste cups of unsweetened green tea, these stand for the '*luxe et volupté.*'[22]

And it would be hard to better the sheer fun of this description of a 'small wayside café': 'Immediately inside the door there was a large bed with a tumble of girls on it and one man emerging from the flurry. I caught sight of a face, a sleeve, a foot. We went through to the café and drank orangeade.' All of this writing is better than its equivalent in the novel. In fact the most fruitful use of this comparison between the work of fiction and the autobiography is the recognition that, although the deeper levels of imagination may have been out of reach in *The Quiet American*, Greene's writing was as fine as ever when it was freed from the problems of fictional creation. This is true even of the dream-world which is such an important part of Greene's private and writing life; *Ways of Escape* contains an extraordinary description of his meeting with the Devil, 'wearing a tweed motoring jacket and a deerstalker cap,' in a 'strange complete dream such as I have experienced only after opium.'[23]

Clearly, then, Greene possesses different levels of creativity. If, as I've suggested, *The Quiet American* is tired and lacklustre, writing contemporary with it sparkles with vivacity. But the novel does contain its own seed of future development, even if its embodiment is perfunctory, in the theme of the transformation of cynicism into commitment. This concern with engagement will bear fruit later on and so perhaps the most positive way to see *The Quiet American* is as the not very successful beginning of an important new phase of Greene's career.

SECTION C: *OUR MAN IN HAVANA*

Our Man in Havana (1958) highlights the problems involved in making a coherent examination of a fertile and complex novelistic career. There is clearly something arbitrary in cutting slices of the fictional cake into pieces labelled belief, politics, and so on. Although not so labelled by Greene, this novel might well, for example, take its place with the entertainments, given the delight it so richly engenders. Presumably the only entirely logical method of discussing a novelist's career would be a rigorously maintained chronological order. But such a treatment may obscure as much as it clarifies. The fact is that Greene has had certain predominant interests at certain points in his development which groupings of novels help to reveal. If such groupings are made with critical tact they may tell us something of the inner growth taking place beneath the apparently formless surface of everyday life, as well as advancing the critical understanding of specific works. Placing a book such as *Our Man in Havana* in its proper category may reveal an essential shade of emphasis crucial to its artistic success. This novel is indeed about politics, although in rather surprising ways. Despite Greene's radical leanings, it disappointed his anti-Batista friends because, in his own words, 'the object was not to talk about Cuba but to make fun of the Secret Service.'[24] The object is certainly splendid enough, especially when Greene's sense of farce is so richly deployed, but lurking behind it are themes which give the novel's comedy a seriousness beyond the reach of the entertainment as a limiting category.

Our Man in Havana clearly belongs to the same phase as *Loser Takes All* (1955), that of Greene's desire to smash the 'death mask' of his previous reputation, but this 'fantastic comedy'[25] is infinitely more suited to the task, in maturity as well as length, than the earlier, slighter work. *Our Man in Havana* is Greene's first novel in an extended comic vein and it triumphantly demonstrates the critical truism that comedy is every bit as serious a form as tragedy. Greene's previous attempt to break the mould, *The Quiet American*, is limp and lifeless whereas *Our Man In Havana* sparkles with vitality, a contrast which prompts one to try to account for the difference. One small sign of Greene's total involvement with a work is his use of a favourite device, absent from *The Quiet American*, of running motifs which make a series of richly interlocking patterns in *Our Man in Havana*. Hawthorne's phrase 'part of the drill', for example, recurs constantly, initially as a signal of how things are done in the Secret Service, but hardening gradually through mechanical, if comic, repetition into the formula of a life without love and spontaneity. Again, a popular song with the line 'My madness offends' is woven throughout the novel in ways which relate to the presentation and development of Wormald's character, the final emphasis occurring in the novel's last line. More important, perhaps, is a motif that counterpoints the book's surface of sparkling comedy and which reveals, yet again, Greene's penchant for the simile. The Secret Service chief in London has 'the appearance of an undertaker, just as the basement room had the effect of a vault, a mausoleum, a grave' (Part 1, 'Interlude in London'); at one point street lamps reveal the vacuum cleaners in Wormald's shop 'standing around like tombs' (Part 4, Ch. 1,i); again, Wormald watches Beatrice leaving his shop, moving 'away from the vacuum cleaners like a mourner in a cemetery' (Part 4, Ch. 1,iv). These motifs add density to Greene's writing, making the reader's involvement more complex than with *The Quiet American* by preparing us for the darkening of farce which occurs through the intrusion of death, above all that of Hasselbacher.

But comedy itself is central to a great part of the novel's success in a way that demands some detailed attention. The wonderful absurdity of the basic situation may well have acquired the authority of its imagined detail from being firmly rooted in the reality of a neutral Portugal in the second world war:

> There those Abwehr officers who had not been suborned already by our own service spent much of their time sending home completely erroneous reports based on information received from imaginary agents. It was a paying game, especially when expenses and bonuses were added to the cypher's salary, and a safe one.[26]

This farcical framework permits the delightful finale of Wormald's reward for services not rendered of a lecturing post and an O.B.E. while, on the way to this triumph, he is forced into such stratagems as basing his drawings of non-existent secret installations on vacuum cleaner parts and fobbing off the inquisitive Beatrice with linguistic fantasties (an imaginary spy's paunch has hurriedly to become "'ponch. It's the local dialect for squint'" (Part 3, Ch. 3,1). But in addition to these incidental felicities, Greene attempts three large-scale comic scenes: extracting the naked chorus girl from her night-club dressing room; Wormald's enforced interview with a bemused Professor Sanchez whom has claimed to H.Q. is one of his agents: and the attempt to poison Wormald at the lunch given by the European Trades Association. The last is, in fact, the best, a beautifully controlled set-piece which moves to its satisfying conclusion through a *tour-de-force* of comic detail. Greene makes hay of the setting's international flavour: the Germans who 'carried the superiority of the deutschmark on their features like duelling scars'; Mr Svenson with his 'dreary laugh like jollity in a long northern night'; Mr MacDougall going on energetically like a Scottish reel' although, such is the force of Wormald's suspicion, there seems something wrong with his 'Scottishness. It smelled of fraud like Ossian.' Some of Greene's favourite insights and uses of language surface here with new freshness. Even under the fear of death, Wormald feels it may be easier to risk that than ridicule, while a moment's kindness from MacDougall puts him 'back in the territory of trust.' A neat in-joke makes the apparently reassuring Carter (the killer, of course) come from Nottwich, the Nottingham of *A Gun For Sale*, while his surname is that of Greene's boyish tormentor from his schooldays. Having betrayed himself through his stammer, Wormald slips the whisky poisoned by Carter to a dachshund which soon collapses 'like a length of offal.' The whole absurd episode is rounded off with a paragraph of vividly precise comic writing:

> The tear-filled eyes so accused him of standing there alive while the dog was dead that he nearly found it in his heart to apologize, but instead he turned and went. At the end of the passage he looked back; the black figure knelt beside the black dog and the white chef stood above and the kitchen-hands waited, like mourners round a grave, carrying their troughs and mops and dishes like wreaths. My death, he thought, would have been more unobtrusive than this. (Part 5, Ch. 3,iii)

If Greene reached new heights of intensity in the cycle of novels beginning with *Brighton Rock*, *Our Man in Havana* reveals a comic gift of a very high order, comedy which acquires seriousness through its relationship both to a development in Wormald's character and to the book's use of a well thought-out contrastive theme. Wormald appears initially as anxiously middle-aged, harassed by small problems, a man who times even his mid-morning drink to the minute. Like a lighter version of Scobie, he is appalled by his responsibility for his daughter Millie, above all the maintenance of her Catholicism although he himself is agnostic, and trapped in a love made all the more intense by the memory of the Catholic wife who has left him. Imprisoned in a decaying Havana whose power cuts render his vacuum cleaners useless, and fearful of the attentions shown Millie by a local police chief, Captain Segura, Wormald daydreams that 'he has amassed savings, bearer-bonds and share-certificates, and that he was receiving a steady flow of dividends like the rich inhabitants of the Vedado suburb; then he would retire with Millie to England' (Part 1, Ch. 3,1). He is thus ripe for recruitment by Hawthorne, a spy-master from the London office, whose financial inducements promise escape from Cuba. Faced with the necessity of inventing a whole network of espionage, however, a vein of joyful irresponsibility surfaces from the depths of his personality, the irresponsibility of the ordinary man, Greene suggests, faced with the inhumanity of anonymous institutions. He is, in fact, irradiated by a kind of madness, a lunacy which Greene sees as the only properly human response to the howling absurdity of a world in which the activities of Hawthorne and his chief are taken seriously. The link with the popular song motif is clear, just as Carter's intended insult, 'You—you clown' (Part 5, Ch. 5,ii), uttered in the moments before Wormald kills him, connects with a passage that leads on to a discussion of the novel's contrastive theme. The clown seen by Wormald at the circus to which he took Millie was 'permanent, for his act never changed. That was the way to live; the clown was unaffected by the vagaries of public men and the enormous discoveries of the great' (Part 1, Ch. 3,iii)

If the change in Wormald's character is induced by his involvement in the absurdities of espionage, so comedy is inseparable from the novel's rich thematic scheme. A key word here (motifs proliferate) is 'real': Wormald's initial response to the almost unknown Beatrice is 'She looks real' (Part 3, Ch. 2,i); later, when they are in love, she implores Wormald to be careful by saying, 'I don't want you murdered. You see, you are real' (Part 5, Ch.3,i). With the lightest of touches the novel pursues the question of what is the true reality in which its characters live by way of a contrast between Wormald's daughter and the spy-master. For Wormald, what Millie says 'had a quality of sense; it was Hawthorne who belonged to the cruel and inexplicable world of childhood.' (Part 1, Ch. 4,ii) Both are enmeshed in 'fairy stories', but while Millie's belong to the humanly dignified world of religious belief, Hawthorne's are 'nightmares, grotesque stories out of science fiction' (Part 2, Ch. 3). This contrast between a girlish Millie whose concerns are the delightful stuff of ordinary living and Hawthorne's underlying allegiance to death and violence is carried through even in minute details. When Hawthorne's chief removes his black monocle in order to polish it, he discloses an eye 'made of glass; pale blue and unconvincing, it might have come out of a doll which said, "Mama"' (Book 1, 'Interlude in London'). He is thus assigned, even physically, to an infantile realm of activites which are meaningless and yet amply capable of inflicting suffering. The extinction of the innocent Dr Hasselbacher is the dark reverse of the farce of non-existent agents and deliberate misinformation. If Millie is child-like, then Hawthorne and his like are childish, playing with a fire which burns others not themselves. What is real for Wormald is his love for Millie and, eventually, Beatrice; the 'evening hour' (Part 1, Ch. 3,ii) when his daft activities, imaginary spying and selling vacuum cleaners, are over and ordinary living can be savoured; the dignified companionship of his friendship with Dr Hasselbacher. All this contrasts with the 'cruel' who 'come and go like cities and thrones and powers, leaving their ruins behind them.' (Part 1, Ch. 3,iii) and the motif is echoed in Hasselbacher's advice that Wormald should take the Secret Service money and lie in return:

> 'They don't deserve truth.'
> 'Whom do you mean by they?'
> 'Kingdoms, republics, powers.' (Part 2, Ch. 1,ii)

It should be clear by now that we have moved a long way from the pleasures of a superficial entertainment. *Our Man in Havana* is a 'fantastic comedy' by virtue of the richness of its language and the seriousness of its themes, clear signs of Greene's imaginative commitment. From being a figure of gentle fun, Wormald is brought to a point where he debates killing Carter in revenge for the murder of Dr Hasselbacher, an inner debate conducted in characteristically Greenian terms to the accompaniment of Beatrice and Millie chatting about make-up:

> He stood on the frontier of violence, a strange land he had never visited before; he had his passport in his hand. 'Profession: Spy.' 'Characteristic Features: Friendlessness.' 'Purpose of Visit: Murder.' No visa was required. His papers were in order.
>   And on this side of the border he heard the voices talking in the language he knew. (Part 5, Ch. 4,ii)

Wormald wants to kill Carter for a 'clean reason . . . because he killed Hasselbacher' and not for the great abstractions of

patriotism, communism, capitalism—the isms which so
clearly arouse Greene's suspicion. The actual assassination is
handled with splended aplomb. After struggling to maintain
his hatred in the face of Carter's pathetic ordinariness,
Wormald exults in having missed with his first shot; 'He had
proved conclusively to himself that he wasn't one of the
judges; he had no vocation for violence. Then Carter fired'
(Part 5, Ch. 5,ii). This chapter ending—Greenian suprise at
its best—leads us with painful suspense into the next to
discover the outcome, that Wormald killed finally in
self-defence. Shortly before he kills Carter, Wormald discovers
that he is beginning to fall into the Secret Service lingo so
characteristic of Hawthorne, a verbal sign of his momentary
corruption by the world of childish irresponsibility represented
by international espionage. But in Beatrice's terms, he has
become part of the 'Boys Own Paper world' for the 'world is
modelled after the popular magazines nowadays. My husband
came out of *Encounter*. The question we have to consider is to
which paper *they* belong' (Part 4, Ch. 1,i). In a media-soaked
universe, the forms of life arise from already existing models
rather than from the ebb and flow of spontaneous living.
Hawthorne and his chief, for example, move in the *ambiance* of
James Bond, although quite unselfconsciously, with their
stress on good living in food and clothes. Their unreality, in
the sense in which the novel examines the term, is stressed by
their total exclusion from an inner life. Even Captain Segura is
allowed a father who was tortured to death by a previous
generation of policemen, a personal fate which removes him
from the gallery of wax figures inhabited by the believers in
thrones and powers. His cruelty has a basis in his personal life
while theirs belongs to a bland placing of institutions before
people.

This sense of a world created at second hand through media
images leads into the novel's most amusing conceit, the nature
of Wormald's activity in creating an imaginary network of
spies. As early as *Stamboul Train*, we saw Greene playing with
reflexiveness in questioning the form of the popular novel from
within. Now he is ready for a full-scale treatment of the novel
within a novel. Greene prepares his thematic ground in many
subtle ways: a tipsy Dr Hasselbacher claims to invent a

character seen crouching dimly in a hotel bar ('I believe, therefore you are' Part 1, Ch. 4,1) while Hawthorne's chief has a 'literary imagination' (Book 1, 'Interlude in London') which transforms the mundane facts of Wormald's existence into what he wants to believe. More importantly, Greene suggests a creative element in Wormald through a passage which a first reading might dismiss as local colour, although critical antennae should quiver at the length of the extract Greene gives us from Wormald's yearly letter to a sister in Northampton:

> The light here is wonderful just before the sun goes down: a long trickle of gold and the seabirds are dark patches on the pewter swell. The big white statue in the Paseo which looks in daylight like Queen Victoria is a lump of ectoplasm now. The bootblacks have packed up their boxes under the arm-chairs in the pink colonnade; you sit high above the pavement as though on library-steps and rest your feet on the back of two little sea-horses in bronze that might have been brought here by a Phoenician. (Part 2, Ch. 2,11)

This is highly evocative writing but, if we avoid the trap of assuming that Greene himself is simply working off some impressions of Cuba, it reveals Wormald as a more complex and talented figure than we had hitherto suspected. The completely ordinary man we first think him would have accepted Dr Hasselbacher's advice and simply lied, or lied simply. For Wormald, however, plain, unvarnished lies are not enough. Like Falstaff in the Boar's Head scene of *Henry IV, Part I*, his lies are in excess of the practical requirements of his situation as when, one morning in his bath 'a creative moment had arrived and he paid no attention to the world beyond the steam. Raul had been dismissed by the Cubana airline for drunkenness. He was desperate; he was without a job; there had been an unpleasant interview with Captain Segura, who threatened . . .' (Part 3, Ch. 3,i). It might be fun to use Coleridge's distinction between fancy and imagination to contrast the spy chief's 'literary imagination' and Wormald's creative activity. The chief uses fancy to embellish an already existing reality while Wormald uses imagination to conjure a completely new reality into existence. He is astonished to discover how much he knows of the detail of his characters' lives and appalled, in true novelist fashion, by their ability to take on a life of their own. Greene twists the knife to dreadful comic effect, rather in the manner of *Six Characters in Search of an Author*, by having one, Raul, take on a death of his own as well. Wormald determines to put an end to H.Q's importunity in demanding aerial photographs of the imaginary platform building in the Oriente mountains by killing off the equally imaginary Raul, his pilot-spy. Horror is entwined with farce, however, because Wormald's unwitting involvement of Dr Hasselbacher leads to his death also, as well as that of a Raul who turns out to have a real existence.

The reality of Hasselbacher's death brings Wormald's creative fantasy to an end with its sickening reminder that it 'was time . . . to pack up and go and leave the ruins of Havana' (Part 5, Ch. 4,1) but not before many memorable examples of Greene's, and Wormald's, exuberant invention. Its randomness, and his love for Beatrice, give a special purity to this passage:

> Passing the Cathedral he gave his usual coin to the blind beggar who sat on the steps outside. Beatrice said, 'It seems almost worth while being blind in this sun.' The creative instinct stirred in Wormald. He said, 'You know, he's not really blind. He sees everything that goes on. . . . As a matter of fact he's one of my best informers. . . . He said slowly as the story grew of itself, 'The beggar's name is Miguel. He really does all this for love. You see, I saved his life once.' (Part 5, Ch. 1)

The benign spirit of Walter Mitty hovers over this, in Wormald's loving enjoyment of his own ridiculous elaboration, a love in every way similar, one feels, to Greene's own loving creation of *Our Man in Havana*. This playfulness, so different from the cruel games of Hawthorne, and mature enough to encompass real suffering, gives the novel a remarkable complexity of form as well as theme. Raul's death in Wormald's novel within the novel is mirrored by the 'real' death of Dr Hasselbacher. But both, like the play within the play of *Hamlet*, are creations of the writer's imagination.

Neither is real, in the simplistic sense, and yet for that very reason they may tell us something about a view of politics that is part of the novel's final achievement.

Greene's life is filled with what he calls his 'commitments,'[27] to small, endangered countries and, above all, to individuals. He reserves a special affection and respect for people who struggle for human rights and freedom against horrific dictatorships such as those of Haiti and pre-Castro Cuba. (It's worth noting his even-handedness in criticising human rights abuses in Castro's Cuba and also his condemnation of what he sees as the terrorism of the Provos in Northern Ireland.) The point needs to be made in order to grasp that Greene's revulsion from international power politics in *Our Man in Havana* is not the response of an ivory-towered intellectual, but that of a novelist who has frequently been as close to world affairs as a creative writer could hope to be. What such involvement leads to in this novel, however, is a politics of the personal life, an implied plea for corners of human experience to be kept free of the influence of kingdoms and thrones and powers. Dr Hasselbacher (a character reminiscent of the eponymous hero of Saul Bellow's *Mr Sammler's Plant*) surely has the weight of authorial endorsement in his advice to Wormald to 'dream more': 'Reality in our century is not something to be faced' (Part 1, Ch. 1,i). The vision at the heart of this 'fantastic comedy' is a profound distrust of power in any of its forms, as when Wormald, through his interrogation in a police station, 'began to realize what the criminal class knows so well, the impossibility of explaining anything to a man with power' (Part 2, Ch. 2,iii).

Such an apparently simple contrast between power and the individual runs the risk of sentimentality, a risk only avoidable if the conflict is embodied in totally convincing novelistic detail. That the possibly banal does live freshly is partly due to a quality in *Our Man in Havana* new in Greene's writing and of great importance for his later development, a tenderness in his attitude to his characters and in the feelings he creates in them for one another. The first version of the novel was written in the 1940s, its hero a 'more besotted character than Wormald'[28], and it is precisely the absence of this driven intensity that makes *Our Man in Havana* a touching as well as a funny and exciting experience. The moving delicacy of Wormald's feelings for his daughter is transferred to his love for Beatrice and the ordinary, but never humdrum, pleasure that they take in one another comes as something of a relief after the anguish of, say, *The End of the Affair*. The charge of sexual disgust levelled against Greene on the basis of such novels as *Brighton Rock* is thus seen to be one-sided. *Our Man in Havana* ushers in a phase where domestic happiness is both possible and worth celebrating. The phase will be interrupted by his next novel, *A Burnt-Out Case*, but it comes to a powerful fulfilment in *The Human Factor* (1978). *Our Man in Havana* smashes the death mask of reputation in more ways than one, then. It proves that Greene can write a deeply serious but also a gloriously funny comedy. It shows him guarding jealously the important privacies of human life from the incursions of a power which is often cruel and always irresponsible. Above all, he conveys his own delight in, and so makes us experience, the pleasures of friendship and the joy of love for people as ordinary, almost, as ourselves.

SECTION D: *THE COMEDIANS*

If Greene's second major period of creativity began disappointingly with *The Quiet American* in 1955, his next three novels testify to a variety of achievement that has lacked full recognition. The move from the splendid, and new found, comedy of *Our Man in Havana* to the pared-down intensity of *A Burnt-Out Case* is remarkable enough. With *The Comedians* (1966) Greene made yet another discovery, of an amplitude rare in his career. Greene has complained of a certain short-windedness in his writing, an inability to make a novel stretch to the requisite 80,000 words or a play last its two hours in the theatre.[29] If this leanness is any kind of limitation—for many readers it clearly isn't—rich amends are made by a ripe expansiveness in *The Comedians* completely at odds with the skeletal power of *A Burnt-Out Case*. The book has an almost nineteenth-century, Jamesian ease of effect despite the apparent didacticism of its genesis: '*The Comedians* is the only one of my books which I began with the intention of expressing a point of view and in order to fight—to fight the horror of Papa Doc's dictatorship.'[30] That Greene achieved this purpose is demonstrated by the vituperation heaped on him by Duvalier and his crew when the book appeared, but nothing could be further from a journalistic exposé than the effect of deeply meditated complexity Greene rises to here. One explanation may be that the horrors of Haiti didn't simply arouse the moral indignation of his conscious mind; Greene felt himself to be in danger on his last visit in 1963 so that fear 'must have penetrated deep into my unconscious . . . for years afterwards Port-au-Prince featured in my dreams. I would be back there incognito, afraid to be spotted.'[31]

Whatever its cause, this richness is to be found everywhere in the novel, in for example the dense clarity of the writing, well illustrated by the opening paragraph:

> When I think of all the grey memorials erected in London to equestrian generals, the heroes of old colonial wars, and to frock-coated politicans who are even more deeply forgotten, I can find no reason to mock the modest stone that commemorates Jones on the far side of the international road which he failed to cross in a country far from home, though I am not to this day absolutely sure of where, geographically speaking, Jones's home lay. At least he paid for the monument—however unwillingly— with his life, while the generals as a rule came home safe and paid, if at all, with the blood of their men, and as for the politicians—who cares for dead politicians sufficiently to remember with what issues they were identified? Free Trade is less interesting than an Ashanti war, though the London pigeons do not distinguish between the two. *Exegi Monumentum.* Whenever my rather bizarre business takes me north to Monte Cristi and I pass the stone, I feel a certain pride that my action helped to raise it.

Greene's perfect ease in the use of the first person singular, through which Brown is made to reveal every aspect of his character to us, is evident here. And something of the Jamesian quality I've referred to may also be felt in the confident complexity with which the book is opened out, its hints of mysteries to be revealed (Brown's 'bizarre business' and the cause of Jones's death), even in a certain absence of the colloquial in Brown's language which is accounted for by his Jesuit education. One small sign of Greene's confidence is his outrageous naming of three major characters Smith, Brown and Jones, especially given his own surname; this adds piquancy to his dedicatory denial that Brown is not Greene, or vice versa, and leads to some moments of delightful comedy, as well as the sense of a writer perfectly in command as he plays with the realistic and non-realistic elements of the fiction he is creating. Greene is also at the top of his bent in characterisation: Dr Magiot is memorably powerful and well contrasted with the funny-tender portrait of the former presidential candidate, Mr Smith, and the transformation of Jones's initial absurdity into something like heroism: these major figures are skilfully juxtaposed by the perfect cameos of Captain Concasseur and Petit Pierre. This faultless assurance is rounded off by the nightmarish power of the novel's setting, its masterly presentation of plot and the ease with which density is given to its handling of time by the insertion of flashbacks.

The density of texture I am trying to isolate is clearly illustrated by the little anecdote describing Brown's loss of virginity. Being assigned the part of Friar Lawrence in a college production of *Romeo and Juliet* gives Brown the idea of getting into the Casino at Monte Carlo; a winning streak leads to feminine company, a delicious tea at the Hotel de Paris and, by a 'gradation of events' Brown can no longer remember, to his seduction. The amusing little episode is, however, rounded off in a surprising manner:

> An odd thing happened as we lay on the bed. She was finding me shy, frightened, difficult. Her fingers had no success, even her lips had failed their office, when into the room suddenly, from the port below the hill, flew a seagull. For a moment the room seemed spanned by the length of the white wings. She gave an exclamation of dismay and retreated: it was she who was scared now. I put out a hand to reassure her. The bird came to rest on a chest below a gold-framed looking-glass and stood there regarding us on its long stilt-like legs. . . . My new friend trembled a little with her fear, and suddenly I found myself as firm as a man and I took her with such ease and confidence it was as though we had been lovers for a long time. Neither of us during those minutes saw the seafull go, although I shall always

think that I felt the current of its wings on my back as the bird
sailed out again towards the port and the bay. (Part 1, Ch. 3,1)

The unnerving strangeness of the moment is then balanced by
a return to the note of comedy when Brown's adventure, which
leads to his expulsion from the college, is discovered through
his inadvertently dropping a roulette-token in the collection-
bag at mass.

We have enough hints to justify a feeling that Brown's
earlier life is made up of such good stories, but he resists the
temptation to tell them with a Jamesian concern for form: 'I
would lose the proper proportions of my subject if I were to
recount every stage of my progress from the casino in Monte
Carlo to another casino in Port-au-Prince' (Part 1, Ch.3,2).
And even the experience we have just glanced at is not simply
a random slice of life; through its language it is woven into the
texture of the whole book by association with one of the richest
patterns of imagery that Greene has ever created. Before tea
and sympathy, Brown is taken into the lady's bathroom where
she helps him to remove his make-up: 'I saw Frère Laurent
disappear wrinkle by wrinkle in the mirror above the shelf
where lay her lotions, her eyebrow-pencils, her pots of
pomade. We might have been two actors sharing a dressing-
room' (Part 1, Ch. 3,1). That Brown and his lady should be
seen as players is linked to the generalising force of the novel's
title in its evident use in the archaic sense of actor rather than
simply funny man. One example makes the point clearly
enough, the moment when Brown finds difficulty in kissing
Martha because the 'corpse in the pool seemed to turn our
preoccupations into comedy. The corpse of Dr Philipot
belonged to a more tragic theme; we were only a sub-plot
affording a little light relief' (Part 1, Ch. 2). This theatrical
motif, worked out with consummate mastery, is of a richness
to preclude detailed discussion of all its appearances, which
range from references to *Hamlet*, *Othello* and *As You Like It*
through phrases such as 'curtain-raiser' (Part 3, Ch. 2,1) to
full-scale scenes such as the grotesque transformation of Jones
into a woman in order to escape detection by the Tontons
Macoute. Even Brown's hotel contains its John Barrymore
suite!

As the novel progresses, this pattern of imagery is displayed in an extraordinarily rich manner. Haiti, for example, is a stage where violence become a media performance as in the (true) incident where schoolchildren are taken to see the televising of a public execution, an event which is then repeated for a week on Haitian television sets. This theatre of cruelty finds its 'perfect spectator' in the British chargé d'affaires:

> The spectator of whom every actor must sometimes dream, intelligent, watchful, amused and critical in just the right way, a lesson he had learnt from having seen so many performances good and bad in indifferent plays. For some reason I thought of my mother's words to me, 'What part are you playing now?' I suppose I *was* playing a part—the part of an Englishman concerned over the fate of a fellow-countryman . . . I temporarily forgot the tangle of legs in the Peugot. I am quite sure that the chargé would have disapproved of my cuckolding a member of the diplomatic corps. The act belonged too closely to the theatre of farce. (Part 1, Ch. 4,2)

Haiti is a setting of monstrous degradation whose performers are instantly identifiable through their costumes: the Tontons Macoute in their black hats and dark glasses, the Voodoo figure of Baron Samedi, stalking graveyards, in his top hat, who by an easy transition becomes a public image of Duvalier himself; even the Voodoo ceremony which Brown attends loses its faint whiff of decorative local colour if it is seen as a ritual of theatrical horror, like the presence of the witches in *Macbeth*, which has its roots deep in Haiti's past. But Haiti is not simply an isolated nightmare. With craftsmanlike cunning, Greene makes Martha's German father a war criminal hanged during his country's post-war occupation, a revelation which prompts the reflection that 'Haiti was not an exception in a sane world: it was a small slice of everyday taken at random (Part 1, Ch. 5,2) so that, by extension, Greene's vision becomes a horrible version of 'All the world's a stage'.

Again, this image permits such ironies as the transformation of 'Major' Jones, a civilian involved in war-time entertainment for the troops, who is trapped by his boasting of guerilla warfare in Burma into joining the anti-Duvalier forces as a potential commander. Having been led by his own weakness and Brown's ambiguous promptings (he is jealous of Martha's relationship with Jones) into playing the part of a hero, he is farcically disabled by his flat feet. In the end, though unable to walk, he holds off the enemy so that Philipot and the others can escape and so, in the last moments of a life of constant role-playing, earns by his death the monument referred to in the novel's opening paragraph. If Jones only steps across the footlights just before his death, the book makes a fascinating distinction between actors and non-actors rather in the manner of James's *Washington Square* whose awkwardly direct heroine is hemmed in by a group of master comedians. I'm not suggesting that James is a direct inspiration here, although we know how importantly he looms for Greene, but rather that *The Comedians* deserves the compliment of being understood in relation to a work of the master. Martha, Brown's mistress, belongs to the line of Greene's heroines (Sarah of *The End of the Affair* and Beatrice of *Our Man in Havana* come to mind) who are seen as 'real'. At one point she breaks out at Brown, Philipot and her husband that *she* is no comedian; her ghastly child, Angel, is ill and the smell of his vomit is still on her hands because she is 'not acting any part. I do something.' Brown agrees when he thinks of her after their affair is over (the novel is a recollection of events in the past): 'She played no part.' And yet back in the present, as it were, he is appalled by her ability to disguise her feelings from her husband at a moment when they have been trying to make love, especially as he 'played my part less well; there was a dryness in my voice which betrayed anxiety' (Part 1, Ch. 5,2). This duplicity doesn't cancel Martha's directness, but it clearly extends our awareness of the complexities of character and behaviour in a penetrating manner.

This hint of ambiguity is, however, absent from the wonderful portrayal of Mr Smith, the presidential candidate who stood against Truman in one state on the vegetarian ticket. Greene's delicate fusion of comedy and tenderness here prompts some thoughts on the special qualities of the popular writer. It is well known that Dickens was especially responsive to the demands of his huge public and that, with no compromise to his artistic integrity, he would on occasion change aspects of his work that seemed offensive or faulty to his readers. He changed the character of the dwarfish Miss Mowcher in *David Copperfield*, for example, in the course of writing the novel, in response to complaints from the lady on whom the figure was partly based. And the saintly Jew, Riah, of *Our Mutual Friend* seems almost like amends for the Fagin of so many years earlier. Similarly, although there's no direct evidence for the point, Mr Smith might be thought of as an apology for the virulent anti-Americanism of *The Quiet American*. Nothing may have been further from Greene's thoughts than this supposition, but if it has any substance at all it suggests one of the most positive features of the good popular writer, a sense of responsibility towards his large and varied audience. In any event, Mr Smith is the 'genuine article, if ever there was one' (Part 1, Ch. 1,1) with 'a continent of difference' (Part 3, Ch. 4,2) between himself and his unpleasant compatriot, Mr Schuyler Wilson. The Smiths as a couple are neatly differentiated in the wife's fierce protectiveness of the gentler husband, but together they make a formidable impression of unsentimental goodness and strength. Just as Jane Austen's irony flickers around all her characters, even the morally superior, with a humanising intention so the smiles provoked by the Smiths' vegetarian fanaticism—their horrible Barmene and Yeastrol—give them the density of real life rather than the attenuation of fictional sainthood. But their good qualities are never in doubt: their physical courage in the face of the comic nightmare of the Tontons Macoute's destruction of Dr Philipot's funeral; Mr Smith's cunning in a good cause which is perfectly compatible with his being born 'with peace in his heart instead of the splinter of ice' (Part 3, Ch 2,5); above all, their mutual loyalty and love which Greene embodies in one of his tenderest moments as they plan to leave Haiti with a sense of failure after the televised executions:

> 'Perhaps we seem rather comic figures to you, Mr Brown.'
> 'Not comic,' I said with sincerity, 'heroic.'
> 'Oh, we're not made at all in *that* mould. I'll say good night to you, Mr Brown, now, if you'll excuse me. I'm feeling kind of exhausted this evening.'

'It was very hot and damp in the city,' Mrs Smith explained, and she touched his hair again as though she were touching some tissue of great value. (Part 2, Ch. 2,3)

In one of the connections with earlier work characteristic of Greene's career, we can see similarities between the Smiths and the puritanical, but kindly, German-American brother and sister who succour the whisky priest in *The Power and the Glory*. But the Smiths are a more complex portrait. They may seek to drive out passion with vegetarianism, and their childlessness is remarked on, but Greene draws a careful distinction between passion and love in showing how the Smiths' lives are suffused with the second. Nor is their love simply an inward-looking emotion; at one point Brown awaits with trepidation the formidable Mrs Smith's response to his adulterous affair with Martha, but she takes it completely in her stride.

A link also exists with the previous book, *A Burnt-Out Case*, on the question of the kinds and nature of belief; this time, however, examining belief in relation to politics rather than religion. The novel's positive characters—Martha, the Smiths, Dr Magiot—draw moral sustenance from a belief in something outside themselves, although it is worth noting that in no case does this come from religion. Martha believes in her love for her child and for Brown, until he destroys it through jealousy; the Smiths believe in their mission to do good in the world; Dr Magiot believes 'in certain economic laws' (Part 2, Ch. 1,5). The novel deals with political questions largely at a personal level, resolving them into the problem of involvement which it clearly illustrated by an exchange between Brown and Mr Smith:

'I wonder if we ought to involve ourselves any further.'
'We *are* involved,' said Mr Smith with pride, and I knew that he was thinking in the big terms I could not recognize, like Mankind, Justice, the Pursuit of Happiness. It was not for nothing that he had been a presidential candidate. (Part 1, Ch. 4,4)

Mr Smith's solemnity provokes a smile, but there is no doubt that we are meant to take his asseveration seriously which becomes rather suprising if we look back for a moment to *Our Man in Havana* where disengagement was presented as a supreme value. We need to remember, of course, that Greene deliberately chose to treat Battista's Cuba in a light-hearted manner in order to prevent his farcical vision of the Secret Service colliding with seriousness. In the face of its absurd and, ultimately, cruel inhumanity, preservation of the self and the private life becomes a major responsibility. The nature of Haiti, on the other hand, in reality and in Greene's presentation of it, is such that retreat into a private life is impossible. Through its hideous agents, the Tontons Macoute, the régime's evil pervades the recesses of private experience. But if Greene has no consistent fictional view of politics this is neither suprising nor blameworthy. The touch of pride with which he mentions his own personal commitment is entirely justified; Greene is outstanding among contemporary writers for his devotion to politically threatened countries and people, above all in the area of human rights, sometimes at the risk of personal danger. In art, on the other hand, he plays variations on the theme of politics, exploring possibilities although with an underlying devotion to the individual that never weakens.

The Comedians plays *its* variation around the duality of action and acting, with the central actor in the comedy the narrator himself, Brown. Nothing establishes the fact that Brown is not Greene more clearly than the former's complete rootlessness as a 'citizen of Monaco.' Greene is utterly rooted in Berkhamsted, even to the sly faces of its inhabitants, while Brown can 'feel no link at all with the hundred or so square kilometres around the gardens and boulevards of Monte Carlo' (Part 3, Ch. 1,2). The emptiness of his background is compounded by his claim that 'somewhere years ago I had forgotten how to be involved in anything' (Part 2, Ch. 2,1), but we need to remember at this point that Brown is very much a created character whose statements about himself must not be taken completely on trust. He remarks on how strangely we must appear to others and it is clear that some of the novel's characters see things in him that he is unaware of. Dr Magiot's friendship is itself a recognition of some kind of distinction and it is hard to know how Brown could have evoked Martha's love, Mr Smith's respect and Joseph's loyalty if he were quite as empty as he believes himself to be. Brown feels shame before the humility of Pineda's tacit admission of his relationship with his wife, Martha ('It was as though he were apologizing to me and proffering me humbly his passport—Nationality: human being. Special peculiarities: cuckold' Part 3, Ch. 1,1). And there is something deeply positive in his capacity for the loving admiration evoked in him by Mr Smith and, above all, Dr Magiot. Despite his own age, it is clear that these older figures answer to Brown's psychological need for the father he has never known, a need made explicit on Dr Magiot's death, but not one which is merely obsessive. The fineness of its recipients testifies to a fineness in Brown himself. And although he ultimately destroys his love for Martha (a passing reference to Othello and Desdemona helps to enforce the reasons) there are moments when his commitment is strong enough to enable him to pass out of himself into absorption with another.

Brown's climactic role in the 'casual comedy' is enacted with all of Greene's characteristic ambiguity. Hatred and disgust at the Haitian régime—Joseph's limp is an ever-present reminder to him, and us, of the barbarities of the Tontons Macoute—fuse with sympathy for the young Philipot and his desire to topple Papa Doc. Jones's boasting of his military background, which Brown genuinely half believes in, appear to make him a natural leader for the rebels, and it is after all the revered Dr Magiot who suggests that he might be trapped by these claims. But Greenian motives are never uncomplicated; Jones's refuge in the embassy and consequent proximity to Martha lead Brown into paroxysms of jealousy as ridiculously inappropriate as those of Othello, so that the removal of his supposed rival becomes at least as important to him as assisting the rebels. Brown risks a great deal in the cause, even torture and death at the hands of Captain Concasseur; the nature of the cause itself, however, remains decidedly questionable.

But despite the novel's uncertain outcome with Jones and Dr Magiot dead, Philipot and his pathetically small band interned in a former lunatic asylum in Dominica, Papa Doc still in command and, on the personal level, the end of

Brown's affair with Martha, Greene is not content to leave us in a morass of ambiguity. His own commitment—political and religious—is powerfully embodied in the brief sermon preached by a young priest at the Mass for Joseph and the others killed under Jones's leadership. Greene dramatises the moment by having Mr Smith shake 'his head sorrowfully: it was not a sermon that appealed to him. There was in it too much of the acidity of human passion' (Part 3, Ch. 4,4) but it seems clear that our sympathies are meant to lie with those who are, in the priest's words, 'moved to violence by the suffering of others.' This is no blanket acceptance on Greene's part: I have already referred to how *The Other Man* makes clear his distinction between freedom fighters and terrorists. But it is difficult to feel that violence is philosophically or morally wrong if it rids the world of a Papa Doc and the suffering he imposed on an entire country. Certainly the extinction of Captain Concasseur and his henchman leaves us no more moved than I believe Shakespeare intends us to be at the deaths of Goneril and Regan in *King Lear*.

Balancing the radicalism of the Roman Catholic church with which Greene is so obviously in sympathy is the rock-like certainty of Dr Magiot, whose political convictions are inseparable from his humanity as a doctor and so the very reverse of fanatical. In his dignity and reserve, Dr Magiot belongs to a by-gone age—his home is almost Victorian in its sense of the past—an amusing reminder that Marx's theories were formulated in Victorian Britain. And Greene's sympathetic creation of the Smiths strengthens all the more the novel's criticism of an American imperialism which can drive a Dr Magiot into the arms of Marx as a refuge from a western world whose values seem totally inverted. Greene is not content in *The Comedians* to leave these political questions at the level of debate through dialogue. He renders them concrete in several memorable scenes, perhaps most strongly in Smith and Brown's visit to Duvalierville (Haiti's Brazilia) and Mr Smith's scattering of his money just before he leaves Haiti a disappointed man. The trip to the unfinished capital city in the company of the crooked Minister for Social Welfare is both wildly funny and a damning indictment of the misuse of misapplied western aid by corrupt régimes:

> Even the sea had receded out of sight; there was nothing
> anywhere but the great cockpit, the cement field, the dust, the
> road, and the stony hillside. Outside one of the white boxes a
> negro with white hair sat on a hard chair under a sign that
> showed him to be a justice of the peace. He was the only human
> being in sight—he must have had a lot of influence to be
> installed so soon. There was no sign of men working, though a
> bulldozer stood on the cement-playground with one wheel
> detached. (Part 2, Ch. 1,3)

This eerily empty landscape is inhabited also by its hideously
deformed beggar with 'very long arms and no legs' who moves
'like a rocking horse.' Mr Smith gives him a tip, but as the
party drives away Brown sees 'the justice of the peace . . .
running fast on long loping legs . . . and the cripple . . .
rocking back with desperation towards the cockpit; he
reminded me of a sand-crab scuttling to its hole. He had only
another twenty yards to go, but he hadn't a chance' (Part 2,
Ch. 1,3). Those who have seen Bunuel's *Los Olvidados* will
recognise instantly the element of surrealist horror in both
works, a horror rooted not in personal obsession but in social
injustice of almost unimaginable proportions.

Beggars of a Bosch-like monstrosity are a motif throughout
the novel, exploding into action most fearfully at the moment
when Mr Smith empties his wife's purse of its Haitian gourdes
and American dollars in the square before the post-office:

> 'For God's sake,' I said. One or two of the beggars gave high
> unnerving screams: I saw Hamit standing amazed at the door of
> his shop. The red light of evening turned the pools and mud the
> colour of laterite. The last money was scattered, and the police
> began to close in on their prey. Men with two legs kicked down
> men with one, men with two arms grasped those who were
> armless by their torsos and threw them to the ground. (Part 2,
> Ch. 3,1)

The scene is a perfect fictional image of a wider political
reality: the charitable Mr Smith scatters his money with the
best of intentions, but this leads merely to a struggle which
encapsulates the worst horrors of an horrific society. Moments
such as these, realised with a totally artistic attention to detail,

justify the few more generalised statements of the problem, as in Dr Magiot's bet to Brown that 'in a matter of months, relations are healed and the American ambassador returns:'

> You forget—Papa Doc is against Communism. There will be no Cuba and no Bay of Pigs here. Of course there are other reasons. Papa Doc's lobbyist in Washington is the lobbyist for certain American-owned mills (they grind grey flour for the people out of imported surplus-wheat—it is astonishing how much money can be made out of the poorest of the poor with a little ingenuity). And then there's the great beef-racket. The poor here can eat meat no more than they can eat cake, so I suppose they don't suffer when all the beef that exists goes to the American market—it doesn't matter to the importers that there are no standards here of cattle-raising—it goes into tins for underdeveloped countries paid for by American aid, of course. It wouldn't affect the Americans if this trade ceased, but it would affect the particular Washington politican who receives one cent for every pound exported. (Part 3, Ch. 2,2)

The Comedians, if not a political novel, is certainly a novel that happens to be about politics in the richest sense; that is, a work which dramatises a passionate outrage at the misuses of power in character, dialogue and action so that we are led with a seeming inevitability towards a political insight, led all the more firmly because of a complete absence of hectoring. Rather in the manner of Bertolucci's *Novecento* we are made to see how the evils of a cruel dictatorship penetrate to the innermost recesses of personal relations. In Bertolucci's film, the attempted reconciliation between husband and wife is wrecked by the monstrous murder of a woman impaled on railings; at a moment just before he fails to make love to Martha, Brown is 'reminded of Dr Philipot's body under the diving board: birth, love and death in their positions closely resemble each other' (Part 1, Ch. 5,2). This interpenetration of the private and public is a masterly achievement in which Greene balances dark comedy and something like tragedy with perfect ease. Dr Magiot's entry into the 'dignified and disciplined ranks' of death leaves Brown in a desolation evoked in some of Greene's finest prose:

I had left involvement behind me, I was certain, in the College of the Visitation: I had dropped it like the roulette-token in the offertory. I had felt myself not merely incapable of love—many are incapable of that, but even of guilt. There were no heights and no abysses in my world—I saw myself on a great plain, walking and walking on the interminable flats. Once I might have taken a different direction, but it was too late now. (Part 3, Ch.4,4)

And the pain of a life beyond amendment is, if anything, intensified by the novel's climactic return to sad laughter in Brown's dream, of Jones trying to remember the lines of his part, which is interrupted by the telephone's 'summoning . . . me to my first assignment'—in Mr Fernandez's undertaking business (Part 3, Ch. 4,4).

NOTES

1. D.E.S. Maxwell, *Poets of the Thirties*, (London: Routledge and Kegan Paul, 1969) and Johnstone, *op. cit.*
2. SL, p.151.
3. WE, p.29.
4. *Ibid.*, p.28.
5. *Ibid.*, pp.28 and 30.
6. Johnstone, *op. cit.*, p.67.
7. Kunkel, *op. cit.*, Ch. 2.
8. WE, p.28.
9. *Ibid.*, p.30.
10. Joseph Conrad, *The Secret Agent* Ch. 5.References to Greene's novels will be given in brackets following quotations.
11. *Little Dorrit*, Book the Second, Ch. 28.
12. OM, p.90.
13. WE, p.167.
14. *Ibid.*, pp.109–10.
15. See John Prados, *The Sky Would Fall. Operation Vulture: The U.S. Bombing Mission in Indo-China, 1954* (New York: Dial, 1983).
16. OM, p.93.
17. WE, p.94.
18. *Ibid.*, p.108.
19. *Ibid.*, p.129.
20. *Ibid.*, p.140.
21. *Ibid.*, p.142.

22. *Ibid.*, p.131.
23. WE, pp.136–7.
24. OM, p.59.
25. WE, p.185.
26. *Ibid.*, p.183.
27. OM, p.60.
28. WE, p.184.
29. *Ibid.*, p.178.
30. OM, p.80.
31. WE, p.206.

CHAPTER SIX

A Burnt-Out Case

As does *Brighton Rock, A Burnt-Out Case* (1961) demands a chapter to itself. Chronologically and thematically it appears to stand outside even the very loose classifications offered by this book. Greene himself is at pains to stress the novel's 'new elements' and believes that it 'marked a turning-point in my work . . . in it I think I succeeded . . . in breaking the pattern in the carpet.'[1] However, this shift is not quite so straightforward as Greene suggests. I have argued that *Our Man in Havana* represents a change of direction in both its comedy and in the tenderness with which it treats human relationships. But, such is the inconvenience of creative writers to critics, this new tone is hardly apparent in the next novel, not at any rate at its artistic centre, the character and situation of Querry. Comedy is present in the savage treatment of Ryker and Parkinson, although of a decidedly dark kind, and there is tenderness perhaps around the edges of the book, in the innocent gaiety of the priests and in what we infer of Dr Colin's relationship with his now dead wife.

So there is continuity as well as development here, and possibly the most interesting link with *Our Man in Havana* is the extension of Greene's creative response to the role of the media in the modern world and, within this, the special place of the serious writer. Personal experience is, once again, relevant to our understanding of the work of art. After what he calls the 'great vulgar' success of *The Heart of the Matter*,[2] Greene was transformed into a public figure, at the mercy of intrusions into his life of every possible kind. This characteristic process of modern civilisation is bound to be trivialising, invariably ignoring the complexities of creative work itself in favour of gossip and personality. Many years ago, the *Daily*

Express newspaper found it necessary to tell its no doubt bemused readers that the once, it its view, monkishly reclusive T.S. Eliot was now taking dancing lessons; a photograph of an equally bemused Mr Eliot was intended to validate his new-found joy in the pleasures of the ordinary man. A favourite target for this colour-supplement treatment was Picasso whose 'life-style' was clearly grist to the mill of bourgeois fantasies of *la vie de Bohème*. The process, dependent on such technological advances as photography and widespread newspaper distribution, began at least as early as the middle of the nineteenth century, one of its first victim-beneficiaries being Dickens. The extraordinary popular success of *The Pickwick Papers* was partly a media event in its own day and led to a whole range of commercial 'spin-offs' in the shape of clothes modelled on those of Dickens's characters, pottery figures, engravings, and so on. Dickens's attitude to all this was clearly much more ambiguous than Greene's; whatever its irritations, he gloried in what he saw as an almost personal involvement with a huge audience. But he was nonetheless public property and so vulnerable to a whole range of demands. Perhaps the most insistent were begging-letters, a source of exasperation in life which Dickens transforms into a great comic fantasy of importunity in the novels. When Greene found himself translated instantly into a Catholic author by the success of *The Heart of the Matter*, he was deluged by letters demanding spiritual comfort (and, on occasion, something more) by hosts of people, above all priests and women, a dilemma transformed into hilariously bitter comedy in *Ways of Escape*. But whatever the laughter this induces in the reader, it was obviously no joke for the recipient. Greene felt himself 'used and exhausted by the victims of religion,' maddened by 'cries for spiritual assistance' in the face of which he felt impotent.[3]

Some of this sense of a world moulded by press and publicity gets into *Our Man in Havana*. In *A Burnt-Out Case*, however, truly savage reprisals are taken against its agents and abettors. The grotesquely fat journalist, Parkinson, draws a vampire-like sustenance from his three million readers of the *Post* which makes him believe that he can manipulate Querry's reputation at will: 'I told you I was going to build you up.

. . . Unless . . . I find it makes a better story to pull you down.' (Part 6, Ch. 2,2). And Greene parodies his yellow-press style with consummate ease, from his muddled use of Conrad's *Heart of Darkness* to his picture of Querry as a St Francis with '"birds shitting in your hair"' (Part 4, Ch. 3,2). But the novel moves beyond this wickedly accurate caricature to reveal how media distortion has its roots in the media-distortions of 'ordinary' life. It is worth quoting at some length Ryker's (the local factory manager) response to Querry's arrival, probably Greene's most repellently critical portrait of a Roman Catholic:

> "In my opinion . . . he may well be the greatest thing to happen in Africa since Schweitzer, and Schweitzer after all is a Protestant. I found him a most interesting companion when he stayed with us. And have you heard the latest story? . . . He went out into the bush two weeks ago, they say, to find a leper who had run away. He spent the whole night with him in the forest, arguing and praying, and he persuaded the man to return and complete his treatment. It rained in the night and the man was sick with fever, so he covered him with his body. (Part 3, Ch. 1,1)

This is language emptied of all personal content, used not in the service of thought and feeling, but as a mould that will force Querry's actions into some preconceived pattern regardless of his own motives or intentions. Just as his wife's romantic, and ultimately disastrous, fantasies are embodied in the language of her women's magazine, *Chantal*, so Ryker's speech and vision of the world are taken from the works of popular theology in which he is so immersed. Spontaneous living is thus nullified by a betrayal of language which instantly hardens it into a series of meaningless gestures and moral clichés.

There is evidently an element of corrosive self-criticism at work here. Parkinson is like a grotesque parody of Greene's journalistic activities, dragging his huge bulk into dangerous places in search of a story while he fires off his absurdly wrongly attributed quotations. With brilliant wit, Greene presents him as the apostle and martyr of a new faith, that three million readers of the *Post* cannot be wrong. His

Remington portable and Rolleiflex camera are placed like the first and second thief on either side of Father Thomas's crucifix and, when he complains of what he has suffered in the cause—'Three times in a restaurant somebody hit me.'—for 'a moment he sounded like St Paul' (Part 6, Ch. 2,2). The cruelly comic deflation of Parkinson is apt and just, but deeper issues are raised also. Parkinson is a user, or misuser, of language, the same medium as that of the novelist, and his apparently widely accepted corruption of the medium of communication between human beings casts doubt on the novelist's ability to rehabilitate the language of the tribe. Perhaps three million readers of the *Post* can't be wrong. However mistakenly, Greene seems to have felt himself to be a part of this debilitating process for he writes of *The Heart of the Matter*, with cruel self-condemnation, that there 'must have been something corrupt there, for the book appealed too often to weak elements in its readers.'[4] The problem is clarified by a passage from *Our Man in Havana* when Beatrice and Wormald sit watching a pornographic film, a 'blue print of love. Similar movements of the body had once meant more to them than anything else the world had to offer. The act of lust and the act of love are the same' (Book 4, Ch. 1,2). The language of the body and the language of words have this much in common, that their outer identity may clothe entirely different feelings and motives. But although the physical movements which express love and lust are the same, it might be argued that the differences between Parkinson's writing and Greene's are obvious enough. Greene, however, refuses to let himself off so lightly at this stage in his career. The crisis engendered by *The Heart of the Matter* was a matter of style in a radically serious sense and he was made agonisingly aware of the pitfalls into which a false style might lure the unwary. My own view is that it is wrong to blame aspirin for the use that fools make of it, but one must admire the sense of responsibility towards his readers, and his craft, revealed in Greene's fear that his novel had proved a spiritual morass for those of uncertain faith.

That these preoccupations were in the forefront of his mind in the period leading up to *A Burnt-Out Case* is demonstrated by his return to Conrad after abandoning him 'about 1932 because his influence on me was too great and too disastrous.'

As he re-reads *Heart of Darkness* on his own journey upriver Conrad's 'heavy hypnotic style falls round me again, and I am aware of the poverty of my own.'[5] Again, the judgement is cruelly harsh, even allowing for Greene's lapses into banal local colour, the over-use of simile, the sometimes mechanical reliance on key words such as 'peace'. But out of this harshness Greene reaps a rich reward, both for *A Burnt-Out Case* and for his later work. His next novel, *The Comedians*, will command a rich expansiveness quite without padding or decoration, but for *A Burnt-Out Case* a kind of stylistic purity seemed perhaps the only way to meet the challenge of human suffering on a plane of complete seriousness. Greene's fertility of invention is remarkable here, for the novel's theme and subject-matter might have suggested a return to the visionary intensity of the period beginning with *Brighton Rock*. Instead of his harking back, however, Greene discovers a totally new manner which answers perfectly to the note he wants to strike in this work. Despite the circumstances surrounding its genesis, there is none of the exhaustion so evident in *The Quiet American*. The burnt-out quality present throughout the novel is, in fact, a telling embodiment of the state of mind and feeling, or absence of feeling, that Greene is seeking to convey.

Querry's, and Greene's, journey is an inner one, a voyage to the interior of the self in a Congo which is a 'region of the mind' (Dedication) and so any hint of mere exoticism in the writing would be totally out of place. Instead of this, setting is touched in only lightly:

> White flowers had opened with twilight on the long avenue; fires were being lit for the evening meal, and the mercy of darkness was falling at last over the ugly and the deformed. The wrangles of the night had not yet begun, and peace was there, something you could touch like a petal or smell like wood smoke. Querry said to Colin, 'You know I am happy here.' He closed his mouth on the phrase too late; it had escaped him on the sweet evening air like an admission. (Part 4, Ch. 2,1)

This delicacy comes from a writer who complains of the poverty of his style! And its sparse beauty is characteristic of every aspect of the novel. The setting is rigorously limited, with just enough trips away from the *leproserie* to avoid monotony. Language is spare, supple, free of clogging adjectives, and similes seem to float naturally to the surface of Greene's prose rather than being snatched from some storehouse of strained comparisons: 'Every rib in the child's body showed. It was like a cage over which a dark cloth has been flung at night to keep a bird asleep, and like a bird his breath moved under the cloth' (Part 2, Ch. 3,1). Characterisation is deft and sure-footed. Dr Colin is beautifully realised through dialogue and action, with only occasional shifts into his point of view, and the sparseness of our information about him in no way impedes his sense of life. Even Querry lacks the tortured complexity of, say, Scobie. His pain is the pain of being unable to feel and his 'case' is fairly straightforward.

This achieved simplicity is, however, the very reverse of simple-minded. Greene made his journey with a novel already beginning to form in his consciousness and the processes lying behind its full realisation are recorded in 'Congo Journal' with an interest, excitement even, that gives the reader an awareness of the joys, as well as the trials, of creation. The journeyings here are manifold: Querry's and Greene's literal and metaphorical journeys, the exploration represented by the completed novel, and then the voyage into the creative process itself experienced through 'Congo Journal'. One moment in this last journey has a peculiar intensity of interest, Greene's discovery of the 'fit' between the novel's various elements, above all between Querry and the setting:

> Leprosy cases whose disease has been arrested and cured only after the loss of fingers or toes are known as burnt-out cases. This is the parallel I have been seeking between my character X and the lepers. Psychologically and morally he has been burnt-out.[6]

Here perhaps one can find an explanation of how the book's pared-down quality is perfectly compatible with various kinds of complexity. The complete fusion of character, setting, theme and language allows a richness and intensity of meaning to arise with unforced naturalness. This intensity, too, has its own special quality in the novel. Intensity may stem from the fusion of levels we find in, say *The Heart of the Matter* and *The*

End of the Affair. The intensity of *A Burnt-Out Case* comes from a stripping away of the surface elements of human life in order to reveal a bedrock of character and theme.

This burning away of inessentials, to put it another way, suggests that Greene's fictional mode here is, in yet another new development, essentially allegorical and many features of the novel substantiate this. Taking a perhaps unconscious hint from Conrad's Kurtz, Greene worries in 'Congo Journey' over the necessity of naming his central character because he is 'unwilling to give him a definite nationality.'[7] The problem is neatly solved in the novel itself: '"My name is Querry," he introduced himself, speaking in an accent which Colin could not quite place as French or Flemish any more than he could immediately identify the nationality of the name' (Part 1, Ch. 2,1). In thus loosing his protagonist at such an early stage from the moorings of realism, Greene opens the way to a voyage of inner exploration through a figure with more than a hint of Everyman. The arresting oddity of his name also pushes one towards an allegorical reading: 'query' and 'quest' come irrestistibly to mind. There's an element of risk and daring here which surely justifies Greene's belief that the novel contains 'new elements.' Another example is the mysterious Pendélé which echoes so strangely throughout the book. We're deeply familiar by now with the importance of 'peace' in Greene's imaginative vocabulary. It's often identifed with a generalised state of being, sometimes it is located in early childhood, but never before has it borne a specific name with its implied avowal of the possibility of an actual place of peace. Querry hears it first when he journeys into the forest in search of Deo Gratias, an experience which he later feels 'seemed a night when things began': 'Deo Gratias grunted twice, and uttered a word. It sounded like "Pendélé". In the darkness the knuckles felt like a rock that has been eroded for years by the weather' (Part 1, Ch. 4,1). The whole episode is a perfect little exemplar of the novel's general method. It is completely acceptable on the realistic level; Deo Gratias falls into a hole and Querry, in whom interest 'began to move painfully . . . like a nerve that has been frozen' (Part 1, Ch. 4,1), goes to look for him. But an allegorical quest fits easily with the vividly realised little adventure just as Deo Gratias's fingerless hand has a rock-like quality completely in keeping with the novel's attempt to reach down to solid foundations. Querry evokes a Pendélé for Marie Ryker, of the simplicities of her family life as an unmarried girl, and dreams of sailing to it himself by going even deeper into the jungle than the *leproserie*, just before his peace of mind is destroyed by Parkinson's newspaper article on him. But Querry's tragedy is that he was clearly in the process of finding his Pendélé within the *leproserie* itself. 'Nouse étions heureux', says Deo Gratias in reply to Querry's questioning about the past he was evidently seeking to rediscover when he was lost and injured in the jungle, and Querry's own admissions of growing contentment, peace, happiness even, suggest that his Pendélé was around him if he could have remained safe from the intrusions of Parkinson, the agent of the gossip column and media publicity.

Yet another allegorical feature is suggested by Greene's Dedication to the doctor of the Yonda Missions where he stayed while gathering material for the novel:

> This is not a *roman à clef*, but an attempt to give dramatic expression to various types of belief, half-belief, and non-belief, in the kind of setting, removed from world-politics and household-preoccupations, where such differences are felt acutely and find expression.

This pin-points the book's element of metaphysical discussion which emerges through its series of fascinating exchanges between Querry, Dr Colin, the Superior, Ryker, and so on. Greene skilfully avoids the dangers inherent in fictional debate: one thinks of those achingly long pages of discussion in *The Magic Mountain* or Stephen's disquisition on aesthetics to Cranly at the end of *A Portrait of the Artist as a Young Man*. Greene's exchanges are pithy without being superficial and they gain complexity from their unforced relationship to a perfectly chosen setting. The characters' arguments about God's existence and nature take place in a context which is both a test of belief and a justification for unbelief for, as we are unobtrusively reminded, they frequently occur within sight of monstrous human suffering. A passage quite early in the book demonstrates a compassion with neither sentimentality nor voyeurism:

> The air in the hospital lay heavily and sweetly upon them: it was never moved by a fan or a breeze. Querry was conscious of the squalor of the bedding—cleanliness was not important to the leper, only to the healthy. The patients brought their own mattresses which they had probably possessed for a lifetime—rough sacking from which the straw had escaped. The bandaged feet lay in the straw like ill-wrapped packages of meat. On the veranda the walking cases sat out of the sun—if you could call a walking case a man who, when he moved, had to support his huge swollen testicles with both hands. A woman with palsied eyelids who could not close her eyes or even blink sat in a patch of shade out of the merciless light. A man without fingers nursed a baby on his knee, and another man lay flat on the veranda with one breast long and drooping and teated like a woman's. (Part 2, Ch. 3,1)

In this context, theological discussion is the reverse of academic, honed to a cutting edge by the implacable presence of the outer limits of human misery.

But however strong the allegorical emphasis of *A Burnt-Out Case*, its meanings are finally worked through in the life of a central personality, Querry, although here too the allegorical mode shapes Greene's characterisation. Querry has gone so far down the road of human nullity that his regeneration is marked not by a melodramatic transformation, but by the simplest evidence of what it means to be human, conveyed in fictional motifs of naked simplicity. Querry detests 'laughter like a bad smell' (Part 1, Ch.1,2) and is, in fact, physically incapable of laughing or even smiling. His capacity for feeling is frozen; as it thaws he begins to develop a 'twitch of the mouth that Colin was beginning to recognize as a rudimentary smile' (Part 4, Ch. 1,1). This most basic form of human communication—we see the baby's smile as one of the first signs of its developing humanity—becomes possible as the atrophied nerves of Querry's emotions and interest in others begin to flicker into life. Greene's art succeeds triumphantly in this area of potential banality by convincing us that the change, simple as it appears, is momentous for Querry. And the danger of over-simplification is avoided by the irony that his new-found capacity for laughter is the direct cause of his death when the murderously jealous Ryker interprets Querry's 'odd awkward sound' (Part 6, Ch. 3,5) as directed at himself.

Given that *A Burnt-Out Case* is such a relatively short novel, Greene is remarkably successful in suggesting the passage of time and, with it, a series of worked-out and believable changes in Querry's character. This is partly achieved by a skilful manipulation of memory, centering on an opposition between discomfort and suffering. Towards the end of the book Querry remarks to Dr Colin '"I suffer, therefore I am." I wrote something like that once in my diary, but I can't remember what or when, and the word wasn't "suffer"' (Part 6, Ch. 3,3). What he did write, in the novel's first sentence, was 'a parody of Descartes: "I feel discomfort, therefore I am alive." ' Discomfort is entirely personal, of course; an itch, an ache, a bad smell are powerful reminders of the self, capable of distracting us from the beauty of art, nature, another person. Suffering, on the other hand, can hardly be entirely egotistical. However self-pitying we may be, suffering brings us inescapably into relation with others, either in what is done to us or in what we do. Querry believes that his moral and spiritual mutilation has gone so far that suffering is impossible for him and asks Dr Colin to teach him how to suffer because 'I only know the mosquito-bites' (Part 5, Ch. 1). Again, this is an echo from something much earlier when the Superior of a mission had remarked, in response to Querry's admission of emotional deadness, 'Oh well, you know, suffering is something which will always be provided when it is required' (Part 1, Ch. 1,2). Querry learns to feel suffering again through the awakening of his personal interest in Deo Gratias, as well as in the general plight of the lepers, but the context in which this is achieved is, once more, crucial. Paradoxically, Querry finds suffering through the peace of the mission. The atheist Dr Colin and the Catholic priests are united in one thing, their overriding involvement in bettering the lepers' existence. Their lives are so dominated by practicalities that they have no time or inclination to badger Querry with either pleas for help or spiritual enquiries. In short, they leave him in peace and this, all unwittingly, becomes a therapy through which

Querry is able to feel his way back into human concerns; a peace threatened and ultimately destroyed by the pestering intrusions of the media-dominated outer world in the person of Parkinson with his determination to turn Querry into the Hermit of the Congo.

Mention of Parkinson returns us to those themes of writing, publicity, gossip and the role of the novelist with which I began and which may help us to see an important link between the novel and Greene's own life. Greene clearly dreads the simple-minded reader's equation of a central character with himself; indeed, one of his most frequently repeated admonitions concerns the necessity of making an absolute separation between author and protagonist. This makes all the more interesting an admission which occurs in a fascinating exchange of letters with Evelyn Waugh recorded in *Ways of Escape*:

> With a writer of your genius and insight I certainly would not attempt to hide behind the time-old gag that an author can never be identified with his characters. Of course in some of Querry's reactions there are reactions of mine, just as in some of Fowler's reactions in *The Quiet American* there are reactions of mine. I suppose the points where an author is in agreement with his character lend what force or warmth there is to the expression. At the same time I think one can say that a parallel must not be drawn all down the line and not necessarily to the conclusion of the line. Fowler, I hope, was a more jealous man than I am, and Querry, I fear, was a better man than I am. I wanted to give expression to various states or modes of belief and unbelief.[8]

The justness of these comments is undeniable and in no way negates the writer/character dichotomy. Eliot's separation of the man who suffers and the writer who creates was surely a stratagem to obscure the personal suffering that lay behind *The Waste Land* rather than a critical dictum of universal value. Can anyone seriously believe that Shakespeare was in a totally equable frame of mind when he wrote *King Lear*? This no more equates Shakespeare with Lear than it does Greene with Querry; rather, it reminds us of a balance of forces necessary for the creation of art. The Turkish-bath of total subjectivism and the icy chill of complete objectivity are equally undesirable.

Personal feeling dramatised in character, image and action is the hallmark of good literature. At any rate, all the evidence suggests that it is this combination that makes *A Burnt-Out Case* such a powerful book.

As with Wormald in *Our Man in Havana*, we are reminded of similarities between Querry and the novelist, sometimes by Querry himself:

> 'A writer doesn't write for his readers, does he? Yet he has to take elementary precautions all the same to make them comfortable. My interest was in space, light, proportion. New materials interested me only in the effect they might have on those three. . . . Materials are the architect's plot. They are not his motive for work. . . . The subject of a novel is not the plot. Who remembers what happened to Lucien de Rubempré in the end? (Part 2, Ch. 3,1)

But these hints of similarity are, finally, only a preparation for the extraordinary 'parable' he recounts to Marie Ryker to pass a sleepless night. The allegorical mode is successfully dominant at this point, in Greene's reliance on a device which seems to echo the interpolated tales of eighteenth and nineteenth-century fiction and which encapsulates his theme with a directness barred to the realist, despite Querry's built-in denial of an autobiographical interest: 'No, you mustn't draw close parallels. They always say a novelist chooses from his general experience of life, not from special facts' (Part 6, Ch. 1,2). The underlying seriousness of this astonishing episode in no way inhibits its brilliance. At one point, Querry accuses Marie of being 'like so many critics. You want me to write your own sort of story', a moment at which Greene's personal exasperation with his own critics surfaces with mordant relish. When Querry's protagonist ceases to believe in the King (God, of course) he fashions exquisite objects for frivolous and morally doubtful purposes, but this makes no difference to the judges of his work who see moral seriousness ('"satires on the age"') despite the protagonist's intentions. Intentionality is a key aspect of the parable, in fact, as it is of *A Burnt-Out Case* itself. In their different ways, Parkinson and Father Thomas totally disregard Querry's motives in coming to the Congo; indeed, there is something maddening in the perversity with which they ignore the reality of his existence in their determination to shape it for their own purposes. The novelist who happens to be a Catholic—rather than a Catholic novelist—has his revenge here as he flicks his scourge over those who perpetrate on Querry's protagonist such critical fatuities as *The Toad in the Hole: The Art of Fallen Man* and who persist in regarding him as 'the Jeweller of Original Sin.'

The despair generated by misunderstanding is, however, not far below this amusing surface. Plato's parable of the perfectly unjust man comes to mind as Querry's ambiguous hero—Marie quickly realises that he is an architect as well as a jeweller and it's not hard for the reader to see that he is also a novelist—moves triumphantly through life: 'articles in the papers praised his jewellery, women cheated their husbands and went to bed with him, and servants of the King acclaimed him as a loyal and faithful subject.' Even his sexual behaviour can be accounted for as a 'great capacity for love', the formula used by the mission's intelligent and sympathetic Superior puzzling over Querry's relationship with Marie Ryker after his death: 'Judging from Parkinson's second article he would seem to have been a man with a great capacity—well—for love' (Part 6, Ch. 3,6).

But if Querry's parable is straightforwardly allegorical in its equation of the King with God and the Jeweller with Querry and, ultimately, Greene himself (the 'time-old gag' cannot be perpetrated here surely), there is nothing schematic about its meaning. Greene excoriates his *bête noire*, the suburban Catholicism which sees the Christian life as a simple matter of rewards and punishments. In Querry's story, the 'good' often apparently suffer in temporal life while the 'wicked' prosper ('the girl was more beautiful with her virginity gone'), but 'that made no difference because the King was the King of the dead too and you couldn't tell what terrible things he might do to them in the grave.' The protagonist's boredom and spiritual emptiness aren't, however, the end of the matter: 'I wouldn't know, but I'm told that there were moments when he wondered if his unbelief were not after all a final and conclusive proof of the King's existence. This total vacancy might be his punishment for the rules he had wilfully broken.'

Querry and Greene himself I think, shy away from this problem which is 'complicated to the point of absurdity', just as Greene himself loathes the labyrinthine complications foisted on such problems as whether or not Scobie is saved as he falls to the floor from the effects of his overdose. What is unproblematic is that telling his 'sad story' gives Querry a 'sense of freedom and release', that his confession—for it is nothing else—leaves him sitting in an 'hour of coolness' with the thought 'the King is dead, long live the King. Perhaps he had found here a country and a life' (Part 6, Ch. 1,2).

In the same way his death leads to a final, unresolved, debate between the Superior and Dr Colin in which each seeks to claim Querry for his own. Uncertainty is followed by horror at the realisation that a child of three, a small and delightful presence in the novel, has become infected with leprosy. These emotions are balanced, however, although not cancelled, by the fact that Querry has left behind something of permanent value, the hospital which had come to play a central role in his existence: 'The roof-tree had been battered and bent by the storm, but it was held in place still by its strong palm-fibre thongs' (Part 6, Ch. 3,6).

NOTES

1. OM, p.64.
2. WE, p.193.
3. *Ibid.*, p.194.
4. *Ibid.*, p.193.
5. 'Congo Journal,' *In Search of A Character: Two African Journals* (Penguin, 1968), p.42.
6. *Ibid.*, p.37.
7. *Ibid.*, p.29.
8. WE, p.195.

CHAPTER SEVEN

The Later Greene

SECTION A: *THE HONORARY CONSUL*

With *The Honorary Consul* (1973) Greene moves on to a plane
of achievement which develops and combines the interests of
earlier work in a fusion that is both a summation and a new
departure. Distinctions such as entertainment, faith, politics
or allegory, which have a certain limited usefulness in
discussing previous novels, lose their separate identity in
becoming the seamless web of a subtly blended whole. Such
freedom from limiting categories may be associated with the
release Greene experienced in writing *Travels with my Aunt*
(1969), the only book he has 'written for the fun of it.' It was
begun in 1966, the year he left England for good to settle in
France: 'I burned a number of boats and in the light of the
flames I began again to write a novel.'[1] Greene himself has a
high opinion of the work, one I cannot share; it strikes me as
episodic in the limitedly picaresque sense, lacking the
thematic richness of *Our Man in Havana* whose absurdities
arouse the liberating laughter of serious comedy. It's a work,
then, about which I can say nothing interesting or useful,
except to note its part in preparing the ground for *The
Honorary Consul*, although, even here, it seems to me that the
truly fertilising process was the creation of *Our Man in Havana*,
A Burnt-Out Case and *The Comedians*.

Equally liberating, however, must have been the discovery
of a uniquely Greenian subject, what we can see by now as an
utterly characteristic clairvoyance in seizing on the topicality
of political kidnapping. Indeed the sensitivity of Greene's
awareness of the contemporary world can be measured by the
fact that, as he finished writing the book, the Tupamaros

kidnapped the British Ambassador in Montevideo. This episode may have reinforced Greene's confidence in the accuracy of his instinct for contemporary events, but one even closer to his subject nearly rendered the novel stillborn. On his first day in Corrientes, a town in northern Argentina where Greene was seeking material, he read in the local newspaper of how a 'Paraguayan consul from a town near Corrientes has been kidnapped in mistake for the Paraguayan Ambassador'![2] How easily by now could Greene have built an entertainment, light-hearted or blackly comic, on the foundation of his grasp of the absurdities and horrors of modern world politics. The distinction of *The Honorary Consul* is, however, to subsume this material in general human concerns, although without in any way emptying it of political interest.

Greene's fertility of invention by this stage in his career is demonstrated by his ability to build into the book, with no sense of deadening repetition, a critique of what he himself is up to as a writer through the *machismo* novelist, Dr Saavedra. Indeed, the portrait of Dr Saavedra is a miniature version of Greene's treatment of the novel's major characters. Beginning as almost a caricature, he develops steadily into a figure of real stature, while allowing Greene to comment reflexively on his own work. Like a parody of Greene, Dr Saavedra has his own Greeneland in the 'mythical region' which is the setting of all his novels, a narrowness of scope which renders him a one-book man with a vengeance: 'The same character appeared again and again in all his books, his history changed a little, but never his strong sad silence' (Part 1, Ch. 1). Plarr is surprised when Dr Saavedra announces that he proposes to write a political novel, a surprise we share when he goes on to sketch his idea of such a work:

'If one is to write a political novel of lasting value it must be free from all the petty details that date it. Assassinations, kidnapping, the torture of prisoners—these things belong to our decade. But I do not want to write merely for the seventies . . . . A poet—the true novelist must always be in his way a poet—a poet deals in absolutes. . . . A novelist today who wants to represent tyranny should not describe the activities of General Stroessner in Paraguay—that is journalism not literature.' (Part 2, Ch. 2)

Greene's intentions are rendered with amusing clarity when Dr Saavedra remarks 'You might as well expect me to write a story about the kidnapping of Señor Fortnum.' (Part 4, Ch. 2) which is, of course, exactly what Greene himself has done. Implied here is a subtle distinction between kinds of political novel. Greene will have none of that comforting view which claims that the novelist can only be politically significant when his work is disguised in the trappings of history. It is clear that, for him, the true political novel must face up to the challenge of contemporary events. But embodiment is everything. The best-seller lists abound in 'novels' which are in essence journalistic exposés of current affairs. Greene's treatment, on the other hand, fuses the specific and the general in a situation that may be contemporary but which, nonetheless, possesses a universal dimension.

Dr Saavedra's absurdities help to lighten the otherwise sombre tone of *The Honorary Consul*. (His name is, of course, the last name of the creator of *Don Quixote* and he shares with the Don himself a tendency to tilt at windmills.) His weekly visit to the brothel run by Señora Sanchez is not merely therapeutic; the brothel is a hunting-ground for fictional material. However, Plarr observes through Theresa, a prostitute whom Dr Saavedra transforms into a heroine of one of his novels, 'how far fiction deviated from reality. It was almost a lesson in the higher criticism' (Part 2, Ch. 3). Again, in the episode when Dr Plarr attempts to form an Anglo-Argentinian Club composed of himself, Dr Saavedra and, an agreeable little joke, yet another doctor, the tetchy Humpries, solely with the purpose of writing to the newspapers on Fortnum's behalf, Greene parodies the convolutions of the literary man called upon to act. Dr Saavedra refuses to sign Plarr's letter because of its stylistic crudity, but his own attempt flounders because 'somehow Señor Fortnum refuses to come alive' (Part 4, Ch. 2). Serious issues lurk below this comic surface: the ambiguous nature of the link between fiction and reality, and the public responsibility of the writer, to name only two. And just at the point when Saavedra's antics are beginning to turn sour because of his refusal to help a man in desperate straits, Greene transforms our response by revealing aspects of the character we had never guessed at. He surprises Plarr, and us, with his insight into Fortnum's underlying melancholy and Plarr's own reason for living near the border—to be close to his homeland and, above all, to the father who may or may not still be alive. Equally sudden is our realisation of Saavedra's capacity for real suffering in the betrayal he feels at an essay critical of his work written by a former disciple. He finally achieves something like heroic stature when Plarr visits his threadbare flat, for the first time, and has an 'impression that the long pursuit of literature had brought the novelist little material reward beyond his tidy suit and his polished shoes and the respect of the hotel manager' (Part 4, Ch. 2). However absurd his work, Saavedra's obsessive involvement in literature commands respect and makes his offer to exchange himself for the kidnapped Fortnum something more than the empty *machismo* gesture it appears at first sight. Significantly, Plarr fails to understand his most perceptive insight because his 'thoughts were elsewhere': 'Dr Saavedra said, "I may not see you again. I have come to you for pills against melancholy, but at least I have my work. I wonder whether you do not need those pills more than I do." ' (Part 4, Ch. 2).

Only writing of high quality can so subtly effect such a complete change in our response to a minor character, and this quality is equally evident in the novel's thematic fusion of politics and religion. Yet again, Greene has chosen a setting, Argentina, of manic corruption and a hideous infringement of human rights, although both are touched in very lightly. Near the beginning of the book a brief, amusing passage sets out clearly the values of the world we are going to inhabit:

> The harbour works before they were abandoned had done a lot of good; they were responsible for a grand piano in one house, a new refrigerator in somebody's kitchen, and perhaps in some small unimportant sub-contractor's cellar, where spirits had hitherto been little known, lay a dozen or two cases of the national Scotch. (Part 2, Ch. 1)

By this stage Greene knows he can take for granted our understanding of the large-scale plunder that lies behind these tiny pickings. Again, he refuses to detail the nightmare by which Aquino lost his fingers, preferring to concentrate on the reactions of a civilised man: 'Dr Plarr listened with nausea. He had been present at many unpleasant deaths which had affected him less. In those cases there had been something to do, some means of helping in however small a degree' (Part 3, Ch. 2). The repetitions of history only make more intolerable the knowlege that these excesses are acceptable to the West for the sole reason that the régimes perpetrating them are anti-communist. But this arena is not simply a political battle-ground; it is also a setting where, in the policeman Colonel Perez's words, 'those third world priests' are so active (Part 4, Ch. 1). And there is ample evidence that this is now the area of the Roman Catholic church's work where Greene's battered faith feels most at home. One senses the suppressed rage behind the novel's small, passing references to the cruel poverty of the *barrio*, which unobtrusively create pictures of every possible kind of deprivation. The *barrio*, a muddy sprawl of hopeless misery, is flown over by a helicopter, in search of Fortnum, which could have been used to survey the area's desperate lack of piped water. Abandoned to its own resources, it becomes a perfect emblem of third-world poverty, the intended recipient of an aid which is creamed off by the fat cats of an old-established or, in some countries, a newly-emergent élite. Greene humanises the *barrio* through the blind José, searching for a priest to anoint his newly dead wife and entranced by the radio he has heard for the first time at the end of a long life, but his main concern is to dramatise the issues that arise from such a setting rather than to depict it in realistic detail.

Extravagant hopes of rapid change are not encouraged by the novel's band of amateur kidnappers who mistake poor Charlie Fortnum for the American Ambassador. Yet its ranks contain representatives of the only forces Greene seems to think capable of making some kind of impact on reactionary third-world dictatorships: Aquino, the violent materialist, and Father Rivas, the priest, his common-law wife only the most extreme example of his total rejection of an institutionalised church whose archbishops dine with leaders who order murder and torture. Like Dr Saavedra, Rivas is initially almost a figure of fun, with his 'protruding ears' standing 'out like little hands raised over an offering'; comically, he makes 'the gesture of

putting his hands against the protruding ears. They flattened
and sprang back' (Part 3, Ch. 3). By the end, the sufferings
engendered by the moral difficulties of his position as priest
and potential murderer have, however, become so moving that
he joins the ranks of those characters who are such a striking
feature of the novel and the major cause of Greene's justified
pride in it. ('I've succeeded in showing how the characters
change, evolve . . . the doctor evolves, the consul evolves, the
priest too, up to a point. By the end of the novel, they have
become different men.')[3]

Broadly speaking, we might say that Greene's first
outstandingly creative period was marked by a visionary
inwardness, a turning in on the self in order to make a fictional
examination of spiritual issues. His second phase involved a
move outwards to the public world of international politics.
Part of *The Honorary Consul*'s distinction lies in its fusion of
these interests. Greene's setting and choice of subject-matter
are skilfully contrived to weave religion and politics into a
unified whole. The moral issues of kidnapping and political
murder are combined with a questioning of the social and
spiritual role of the Roman Catholic church in a debate that
combines a high degree of seriousness with fictional excitement. In the moments before they discover that their hut is
ringed by troops, for example, Dr Plarr and Father Rivas argue
out their situation—a matter of life and death to both of
them—in such a way that religion and politics become
inextricably combined, facets of the same basic dilemma. This
is advanced, at the purely artistic level, by Greene's
deployment of the most complex motif he has ever given us,
one that perhaps justifies the word profound. Psychologically,
socially and spiritually the novel is unified around the concept
of the father, a time-honoured notion but one that Greene is
able to renew for his own purposes.

He has, of course, a great tradition to draw on. The
importance of the father in western culture (until recently, at
any rate) is no doubt related to the male-oriented structure of
Christianity as well as the patriachal organisation of European
society. The importance of the father, often as a figure highly
criticised, is clear from even a brief examination of one small
segment of European culture, the English novel. Richardson

(in *Clarissa*), Jane Austen and Dickens all make use of fathers in highly interesting ways. Clarissa's is a tyrant, a patriarch run mad with the abuse of power. Mr. Bennet, of *Pride and Prejudice*, is a very different figure in his wit and intelligence, but his culpable unwillingness to accept familial responsibility has devastating consequences for those in his care. Dickens is the most complex example here, with fathers and father-figures who range from simple benefactors to the ambiguous influence of the childless Mr Jarndyce of *Bleak House*. With the latter, it becomes clear that Dickens sees an equation between the father and society as a whole, and that for him the social world depicted in the later novels is fatherless in its lack of compassion and absence of purpose.

These are possibly heady predecessors to compare with Greene, but he undeniably does justice to the theme within his creative limits. Although Plarr's is the more elaborately worked-out case, he and Fortnum are connected by a psychological dependence on their fathers which is an integral part of the crisis of development to which they are forced by the novel's events. Charlie Fortnum's shiftless, boozy life is dominated by hatred of his father, a hatred focused on his loathing of horses. Despite his age, he still has a photograph on his bedroom wall of 'a man with a heavy moustache in riding kit' (Part 2, Ch. 1) and his memories of childhood are concentrated on an incident when, a frightened child of six who had just fallen off his horse, he realised that his father was too drunk to know who he was. This rejection is inseparable from an empty life and a failed first marriage, modified only by a last-moment hope of happiness with the prostitute, Clara, whom he has made his wife. Charlie's precarious joy centres on the fact that he is to be a father himself, but during his kidnapping he makes the bitter discovery that the child is, in fact, Plarr's. It is one of Greene's triumphs to show us this vulgar, commonplace man developing slowly, and with complete credibility, through suffering and love for Clara towards compassionate acceptance. By the end, he is even willing to take Plarr's child as his own, but an earlier sign of change, and one that relates to this major theme, is his coming to terms with his own father immediately after he has tried to offer comfort to Father Rivas: 'Father, Father, Father. The word repeated itself in his mind. He had a vision of his father sitting bewildered, not understanding, not recognizing him, by the dumb-waiter, while he lay on the ground and the horse stood over him. Poor bugger, he thought' (Part 5, Ch. 4). 'Poor bugger' is not a very exalted expression of reconciliation, but here it has the force of an ordinary man going to his limits in understanding and love.

The moment is echoed by Plarr's 'God help you, father, wherever you are' (Part 4, Ch. 2) which has a dignity marking the differences between the characters as individuals as well the nature of their memories. Plarr's worship of his father, however, has marked his personality as deeply as Fortnum's hatred. And, with a complexity entirely characteristic of this fine novel, the effect of his loving admiration is double-edged. His father's English reticence has made Plarr wary of any show of emotion, a trait intensified by the disparity between his parents: 'His first years in Buenos Aires, while his mother complained, dramatized and wept over his missing father's fate, and the later years when she became volubly content with sweet cakes and chocolate ices had given Dr Plarr a suspicion of any emotion which was curable by means as simple as an orgasm or an éclair' (Part 2, ch. 2). This dichotomy of responses atrophies Plarr's emotional life, so that he is embarrassed by Charlie's direct expressions of sentiment (he's a 'cold fish', according to Fortnum, Part 5, Ch. 1) and believes that 'Caring is the only dangerous thing' (Part 5, Ch. 3). His dilemma centres, then, not on learning to love his father but on making his own actions conform to his father's compassionate heroism.

As always with Greene, his characters' moral and spiritual dilemmas are intensified by the constrictions of plot woven around and through them. For a complex of motives, but above all in the hope of freeing his father from political imprisonment in the neighbouring country, Plarr agrees to give the kidnappers information on the movements of the American Ambassador. In the event, these amateurs take Charlie Fortnum instead. Plarr is then free, in a sense, to continue his affair with Clara uninterrupted. But when Charlie recognises Plarr giving him medical assistance at the hide-out, Plarr is drawn irresistibly into a situation from which he had planned to remain aloof. Also, on the personal level, a Charlie unimprisoned, boozy and cuckolded is a different proposition from a Charlie in captivity; kidnapped, he takes on 'the appearance of a serious rival' (Part 3, Ch. 1). Plarr pursues Clara out of what he thinks is an obsessional whim that will disappear once he possesses her sexually. He discovers instead that his obsession intensifies with possession and that the seemingly impassive Clara is capable of love as well as compassion for Charlie. Above all, he comes to understand the depth of feeling in Fortnum for his wife. All of this destroys the apparently calm surface of the life Plarr has constructed for himself: 'The small patch of marble floor on which he stood seemed like the edge of an abyss; he could not move one step in either direction without falling deeper into the darkness of involvement or guilt' (Part 4, Ch. 2). Eventually, hopelessly trapped in the hut with Fortnum and his kidnappers, and overheard by Charlie admitting to the others that he is the father of Clara's child, he is forced to the acceptance of Rivas's charge that he is jealous of Charlie because of his capacity for love. Compelled by self-knowlege to an act of commitment, he steps outside in an attempt to bargain for Fortnum's life with Colonel Perez, and is shot. Dying, he cannot hear the words of León Rivas who comes out to his own death in trying to help him: 'The voice said a word which sounded like "Father."' As with Querry, laughter is a sign of restored humanity for Plarr and, in the moment of death, the memory of a schoolboy joke with León prompts an attempt at mirth, 'but he was too tired and the laugh shrivelled in his throat' (Part 5, Ch. 4).

It had never been Plarr's intention to follow 'in his father's steps' (Part 5, Ch. 2). The ironies of Greene's plot and Plarr's own development as a character conspire, however, to lead him in that very direction. Psychologically, Plarr and Fortnum find a resolution of the dominance of their lives by fathers. But what of fathers in the wider, social and political, sense? Rivas's father was a wealthy lawyer '"who never worked for a poor client"' and consequently '"everyone said he was a good father because he left plenty of cash behind him."' León then reflects, 'Oh well, I suppose he was, in that way. It is one of the duties of a father to provide' (Part 5, Ch. 3). This familial duty clearly reflects the father in his social role, one that may be fulfilled by individuals but is signally absent at the wider national level. The general who governs the nearby state—contemporary examples come readily to mind—is a father to his people only in the sense that he wields total, arbitrary power over them. As when a child is maltreated, this father towers over his country in cruel omnipotence. Argentina, and its neighbouring dictatorships, is a place of absolute terror, of a degradation reaching from the bottomless misery of the *Barrio* to Plarr's mother stuffing herself with cream cakes in Buenos Aires. The wealthy are presented by Greene as living lives of complete vacuity, the men obsessed with *machismo*, the women with gratification of their over-fed bodies: both are caught in the comic grossness of the scene when one of Plarr's mistresses makes love to him on a sofa behind the back of her, presumably, sleeping husband while Plarr mutters cruelly appropriate nursery rhymes as a substitute for conversation.

Such a world seems to demand the question posed by Plarr after Father Rivas has been telling him of his father, the wealthy lawyer: 'And God the father, León? He doesn't seem to provide much. I asked last night if you still believed in him. To me he has always seemed a bit of a swine. I would rather believe in Apollo. At lease he was beautiful' (Part 5, Ch. 3). Plarr has the cruel, even frivolous, intention of goading Rivas, but the conversation that follows moves him, with a 'sense of some obscure grievance', to a level of real seriousness. He instances having seen a child born 'without hands and feet': 'The Jesuits used to tell us it was our duty to love God. A duty to love a God who produces that abortion? It's like the duty of a German to love Hitler. Isn't it better not to believe in that horror up there sitting in the clouds of heaven than pretend to love him?' (Part 5, Ch. 3). Plarr is oppressed with the sense of not having intended the things he does, of following in his father's footsteps, of having a child with Clara, of blurting out the truth so that Fortnum overhears; '"You would almost think there was a great joker somewhere who likes to give a twist to things"' (Part 5, Ch. 3). God may well be a joker or, just as easily, not exist at all—by this stage Greene is content to leave these problems unresolved. In their final moment of reconciliation, Plarr and Fortnum respond to the mass that Rivas is about to take in interestingly different ways. Charlie is physically incapable of getting through to the next room, but remarks with admirable stoicism, 'Why should I anyway? I wouldn't want to curry favour at the last moment. Take me back to the whisky. That's my sacrament.' Questioned by Fortnum about his religious beliefs, Plarr qualifies his first 'No': 'Now that the personal truth was out between them Doctor Plarr felt a curious need to speak with complete accuracy. He added, "I don't think so"' (Part 5, ch. 4).

The reader feels something almost like gratitude that Greene mitigates the blackness of his vision in the novel's closing pages. Plarr dies absolving Rivas in 'a flash of memory' of their schoolboy joke when he asks for forgiveness, but his sacrificial death is nullified by the lie that he was killed by the kidnappers instead of the authorities. Charlie sticks to the truth despite the polite evasions of a chinless wonder from the British Embassy although, in a masterly touch of characterisation, he is overwhelmed with delight at the thought of receiving an O.B.E. But the new Charlie, wrought by suffering and love, still exists below the surface, emerging in this magnificent novel's conclusion. Clara's pain at the death of Plarr, far from being unwelcome to Charlie, validates her capacity for love in his eyes and gives him a 'sense of immense relief':

> It was as though, after what seemed an interminable time of anxious waiting in the ante-room of death, someone came to him with the good news that he had never expected to hear. Someone he loved would survive. He realized that never before had she been so close to him as she was now. (Part 5, Ch. 5)

SECTION B: *THE HUMAN FACTOR*

The literary critic, always on the look-out for beginnings, middles and ends, would have enjoyed a keen satisfaction if *The Human Factor* (1978) had been Greene's last novel. The book undeniably achieves new things, at least the deepening of a note already sounded, but it makes a much richer resumé of his literary career than that claimed by some critics for *Travels with my Aunt*. This quality of summation persists throughout the novel. For his epigraph Greene returns to the Conrad whom he had self-protectively thrown off so many years before and rediscovered, perhaps rather tentatively, with *A Burnt-Out Case*. The authority with which one of Conrad's most troubling utterances—'I only know that he who forms a tie is lost. The germ of corruption has entered into his soul.'— becomes part of the bloodstream of Greene's book is a sign of complete artistic assurance. We find echoes, too, of his own work; in the naming of his married couple Sarah and Maurice, for example, a duplication of the adulterous lovers of *The End of the Affair* whose agonised intensity is such a profound contrast with the depths of domestic tenderness in the later book. The 'flaming strawberry mark' (Part 1, Ch. 2) on the cheek of Dr Barker is surely a hint that this link is not fortuitous. We have reminders of some of Greene's favourite boyhood reading in references to Rider Haggard and Allan Quatermain as well as a reprise of several of his most persistent verbal motifs: the role of acting in human life is carried on from *The Comedians*; his daughter's impending marriage makes Colonel Daintry feel 'like a man who was departing into a long exile' (Part 3, Ch. 1, 2); and Castle's resistance to friendship with Muller is because 'an enemy should never come alive. The generals were right—no Christmas cheer ought to be exchanged between the trenches' (Part 4, Ch. 1,2). Religion surfaces in the materialist Castle's desire to utter a prayer for Sam's complete recovery from illness to a God he believes to be non-existent, while his relationship with his espionage control, Boris, is like that of a Catholic to his priest, 'a man who received one's confession whatever it might be without emotion' (Part 3, ch. 5,1). The last of these small details is the novel's rewording of the father theme from *The Honorary Consul*. The spy-chief, Sir John Hargreaves, and his wife are deliberately childless; the murderous Dr Percival is not merely unmarried, but without any conception of the ties involved in such a human relation as parenthood; the infinitely lonely Colonel Daintry is separated from his wife and has a grown-up daughter who is practically a stranger to him. Castle, on the other hand, does have a 'son' for whom his feelings are almost as deep as those for Sarah, but he loves him because 'he's not mine. Because I don't have to see anything of myself there

when I look at him. I see only something of you. I don't want
to go on and on for ever. I want the buck to stop here' (Part 1,
Ch. 2). The novel's roll-call of solitary men would be
incomplete without Davis who is 'taken out' with ruthless
efficiency on the, mistaken, chance that he is the leak in
Castle's section. Despite his act as the carefree bachelor, Davis
longs for marriage, a feeling for the domestic he disguises by
his joking references to Sam as 'the little bastard'. The joke is
characteristically Greenian, of course, because a bastard,
technically speaking, is precisely what Sam is, the child not of
Castle, but of a mysterious figure from Sarah's earlier life.

These links with the past give *The Human Factor* a very
special resonance in Greene's output, but its major contribution to the intermingling of ends and beginnings is its setting,
the return to the loved and hated Berkhamsted of Greene's
childhood. When Castle thinks of praying for Sam, it is to the
'God of his childhood, the God of the Common and the castle'
(Part 2, Ch. 2), a fusion which evidently stirred Greene to his
depths. His hero's surname is clearly a tribute to the castle
which loomed so powerfully in Greene's childhood, as well as
hinting at 'an Englishman's home is his castle,' a tag entirely
appropriate to Maurice's desperate urge for domestic peace and
privacy. Like Wemmick's Castle in Dickens's *Great Expectations*, itself a distinctly shaky edifice, the insecurity of Castle's
personal solution to public dilemmas is revealed by the entry
into his home of Muller, the man from BOSS, and, later, of
Colonel Daintry who comes to investigate Castle at the point
when his home has become a house because of Sam and Sarah's
departure. Although Castle and Greene share Berkhamsted as
a birthplace as well as a hatred of school, it would be a mistake
to identify the character with his author. The novel's
emotional charge is generated, rather, by the nostalgia aroused
in Greene by its setting, a feeling richly present in the novel's
second chapter when Castle, like any other commuter, cycles
home from the railway station. The detail here is not
vivid—Berkhamsted requires no local colour—but its un-
erring precision creates the sense of familiarity which gives
Castle the 'security that an old lag feels when he goes back to
the prison he knows' (Part 1, ch. 2).

Greene has complained, in *The Other Man*, of a general

failure to recognise the element of fantasy in his work in favour of a straightforward realism. Interestingly, he twice mentions *The Human Factor* as a novel in which fantasy is of particular importance, above all in the scenes on the common and the story of the dragon which Castle tells to Sam. This seems another clear sign that setting the novel as he does creates in Greene an especially painful imaginative response to the book. One small sign of this is its careful manipulation of a motif of references to spying centred on Sam. Castle tries to draw Sam back into his boyish fantasy world of a common inhabited by a genial dragon who, hunted and alone, befriends a Castle who feels himself to be in the same plight. He is disappointed, however, by Sam's response to his talk of 'private signals, codes, ciphers . . . . "Like a spy," Sam said' (Part 2, Ch. 2). There is every reason why the imaginative life of a boy living in the 1970s should be inhabited by spies rather than dragons and Greene uses this realistic touch in Sam's unconscious unmasking of secret lives. His hero-worship of Davis, a powerful factor in the distress we feel at the latter's hateful elimination, is rooted in his skill at hide-and-seek which leads Sam to ask, 'Are you a real spy?' (Part 3, Ch. 2,1). Again, Sam badgers Muller, 'Can you play hide-and-seek. . . . Are you a spy like Mr Davis?' (Part 3, Ch. 3.1). This link between Castle's professional life and Greene's is obvious. Greene has repeatedly stressed the novelist's role as a kind of spy and so the opening sentence of his first volume of autobiography, *A Sort of Life*, could apply equally well to his own character: 'If I had known it, the whole future must have lain all the time along those Berkhamsted streets.' In most ways Castle is utterly unlike his creator, but the shared secret life of the spy-novelist is so powerful a link that it suffuses *The Human Factor* with the anguish of tenderness and nostalgia, although these emotions are dramatised in a story that fully accounts for them. The novel contains none of the excess of feeling, stemming from a writer's indulgence in purely private emotion, that we call sentimentality. *A Sort of Life* makes us see the otherwise genteel Berkhamsted as the perfect training ground for the kind of novel Greene was to write, its inhabitants with their 'pointed faces like the knaves on playing cards, with a slyness about the eyes, an unsuccessful cunning.'

Finally, there is something deeply satisfying in Greene bringing his life's work full circle as he does in *The Human Factor*, back to a world where violence lurks just below the surface of middle-class respectability. We remember, from *A Sort of Life*, that Greene's first memory is of 'sitting in a pram at the top of a hill with a dead dog lying at my feet',[4] followed at the age of about five by the incident of the man cutting his throat at an alms-house window. The themes of international politics which have preoccupied him for so many years, and which are dealt with richly here in the Uncle Remus plot and the coda in Moscow, are finally brought home with understated yet devastating power. The Kim Philby whom Greene is not afraid to call 'my friend' thought that Dr Percival was more a figure of the C.I.A. than the British Secret Service; Greene agrees, feeling that the book's element of violence detracts from what he finds most valuable, its 'married-love' story.[5] Philby and Greene have a formidable knowledge of espionage between them but fantasy, in the sense of visionary experience, may apply to the novel's presentation of the Secret Service as much as to Berkhamsted Common. At this level, of the terrifying intervention of the unthinkable into the everyday, the novel is grippingly successful. Indeed Dr Percival is, for me, Greene's most persuasive portrait of an evil which is as absolute as it is unmelodramatic. Percival's fishing, his greedy enjoyment of food, his appreciation of abstract art add up to a totally convincing and unified character whose evil, like Iago's, stems from a moral blankness incapable of understanding the ties of love, fellowship and decency which bind human life together. The scene in which he insinuates to Sarah, over an expensive lunch, the impossibility of her getting with Sam to Moscow is a masterly exposure of a mind unruffled by the enormity of its own actions. For the Sarah who is impressed by the apparent decencies of English life—the friendly bobby, the quiet country town—from her perspective of a black South African liable to the attentions of BOSS, this represents an awakening to the true nature of modern life as it is envisioned in *The Human Factor*. In a world dominated by the media and computer technology no individual is safe from the institution, whether it be the multi-national corporation or the spy network.

But if *The Human Factor* reworks Greene's past into a new synthesis, it also contains elements which are new in an absolute sense. One is a quality of total simplicity in everything but its plot. This is as convuluted as ever (it's perhaps unwise to confess that, on the first reading, I got as far as page 117 before realising that Castle was a double agent) and these complications are unavoidable if we are to experience directly the shifts and stratagems inseparable from Castle's life. Apart from this, however, the other elements of the novel are marked by a lucid simplicity. Its opening paragraph may serve as an example:

> Castle, ever since he had joined the firm as a young recruit more than thirty years ago, had taken his lunch in a public house behind St James's Street, not far from the office. If he had been asked why he lunched there, he would have referred to the excellent quality of the sausages; he might have preferred a different beer from Watney's, but the quality of the sausages outweighed that. He was always prepared to account for his actions, even the most innocent, as he was always strictly on time.

Writing such as this comes only from a lifetime's exacting practice of a craft. Everything is spare, direct and self-denying, a style which draws no attention to itself, content to expose with maximum force the book's human factor. Its simplicity is thus organic, embodying the values which lie at the heart of the novel. The tenderness which I noted as something new in *Our Man in Havana* is here brought to its fullest expression in the celebration of a domestic love which has sometimes in the past aroused Greene's contempt. We can't escape a touch of complexity even at this still centre of beauty, however. Castle's domesticity is part of his cover as a double agent, but also a quite genuine aspect of his character: 'There were times . . . when he day-dreamed of complete conformity, as a different character might have dreamt of making a dramatic century at Lord's' (Part 1, Ch. 1). Although not without passion, the deepest pleasures of Castle's life are the evening drink and chat with his wife, the walk on the Common with the dog and Sam. (We can be sure that if he allowed himself a car, he would wash it on Sundays.) Castle is the culmination of a line of Greenian heroes whose deepest desire is for peace, a longing expressed in *The Human Factor* with the peculiar charge of emotional intensity I have already tried to analyse, as at a moment when Castle has been staying awake until he is sure that Sarah is asleep:

> Then he allowed himself to strike, like his childhood hero Allan Quatermain, off on that long slow underground stream which bore him off towards the interior of the dark continent where he hoped that he might find a permanent home, in a city where he could be accepted as a citizen, as a citizen without any pledge of faith, not the City of God or Marx, but the city called Peace of Mind. (Part 3, Ch. 3,2)

Castle desires a secular peace which passes all understanding, a longing for the minimal, yet all-important, joy of a private life in a world riven by abstractions and violence: the creation of a world within a world. Sarah's response to his confession ('I'm what's generally called a traitor,') enforces this primacy of the personal: 'We have our own country. You and I and Sam. You've never betrayed that country, Maurice' (Part 5, Ch. 1,2). And so the novel centres on a love at the opposite extreme from that of *The End of the Affair* with its spectacular eroticism, but fated just as much to carry the seeds of its own special destruction.

Castle's espionage activities are restricted solely to giving the Russians information about Africa, an act not of ideological conviction but of gratitude to the communist, Carson, for his part in helping Sarah to escape from the South African secret police. His dream of abandoning this double life is shattered on the appearance of Muller who has come to Britain to further the Uncle Remus plot, an arrangement between Germany, America and Britain to allow South Africa to use tactical atomic weapons in the event of a black uprising as a 'kind of Final Solution to the race problem.'[6] This horrific plan takes Castle down the well-trodden Greenian path of commitment and he copies Muller's notes for the Russians in the knowledge that with Davis dead, any leak will expose him as the only possible source of information. He then activates his escape route and is spirited off to Moscow leaving Sarah and Sam behind, temporarily as he believes.

The novel ends with an unforgettably depressing picture of exile in Moscow, as Castle endures a parody of his former domestic existence in a tiny flat with a 'large stout middle-aged woman' as a daily help and teacher of Russian (Part 6, Ch. 2,1). Castle passes the time in reading, amongst other books, an accidentally acquired but significant *Robinson Crusoe*. He could not be more cast away than Robinson himself and his loneliness is hardly tempered by a visit from a homosexual fellow-spy, Bellamy (Burgess, of the inevitable pairing, one wonders). The Boris who finally comes to Castle's aid is now a menacing figure who warns him of the difficulty of extricating Sarah and Sam from Britain, and reveals that the information he passed was of no direct value: 'You have never been given the real picture, have you? Those bits of economic information you sent us had no value in themselves at all. . . . Your people imagined they had an agent in place, here in Moscow. But it was we who had planted him on them. What you gave us he passed back to them. Your reports authenticated him in the eyes of your service. . . . That was the real value of your reports' (Part 6, Ch. 2,5). Nothing reveals more clearly Greene's vision of individual helplessness at the hands of the large organisation. Led into action by a profoundly human emotion, Castle is manipulated by a power struggle that takes no account of the personal life. Boris's final protestations ('I want to stay your friend. One needs a friend badly to make a new life in a new country.') have a hollow ring:

Now the offer of friendship had the sound of a menace or a warning. The night in Watford came back to him when he searched in vain for the shabby tutorial flat with the Berlitz picture on the wall. It seemed to him that all his life after he joined the service in his twenties he had been unable to speak. Like a Trappist he had chosen the profession of silence, and now he recognised too late that it had been a mistaken vocation. (Part 6, Ch. 2,5)

The novel closes with a telephone conversation between Sarah and Maurice which is almost unbearably painful. In the spirit of the entire novel, nothing could be more simple and yet more anguished than their desperate avowals of love and hope. The human factor which was the centre of their lives, and which led Castle to do 'more than I ever intended to do', is only one element in the machinery of modern institutions, and dispensable when it has outlived its usefulness:

> 'When the spring comes,' he repeated in a voice she hardly recognised—it was the voice of an old man who couldn't count with certainty on any spring to come.
> She said, 'Maurice, Maurice, please go on hoping,' but in the long unbroken silence which followed she realised that the line tc Moscow was dead.

NOTES

1. WE, p.220.
2. *Ibid.*, p.224.
3. OM, p.136.
4. SL, pp.11 and 13.
5. WE, p.229.
6. OM, p.102.

CHAPTER EIGHT

The Achievement

SECTION A: THE MAN OF LETTERS

I hope it is clear by now that with Greene we are dealing with one of the more remarkable careers in twentieth-century fiction. Its sheer longevity is worthy of comment. In very recent years, Greene has published two short novels, *Dr Fischer of Geneva or The Bomb Party* (1980) and *Monsignor Quixote* (1982), both chamber works compared with *The Honorary Consul* and *The Human Factor*, but interesting in their pared-down treatment of such continuing themes as the nature of power and the problem of belief. Neither, however, has the power to dislodge *The Human Factor* from its place as the work which seems the culmination of Greene's writing career and so I have not attempted any discussion of them. Another aspect of his total achievement, one possibly ignored by that general public which so avidly consumes the novels, is the range of Greene's output as a man of letters. The correspondence is yet to be collected and his early volume of verse is, mercifully, hidden from view, but apart from this Greene has contributed to all the major literary genres: novels, short stories, travel books, essays and literary criticism, autobiography and biography, and books for children. None of these areas is without interest—even the mechanical hero of *The Little Train* is propelled on his adventures by the fact that he 'was sometimes bored to tears!'—although none can shift Greene the novelist from the centre of our attention. They testify, however, to a creative energy that has sought to explore the forms open to the literary imagination, and to the fact that Greene is a writer in the deepest, as well as the widest, sense of the term, that the placing of words on the page is as necessary to him as breathing. The point is made in amusing detail by Philip Stratford; 'For the sake of statistics, in the ten years from 1932 to 1942 he published 44 essays and stories in the *Spectator* alone, plus 384 review articles covering 860 books, films and plays.'[1] And despite his unfailingly modest estimate of his place in literature the range of his output signifies, also, to an ambition to scale at least the lower slopes of greatness. One suspects that Greene's masters are never far from his thoughts and the example of James, the supreme story-teller and failed playwright, is relevant here.

Courage, too, is an aspect of this phenomenon. It would have been easy enough for Greene to remain within the successful world of his novels, especially as these forays across the frontier have sometimes exposed the weaker side of his talents. None of the short stories and plays, for example, is on the level of the very best of the novels and some fall painfully below the standards of even the poorest of the longer books. 'The Blue Film' from the *Twenty-One Stories* of 1954 centres on the infinitely depressing Far Eastern holiday of an infinitely depressing couple, the Carters. In an attempt to placate his wife's frigid hunger for sexual excitement, Carter takes her to a pornographic film through a setting that reads like a parody of Greeneland: 'They drove a long way and came to a halt by a bridge over a canal, a dingy lane overcast with indeterminate smells.'[2] In a preposterous coincidence that outdoes even Dickens in sheer unlikeliness, Carter turns out to be the young man in the film, sexually fulfilling himself with a girl he loves while simultaneously helping her to a much needed £50 for appearing in the movie. The climax, in every sense, occurs on the couple's return to their hotel:

> She was dry and hot and implacable in her desire. 'Go on,' she said, 'go on,' and then she screamed like an angry and hurt bird. Afterwards she said, 'It's years since that happened,' and continued to talk for what seemed a long half hour excitedly at his side. Carter lay in the dark silent, with a feeling of loneliness and guilt. It seemed to him that he had betrayed that night the only woman he loved. (p.34)

This is popular writing of quite the wrong sort, surely. The story's revelation has all the mechanical slickness of magazine fiction—a whiff of O. Henry permeates the atmosphere. And the twin lures of so many best-sellers, cynicism and sentimentality, are shamefully exploited in the wife's externally contrived excitement and the husband's odious nostalgia. These only superficially opposed qualities form the keynote of an entire volume of stories, *May We Borrow Your Husband?* (1967), described in its sub-title as 'Comedies of the Sexual Life'. The offerings here range from the taking over of a young husband on his honeymoon by a homosexual couple, in the title story, to the 'things might have been different' encounter of 'Two Gentle People,' whose central characters are married to an ageing homosexual and a middle-aged invalid.

Works of this kind are, of course, annihilated by the best stories, the well-known 'The End of the Party' (1929) and 'The Basement Room' (1936), the dating of which suggests that this is not an area where Greene's talents have matured with age. Less famous, but very fine, is 'A Drive in the Country' (1937) which shares with *Brighton Rock* (1938) not merely a suicide pact but something also of that novel's visionary intensity; their close proximity suggests, in fact, that story and novel both have their imaginative roots in that deepening of experience I discussed in Chapter Three. The pervasiveness of Greene's vision, at this period, of a social world emptied of almost all value is reinforced by its embodiment in a quite different milieu from that of *Brighton Rock*. The story's boy and girl who drive out into the night for what he plans as a suicidal end to a doomed relationship are from the world of jerry-built villas, rather than the degraded poverty of Pinkie and Rose, but their future in an Orwellian world of lower middle-class gentility is every bit as hopeless. Orwell's social detail is, however, replaced by a landscape of allegorical power. The country into which the young people drive is a waste-land to them because they haven't 'a name for anything round them; the tiny buds breaking in the bushes were nameless' (pp. 100–1). And although the boy's irresponsibility is related to a social context of unemployment and support by reasonably well-to-do parents, it eventually comes to be synonymous with evil because it is 'without any limit at all' (p. 103). In this context, the girl's unwillingness to accept death at his hands and her return to her father's endlessly 'improved' property—a shelter from life's storms every bit as flimsy as Wemmick's Castle in Dickens's *Great Expectations*—acquires the complexity of real choice.

Greene's most ambitious collection of stories is probably *A Sense of Reality* (1963), 'A Visit to Morin' being a particularly notable exposition of those themes of faith and the nature of writing which I have already discussed in detail. Pierre Morin is a once famous Catholic writer who, before his loss of public favour, 'offended the orthodox Catholics of his own country and pleased the liberal Catholics abroad.'[3] Morin's similarity to Greene himself seems unmistakeable, especially when we hear of his readership among 'non-Christians once they had accepted imaginatively his premisses' (p.65), and his exposition of his life to the story's narrator, Dunlop, bears a close relationship to Greene's explanation of his religious position in *The Other Man*. Both have broken rules they respect and live irregular private lives, so they prefer to excommunicate themselves rather than seek the Church's help. Greene's distinction between belief and faith, 'Faith is above belief,'[4] is reinforced by Morin's conclusion:

> 'I can tell myself now that my lack of belief is a final proof that the Church is right and the faith is true. I had cut myself off for twenty years from grace and my belief withered as the priests said it would. I don't believe in God and His Son and His angels and His Saints, but I know the reason why I don't believe and the reason is—the Church is true and what she taught me is true. For twenty years I have been without the sacraments and I can see the effect. The wafer must be more than wafer.' (p.78)

The story exerts its own fascination within the context of Greene's life, but taken in isolation as a work of art it appears somewhat schematic. It hardly seems accidental, for example, that it should be composed almost entirely of dialogue, a device which in the hands of Henry James is capable of imaginative involvement, but which here remains largely at the level of statement.

The skeletal quality of many of the stories and plays may, in fact, hint at an explanation of the superiority of the novels, where the pressure towards the detail of the longer form enforces a qualifying flesh and blood on the bones of theme and idea. This seems true, at any rate, of *The Potting Shed* (1958), the second out of the five plays Greene has published so far. His move towards the theatre, at least as far as production was concerned, occurred in the 1950s as a 'novelty, an escape from the everyday.'[5] Greene writes with affection of his involvement with actors as almost a holiday from the solitary pressures of the novelist and, although he doesn't make the point himself, one is tempted to see a Jamesian link between this venture into the world of dialogue and action, and a novel such as *The Comedians* which is theatrical in a wider sense than its reliance on acting as a controlling metaphor. And yet works which have held their place in the theatre are clearly of interest in their own right, not simply as aids to improvement in the fiction. *The Potting Shed* is undeniably of real power in its opposition between a successfully created rationalism of the Wellsian variety and the intervention of the miraculous. Coming some seven years after *The End of the Affair*, it reworks that novel's incident of a life 'saved' through prayer, but in a significantly unsatisfactory manner. In the novel, we don't actually know whether Maurice is dead or not, just as the 'miracles' after Sarah's death are susceptible of a rational explanation. This necessary ambiguity is compounded by the book's wealth of detail which deflects the mind from too direct a contemplation of what for many would be the sheerest impossibility. This creation of embodying detail is a basic function of narrative, a technique barred to drama by its very nature, of course. Although James's suicidal death by hanging is only reported in dialogue by the widow of the gardener, Potter, who cut the boy down and thought him 'beyond human aid' (Act II, sc.i), the audience is left little leeway seriously to doubt the fact, especially when it learns that the boy's rationalist father comes to take the same view. What I'm suggesting is the presence of a strongly allegorical bent in Greene's artistic make-up, particularly in the more ostensibly Catholic works, which is mitigated by the demands of realism in the modes of fiction he has opted for. This lack of a qualifying element in at least some of the stories and plays allows the bare bones of religious conviction to show through too clearly, so that *The Potting Shed* must be seen as an ideological work rather than a play of doubt and belief. Humanity stakes its claim briefly in the moving words of yet another Sara (although spelled differently this time) in response to her former husband's new-found discovery that God is in his 'lungs, like air':

> 'He's not mine. I'm sorry, James. You believe in God and life eternal. But I don't want to be that important. I wasn't kissing God when I was kissing you. I was only saying, "I have remembered to order the steaks. And I know you don't like water-cress. And I'll be here tonight, and next night, and the night after" . . . . I don't want eternity. I hate big things— Everest and the Empire State Building." (Act III)

But movement in this direction is left undeveloped and it is worth noting that the play is a very optimistic work by Greene's standards. This may have something to do with the demands of operating within the West End theatre but more, I think, with an ideological purity uncontaminated by the pressures of ordinary living. These problems are exacerbated by a curious lack in the plays, that of memorable characters. There are no Scobies or whisky priests here, only rather dimly remembered figures who perform their parts adequately enough in the dramatic puzzle, but who fail to live on as part of one's inner life as so many of the novels' characters do. My point is obvious enough: that the fully realised character is capable of embodying within himself the ambiguities of whose absence I am complaining. The Father of *Carving a Statue*, based on the manic yet absurd figure of Benjamin Robert Haydon, a sculptor with a 'true daemon and . . . no talent at all' (Epitaph to *Carving a Statue*), is clearly intended as a figure of Ibsenite grandeur, but he remains inert, at least in a reading of the play. Yet one can hardly regret Greene's adventure into the theatre. None of the plays is truly negligible, all have their moments of theatrical excitement and wit, and as a body of work by a writer whose major talents clearly lie elsewhere they constitute a formidable threat to the standard, serious West End fare of the 1950s and 1960s.

If reservations have to be expressed about the stories and plays, one turns with unqualified pleasure to the *Collected*

Esssays (1969), over 300 hundred pages of unalloyed delight. In fact, my own claim is that this is the area of Greene's non-fictional writing which has been most clearly under-valued. Beautifully framed by the autobiographical fragments, 'The Lost Childhood' and 'The Soupsweet Land' (Greene's evocation of his return to Sierra Leone in 1968) are two major sections on 'Novels and Novelists' and 'Some Characters'. The first section ranges from 'Fielding and Sterne' to Ford Madox Ford by way of Mauriac, Rider Haggard, Beatrix Potter and many others. The second contains pieces serious and comic (and both) on Samuel Butler, Herbert Read, Simone Weil, Kim Philby—again the full list is a long one. 'Film Lunch' is a mordant recreation of Hollywood's lure for writers who 'a little stuffed and a little boozed, lean back and dream of the hundred pounds a week—and all that's asked in return the dried imagination and the dead pen;'[6] 'The Marxist Heretic' gives a beautifully precise account of Castro and his Cuba; while 'Sore Bones; Much Headache' establishes a sympathetic bond between Greene the traveller and another, David Livingstone. The reader may safely be recommended to these treasures for himself. What is perhaps more illuminating for this book is the charting of Greene's path through his fellow novelists as a way of establishing something of his own conception of his function as a writer.

It is amusing, for example, to see him playing the role of literary sociologist as early as 1937 in his essay, 'Fielding and Sterne':

> One cannot separate literature and life. If an age appears creatively, poetically empty, it is fair to assume the life too had its emptiness, was carried on at a lower, less passionate level. (p.67)

I have chided those who would restrict Greene to a limitingly realistic conception of the novel, but my own view of his sometimes visionary quality must be qualified in the light of this assertion. Certainly no writer could have drawn more richly than Greene on a turbulent historical period for his subject matter. He may have chosen largely to ignore the almost equally turbulent artistic developments in his forma-

tive period, but this is a decision I have tried to explain in my
first chapter, and a word more will be said on it in the next
section. Greene's skirting of the headier technical developments in modernist fiction is certainly no indication that he
draws his material from the contemporary world in a purely
unmediated fashion. World events gain their special inflection
from his own peculiar blend of technique and vision, as George
Woodcock recognised as long ago as 1948 in *The Writer and
Politics*:

> Greene's novels form, within obvious limits, one of the most
> comprehensive surveys of modern social violence that has yet been
> made in European fiction. They show clearly the nature of the
> class struggle in modern society, and also go beyond the Marxists
> to a realization of that even more fundamental struggle . . .
> between the individual and the collective.[7]

As a much travelled man and a creative writer truly in touch
with public affairs Greene does, then, seize the modern world
eagerly as a major field of action but, with characteristic
subtlety, his final justification for the substantiality of the real
world in fiction is based on its spiritual value rather than its
documentary surface. Greene's position is elaborated most
fully in his essay on François Mauriac, a piece of such central
importance that it demands lengthy quotation:

> For with the death of James the religious sense was lost to the
> English novel, and with the religious sense went the sense of the
> importance of the human act. It was as if the world of fiction had
> lost a dimension: the characters of such distinguished writers as
> Mrs Virginia Woolf and Mr E.M. Forster wandered like
> cardboard symbols through a world that was paper-thin. Even in
> one of the most materialistic of our great novelists—in
> Trollope—we are aware of another world against which the
> actions of the characters are thrown into relief. The ungainly
> clergyman picking his black-booted way through the mud,
> handling so awkwardly his umbrella, speaking of his miserable
> income and stumbling through a proposal of marriage, exists in a
> way that Mrs Woolf's Mr Ramsay never does, because we are
> aware that he exists not only to the woman he is addressing but
> also in a God's eye. His unimportance in the world of the senses is

only matched by his enormous importance in another world. (p.91)

Amongst other things this constitutes a brilliant critical evocation of Trollope and its central argument, akin to that of Bishop Berkeley, that the real world is invested with its reality by its presence in the eye of God leads Greene to a searching critique of modernist fiction:

> The novelist, perhaps unconsciously aware of his predicament, took refuge in the subjective novel. It was as if he thought that by mining into layers of personality hitherto untouched he could unearth the secret of 'importance', but in these mining operations he lost yet another dimension. The visible world for him ceased to exist as completely as the spiritual. Mrs Dalloway walking down Regent Street was aware of the glitter of shop windows, the smooth passage of cars, the conversation of shoppers, but it was only a Regent Street seen by Mrs Dalloway that was conveyed to the readers. . . . But, we protest, Regent Street too has a right to exist. (p.92)

It is interesting to note at this point, if only as an example of how extremes meet, the similarity between the position of the Catholic Greene and the Marxist Lukács on the modernist novel, although their premisses are so different. The central point for both is its lack of substantiality compared with the classic realist novel of the nineteenth century. It is from this ground that Greene reaches his life-long admiration for Henry James, a writer of no discernible religious persuasion whatever. Greene is drawn to James by a quality that illuminates some of the most powerful aspects of his own work, what he calls 'the ruling fantasy that drove him to write: a sense of evil religious in its intensity' (p.21).

Here, then, is one explanation of Greene's power as a writer and also of his popularity. He discovered for himself the deepest truth about human life as it appeared to him, and so too his major theme as a novelist, at the age of fourteen when he read Marjorie Bowen's *The Viper of Milan* which gave him his 'pattern': 'perfect evil walking the world where perfect good can never walk again.' Religion 'might later explain it to me in other terms' and he would find it powerfully reinforced in Conrad and, above all, Henry James, but 'the pattern was already there' (p. 17). Clearly this pattern of evil—especially in its form as various kinds of betrayal: spiritual, sexual, political—recurs in his work again and again. And accompanying it are the essential Greenian components of guilt, attempted expiation and substitutionary sacrifice. But it is here that he decisively parts company with his literary masters. A well-established complaint against Henry James centres on the stratospheric level of material comfort enjoyed by many of his characters, a wealth that cuts them off from the pressures of ordinary living. This may have its suspect side; at its best, however, it enables James to concentrate on the moral dilemmas of the personal life in almost laboratory conditions, a fact which gives his greatest novels their special distinction of the minutest possible analysis of thought, feeling and action. For those attuned to it, the Jamesian world is infinitely fascinating and yet the elaboration of these insights must be acknowledged as a hindrance to his wide general popularity with even the educated public. Greene was rescued from this dilemma by the opposite side of his creativity to the spiritual: his interest in and knowledge of the public world. It is this conjunction that has enabled Greene to bring serious issues before a wide public in an entertaining form. That this may have been a cause of tension to him is suggested by the brilliant essay, 'The Young Dickens', where he says that *The Pickwick Papers* 'was enormous, shapeless, familiar (that important recipe for popularity)' and goes on to ask, 'How many in Dickens's place would have withstood . . . the popularity founded, as it almost always is, on the weakness and not the strength of an author?' (p. 80). I have tried to show in my discussion of specific novels that in seeking his own serious popularity Greene did not succumb to the failure of repetition. His concern for popularity itself may acquire a little more light in the next section.

SECTION B: GREENE AND CINEMA

Greene's involvement with film has been closer than that of any other serious twentieth-century writer. Scott Fitzgerald,

Faulkner and, at a lower level, Chandler, all had their contact with Hollywood, a relationship by no means as disastrous as is sometimes made out. By contrast with Greene, however, their baptism has the appearance of a mere sprinkling on the forehead compared with the total immersion of a once fanatical devotee. With the exception of direction itself, Greene's involvement has been as total as it could well be: at least eighteen films have been made of his work, beginning as early as 1934 with *Orient Express*, a version of *Stamboul Train*. His screenwriting has ranged from adaptations of his own and others' material, to the creation of original screenplays, most notably *The Third Man*; he has been a producer; for four and a half years, from 1935 to 1940, he was one of the most brilliant film reviewers ever; even film 'acting' has not eluded him, in the shape of a walk-on part in Truffaut's *La Nuit Americaine*, a film concerned with the act of film-making, as so many of Greene's novels comment reflexively on the act of writing. At the level of content, many of the novels make references to film, however passing—perhaps only in the visit of a character to the pictures. If Dickens's David Copperfield is 'saturated' in his love for Dora, it seems fair to say that Greene was saturated in cinema for a large part of his career. Although he apparently remains a film-goer, the love affair cooled in Greene's later years, as an essay of 1958 makes clear:

At least the cinema, like a psychiatrist, has enabled one to do without it. But that last sentence which slipped off the pen has a certain sadness. Am I the same character who in the 1920s read *Close-up* and the latest book on montage by Pudovkin with so much enthusiasm, who felt in *Mother*, *The Gold Rush*, *Rien que les heures*, *Souvenirs d'automne*, *Warning Shadows*, even in such popular Hollywood films as *Hotel Imperial* and *Foolish Wives*, the possibility of a new kind of art? of a picture as formal in design as a painting, but a design which moved?[8]

Despite this later qualification, an involvement once so complete must have had some effect on Greene's general outlook and, even, on the novels themselves.

That a major history of the influence of film on British social life still remains to be written becomes all the more remarkable when one considers the figures quoted by Angus

Calder for cinema attendances in the mid 1940s: 'Every week in Britain, some twenty-five or thirty million cinema seats were sold . . . a third, overall [of the whole population] went once a week or more often still.'[9] It is clear that the social, familial and personal effects of this experience must have been profound and yet as an area of enquiry it has remained the domain of narrow specialism of a mainly sociological kind, or of unsubstantiated impressions. There is a phase of modern British intellectual history to be explored here also, in the response of artists and thinkers to this amazing phenomenon of the largest mass entertainment in human history. Several strands of response can be disentangled, of course, but one of the most influential for British literary life, and for generations of academics and schoolteachers, is that associated with the periodical, *Scrutiny*. In his careful study, *The Moment of 'Scrutiny'*, Francis Mulhern has this to say of its attitude to cinema:

> The consensual judgement of the *Scrutiny* group on the subject was crushingly negative. Q.D. Leavis saw the cinema as one of the 'disruptive forces' that now threatened to extinguish the traditional culture of the working class. For L.C. Knights, it was part of a coalition of interests that stood ranged against valid cultural ideals. And in the writings of Denys Thompson, as in those of F.R. Leavis, cinema figured in the company of the Press, radio and motoring as a familiar of 'the machine.'[10]

Such views represent the literary-oriented nature of British culture, even in the twentieth century. British contributions to music and the visual arts are hardly negligible, but the domination of our cultural life by the undoubted greatness of English literature (Shakespeare casts a very long shadow) has resulted in a deeply, and sometimes unthinkingly, held conviction that literature is the norm of artistic creativity. In its turn, this has played a large part in creating the well-established fact that it is only in very recent years, if at all, that cinema has achieved in Britain the artistic respectability it has long enjoyed in the rest of Europe.

A figure of particular interest here is Raymond Williams who is of a younger generation than the major *Scrutiny* figures and yet old enough to have experienced the social impact of cinema in its hey-day. Williams has not merely explored the roots of modern British cultural life with sensitivity as well as intellectual power, but he has also celebrated the rise of a distinctively popular and urban culture in nineteenth-century literature, above all in the work of Dickens. Williams's engagement with contemporary culture is marked by a brilliant book on television and, at an earlier stage, a collaboration, with Michael Orrom, *Preface to Film*.[11] What, in the light of all this, is one to make of the following disagreement with his collaborator?

> In the end the biggest argument I had with Orrom was over Hollywood. When we were discussing what we meant by a film of total expression, I asked him to cite an example of his version of one. He answered: *Singing in the Rain*. [The title is *Singin'*, of course!] At first I was completely uncomprehending—I thought it was a joke. Then the emphasis on technique, abstracted from any content, totally turned me off.[12]

Despite his passionate commitment to cinema (above all, Eisenstein and the other early Russians), Williams's mind seems quite closed to a work of immense popularity which, in Greene's words, is able to give 'a sense of absurd unreasoning happiness, of a kind of poignant release.'[13] A left-wing hostility to Hollywood is obviously present, but it is also worth noting that Williams's intense involvement with film was part of his undergraduate experience; his semi-rural boyhood in the border county of England and Wales provided none of the picture-going opportunities available to even the poor urban child.

Professor Williams provides, then, a particularly fascinating example of hostility to cinema as a manifestation of popular culture all the more startling from his standpoint of personal as well as political sympathy with working-class life. The *Scrutiny* position can, of course, be contrasted with the response of another major grouping in British culture, with those who formed the London Film Society in 1925 and helped to create the G.P.O. Film Unit. Artists in the traditional forms played their part in this activity—W.H. Auden and Benjamin

Britten, for example. But the major creators, figures such as Norman McLaren and John Grierson, Basil Wright and Humphrey Jennings, appear as a beleaguered minority standing, with passionate attachment, for the art form of the modern world. Jennings is of outstanding interest in this group. A man of diverse talents—a painter and poet as well as a film-maker—his true genius flowered only under the pressure of the second world war in a manner that suggests that his earlier artistic activities were an unconscious preparation for his true *métier*, that he was training himself to be that new kind of artist, the artist in film.

And so it would be an absurd mistake to see Greene as alone in his enthusiasm for cinema; rather, he joined the already existing ranks of an excited minority within the broadly literary culture of Britain in the 1920s. The sense of daring that clung to this interest, like that of the early jazz enthusiasts, was undoubtedly a factor in the excitement it generated, and the older world against which it was reacting is caught amusingly in Greene's story of his father's confusion over the first Tarzan film. As headmaster of Berkhamsted School, he allowed his senior boys to see it 'under the false impression that it was an educational film of anthropological interest . . . ever after he regarded the cinema with a sense of disillusion and suspicion.'[14] This almost clandestine feeling of involvement emerges vividly in Greene's reminiscences of Oxford:

> I had appointed myself film critic of the *Oxford Outlook*, a literary magazine which appeared once a term. . . . *Warning Shadows*, *Brumes d'Automne*, *The Student of Prague*—these are the silent films of the twenties of which I can remember whole scenes still . . . I was horrified by the arrival of 'talkies' (it seemed the end of film as an art form), just as later I regarded colour with justifiable suspicion.[15]

But despite his membership of this freemasonry, Greene still remains an interesting individual 'case' in his relationship to film. I have already mentioned, in my discussion of the novel, that *Stamboul Train* was written in the hope that it might be filmed, surely one of the earliest examples of what has become a widespread phenomenon. And he remains unique as an example of a major writer involved in almost the full range of activities associated with cinema, a relationship that has borne fruit in two major ways: in its effect on his writing and in a theory of film, sketched through his reviewing, which has a direct bearing on his own work as a novelist.

An element of critical wittering seems inseparable from discussions of the filmic elements in Greene's novels. Ah yes, the critic murmurs, the influence of cinema, and one has the sense of hands moving rather ineffectually. Even such a distinguished film writer as James Agee falls victim to this vagueness, as in a review of *The Confidential Agent* in 1945:

> Greene's greatest talent—which is, I think, with the look and effluence of places, streets, and things . . . in these respects Greene achieves in print what more naturally belongs in films, and in a sense does not write novels at all, but verbal movies.[16]

As so often in this area, the point remains undeveloped and unexplained. The look and feel of places, streets and things is as much the province of Dickens as it is of Greene and while it may be true that Dickens, as part of a whole popular culture rooted in melodrama and sentimentality, did have a traceable effect on at least silent cinema, the opposition between writing and film which Agee suggests is a false one. We may get a little closer to the issue if we glance at Greene's reviews themselves, although it is impossible not to spend a digressive moment on their many joys. They are, of course, incomparably witty and intelligent, castigating absurdities with delightful savagery, but also—for the mid-1930s—giving somewhat unexpected praise. Noteworthy, for example, is the attention paid to Howard Hawks, a central figure for a later generation of critics, who was regarded mainly as a journeyman in Greene's day. Also, the cutting edge of Greene's intelligence is sometimes more than brilliant as in an extraordinarily prophetic judgement on Russian cinema by way of a review of *Lenin in October* which takes issue with the 'curious gritty hyphenated prose which seems to go with ideological convictions' of a Film Society programme note. The note contrasts *Lenin* with Eisenstein's *October* in its concentration 'upon a particular figure' as opposed to certain 'mass scenes' in the earlier film. Greene's comment is devastatingly exact in its foreseeing of the rise of the personality cult, in Soviet society as well as in cinema; 'we have reached the end of the Communist film. It is to be all "Heroes and Hero-Worship" now: the old films are to be remade for the new leaders: no more anonymous mothers will run in the van of the workers against the Winter Palace. The USSR is to produce Fascist films from now on' (p.206). The implication behind this judgement is an aesthetic of generalisation as distinctively cinematic and the point is carried through in a variety of interesting ways. In his review of a little Russian comedy Greene suggests that 'one is inclined to believe that characters can all be left to the stage; the cinema generalizes. It is not one man called Kostia who sings his way through *Jazz Comedy*, but all brave, coarse and awkward simplicity' (p.24). The point is carried a stage further in his comments on a French thriller:

> It is an excellent illustration of the main advantage the film possesses over the ordinary stage play; the means it has to place the drama in its general setting. We have almost given up hope of hearing *words* with a vivid enough imagery to convey the climate of the drama. *La Bandéra* on the stage would be only one more melodrama of African heat and brutality and death. . . . But the camera, because it can note with more exactitude and vividness than the prose of most living playwrights the atmosphere of mean streats and cheap lodgings, gives the story background and authenticity. We recogize the truth of the general scene and are more prepared to accept the truth of the individual drama. (p.39)

This, no doubt, is the area Agee had in mind in the passage I have just quoted although, as I argued, there is nothing specifically non-novelistic in Greene's treatment of similar material. The point is crystallised in his fine evocation of a Hollywood melodrama, *Barbary Coast*, directed by Howard Hawks:

> There are moments as dramatically exciting as anything I have seen on the fictional screen. *Sous les Toits de Paris* contained a sequence in which Préjean was surrounded by a gang with drawn

razors in the darkness of a railway viaduct; the smoke blew continually across, and the dialogue was drowned in the din of shunting trucks. The steamy obscurity, the whispers, the uproar overhead combined to make the scene vividly sinister. There is a moment in *Barbary Coast* that takes its place with Clair's, when the Big Shot's gunman, on his way to commit another murder in the San Francisco of which he has long been one of the undisputed rulers, feels the pistols of the vigilantes against his ribs. They walk him out to the edge of the acetylene-lighted town along streets ankle-deep in mud, holding a mock-trial with counsel and witnesses as they go; the low voices, the slosh of mud round their boots, the rhythmic stride are terrifying because they have been exactly imagined, with the ear as well as the eye. (p.32)

For readers of the novels this provides a moment of instant recognition: where are we, if not in Greeneland? *Barbary Coast* was made in 1935, the year of *England Made Me*: it was preceded, apart from the three earliest books, by *Stamboul Train* (1932) and *It's a Battlefield* (1934); *Sous les Toits* belongs to 1930. I'm not, of course, suggesting anything as reductive as a one-to-one influence at this point. But it seems entirely credible, given the amount of film-going Greene indulged in long before he became a professional reviewer, that this kind of film should take its place in the complex of influences which led him towards his own style and subject-matter. Greene's youthful liking for the adventure story is so well known that there is little reason to doubt that this interest was reinforced by a cinematic genre which took over many of the functions of such earlier literary entertainments, often placing them in a sharply observed contemporary setting.

The role of cinema in Greene's imaginative life is further substantiated if we turn to the example of a specific director, even one that Greene disliked, Hitchcock.[17] In *Ways of Escape* Greene describes an encounter with Alexander Korda at which he was asked if he 'had any film story in mind. I had none, so I began to improvise a thriller—early morning on Platform 1 at Paddington, the platform empty, except for one man who is waiting for the last train from Wales. From below his raincoat a trickle of blood forms a pool on the platform'.[18] Pure Greene or pure Hitchcock: it's hard to know which is the more accurate. The shock of the unexpected arises from the setting's banality, the keynote being the eruption of pain and terror in the everyday. Such moments are to be found everywhere in Greene's earlier work, from the tiny detail to the large set piece. Both are present in the comic excitement of D's pursuit of K in *The Confidential Agent* when he persuades a policeman and a crowd of onlookers that K is drunk rather than in the abject terror of D from which he is attempting to escape by getting himself arrested.[19] But, again, the interesting questions here have nothing to do with direct influence. It is, at the very least, amusing to note that the cricket bores of Hitchcock's *The Lady Vanishes* (1938) appears to be anticipated by the 'Hobbs and Zudgliffe' nonsense of *Stamboul Train* (1932), although the complex and collaborative genesis of film-making makes this impossible to prove. (*The Lady Vanishes* was adapted from a novel by two screenwriters and Hitchcock no doubt made his own contribution at this level; the actors concerned may have suggested the cricket business themselves, either directly or through the cricketing image they seem to personify.) .What can be said is that the 'entertainments' side of Greene's creative personality was deeply in tune with the world of cinema and the complex of forces out of which it emerged, and I have tried to show earlier that this has important implications for his 'serious' work. T.S. Eliot once remarked that the modernity of poetry is to be judged not by its subject matter, its references to electricity pylons or skyscrapers, but by its assimilation of the rhythms of modern life and of the car; and—I would add—of cinematic montage. We have seen that Greene's work is filled with references to film at the level of content; he himself has suggested the stylistic effect of this in *The Other Man*:

> When I describe a scene, I capture it with the moving eye of the cine-camera rather than with the photographer's eye—which leaves it frozen. In this precise domain I think the cinema has influenced me. Authors like Walter Scott or the Victorians were influenced by paintings and constructed their backgrounds as though they were static and came from the hands of a Constable. I work with a camera, following my characters and their movements. So the landscape moves. . . . I realize the extent of this influence of the cinema, especially since *It's a Battlefield* . . .

because films and film reviewing interested me very early. . . .
But the impact of the cinema on my way of writing comes from
the films themselves rather than from my reviewing.[20]

A small, but representative, example is provided by the novel
Greene refers to here, *It's a Battlefield*:

> The car climbed a hill and crossed the railway line by an hotel.
> Turning, the beams of the head-lamps caught a few bare trees,
> and a sandpit where children played in the dark. The car followed
> a long straight road beside the cutting, and a train overtook
> them, tearing south, dropping sparks on the roof. (Ch. 1)

The use of the gerund ('turning,' 'tearing,' 'dropping') is
perhaps the key factor, rather than any so-called 'visual' detail,
in creating a mimesis of movement within the rhythms of the
prose itself.

This, then, is the distinctively cinematic element in
Greene's work, a sense of movement in the prose of his
descriptive writing which captures the restless activity of a
great deal of modern experience. Assimilating at such a level,
Greene may well have been unconscious of the influence, at
least initially. His fascinating attempt to sketch a theory of
cinema through his reviewing is clearly, however, the work of
a self-aware intelligence playing over a mass of material for
which it has a fundamental sympathy as well as understanding. Once again, Greene's sensibilities run strongly counter to
the unthought-out position of the supposedly culturally
advanced. We are all familiar, especially in Britain, with the
easy opposition of the European art film to the mere
entertainment of Hollywood. But Greene's chief objection to
the popular film of his own day is that it is not popular, and
vulgar, enough. He rebukes an evidently rather arch experiment in cutting a film to music, *The Robber Baron*, for 'a
certain complacency, a conscious withdrawal from the corruption of the commercial film, in its painstaking irresponsibility. Virtue can afford to be charitable, and all those who have
occasionally enjoyed the corrupt pleasures, the bright facile
excitements of popular entertainment will feel as if an old
friend (vicious, of course, but not always unamusing) has been

too priggishly reprimanded' (p.76). His response to 'Bing Crosby crooning a prize bull to sleep on a freight car' is to long for a 'genuinely vulgar art':

> The novelist may write for a few thousand readers, but the film artist *must* work for millions. It should be his distinction and pride that he has a public whose needs have never been met since the closing of the theatres by Cromwell. But where is the vulgarity of this art? Alas! the refinement of the 'popular' novel has touched the films; it is the twopenny libaries they reflect rather than the Blackfriars Ring, the Wembley Final, the pin saloons, the coursing. (p.93)

Greene constantly hopes to see cinema rise to a 'simple and popular poetry.' He changes his ground slightly in a comment on *The Plainsman*, although in a way that shows his grasp of the economic underpinning of cinema: 'A few great spectacular moments in the history of the film remain as a permanent encouragement to those who believe that an art may yet emerge from a popular industry: the long shots of the Battle of Bull Run in *The Birth of a Nation*, the French attack in *All Quiet*. Some of the scenes in *The Plainsman* belong to that order' (p.131). A slightly regretful note is struck here, as though Greene doubts that the miracle he hopes for can ever occur and yet as late as January 1940, only two months before he gives up reviewing, he writes with lyrical enthusiasm of Capra's *Mr Smith Goes to Washington* and states baldly; 'It is a great film' (p.261).

Greene's enthusiasm for the cinema is an aspect of the sensibility I tried to analyse in my first chapter with its absence of an apocalyptic condemnation of the modern world, and it helps to explain his modest claim, 'I suppose I am a good popular writer.'[21] His best novels are, of course, on a different artistic level from most of the films he praised as a reviewer, although a real link exists between, say, *The Ministry of Fear* and his recognition that *Pépé le Moko* raises 'the thriller to a poetic level' (p.145). One reason why even Greene's best work has reached a large public is his avoidance of the experiments in fiction associated with the names of Joyce, Faulkner and Virginia Woolf. The explanation of this is no easy matter, but I hope to have shown that one factor was his sympathetic involvement with the major popular art of the twentieth century.

SECTION C: THE TERRITORY OF ANGUISH

It remains only to attempt a final word on this remarkable writer. Summings-up often hover on the edge of banality and this is a peculiar danger in Greene's case. The standard critical moves are commonplace by now: Greeneland, the deft sketching of character and setting, economical writing. I have tried to show that however adequate these gestures may be for the lesser entertainments, they cannot do justice to *The Ministry of Fear* and the best of the novels. Greeneland as a setting has visionary power, at its best, rather than the mechanical exoticism of local colour. Scobie and Charlie Fortnum, to take very different examples, are too richly realised, live too deeply within themselves and for us, to be the fictional counters common to the bestseller. And whatever its dangers, Greene's fascination with simile frequently adds texture and density to his writing. The most distinguished critical book on Greene so far, Allott and Farris's *The Art of Graham Greene* cuts much deeper than this, as one would expect. For it, the 'terror of life, a terror of what experience can do to the individual, a terror at a predetermined corruption, is the motive force that drives Greene as a novelist.'[22] I would agree, with the sole qualification that a writer as interesting as Greene is capable of being motivated by more than a single obsession. Perhaps my own emphasis is best seen as the effect of this terror, the emotion it generates within the books and for the reader.

In his wonderful appreciation of Fritz Lang's great film of 1936, *Fury*, Greene evokes the painful parting of two lovers, one of whom is soon to be made the object of an apparently successful lynching, as 'the ordinary recognizable agony, life as one knows it is lived.'[23] It is surely an aspect of Greene's distinction that the territory he explores is part of the landscape of so much of the greatest literature: the terror of life's unpredicatability and the anguish of its victims. This theme's resonance for Greene stems from his conviction that anguish is inseparable from the daily experience of human life; like the act of breathing it amounts almost to an involuntary accompaniment to existence. The conviction is partly theological: the unbridgeable gap between man's fallen nature and Christ's perfect goodness is, for him, a source of continual pain. For some Christians the stress clearly falls differently, on God's beauty rather than man's ugliness, for example; again, the gulf between man and God may be a spur to spiritual achievement instead of a daily reminder of inadequacy. Greene's sensibilities are adjusted so finely—some might say morbidly—to what man inflicts on God through his betrayals that Christ's sufferings on earth are re-enacted with an intensity that never decreases. The curse, the spit, the blow pervade Greene's world with a completeness akin to George Eliot's spectre of a consciousness attuned to the suffering of flowers being picked and grass cut.

But this theological dimension is the centre of a perhaps more widely acceptable sense of the sheer poignancy of our ordinary experience of living. Self-consciousness and temporality are inescapable burdens, suffusing life with its inextricable confusion of levels: our awareness that growth towards maturity is simultaneously a movement towards death is only the most obvious example. Greene's treatment of personal relations is also permeated by the fear of betrayal, self-knowledge too long delayed, the missed opportunity, the offer refused. That novel of marriages, *Middlemarch*, is haunted by the unspoken certainty that Dorothea and Lydgate were 'made' for each other, and that they miss one another partly through mere accident but also through aspects of their characters which change only under the pressure of marriage to the wrong partners. This ache of incompleteness at the paradoxes and missed opportunities of human life is central to Greene's vision of ordinary living. Writers, like everyone else, respond differently to the phenomena presented to our intelligence, feeling and spirit by the spectacle of existence. The endlessly repeated cyle of birth, growth, extinction is a deadening repetition to T.S. Eliot ('dung and death')[24] while for D.H. Lawrence, in the opening pages of *The Rainbow*, it is a source of ecstatic celebration. Dylan Thomas may sing in the chains of time and mortality, but Greene's melody is elegiac. Even great happiness is stress in his world, never more so than in the passionate involvement of Sarah and Bendrix in *The End of the Affair*, as Sarah's diary makes clear:

> Sometimes I get so tired to trying to convince him that I love him and shall love him for ever. He pounces on my words like a barrister and twists them. I know he is afraid of that desert which would be him if our love were to end, but he can't realize that I feel exactly the same. What he says aloud, I say to myself silently and write it here. What can one build in the desert? . . . If only I could make him feel secure, then we could love peacefully, happily, not savagely, inordinately, and the desert would recede out of sight. For a lifetime perhaps. (Book 3, Ch. 2)

The pervasiveness of anguish in Greene's view of things is such that it surfaces in the most apparently unlikely places, in his witty and seemingly rather superficial play, *The Complaisant Lover*, for example. The boring, decent husband, the loving wife who needs the fulfilment that has disappeared from her marriage, the lover whose complaisance is so amusingly contrived, go through their little dance in a manner that arouses pain as well as laughter because the play creates the pressure of real suffering. This response is developed through the character of the husband, Victor, perhaps Greene's most successful dramatic creation, in his capacity to surprise the audience as well as the play's other characters. The hearty practical joker is suddenly revealed in a new light when his wife claims that they

> 'haven't been married properly for years':
> Oh yes we have. Marriage is living in the same house with someone you love. I never stopped loving you—I only stopped giving you pleasure. And when that happened I didn't want you any more. I wasn't going to use you like a pick-up in the park. How did you know that?
> You were always very quiet when we made love, but you had one habit you didn't know of yourself. In the old days just before going to sleep, if you had been satisfied, you would touch my face and say 'thank you'. And then a time came when I realized that for months you had said nothing. You had only touched my face.

(*In sudden pain.*) Do you say thank you to Root?
I don't know. Perhaps.
You are always so damnably honest—that's the awful thing about
you . . .
I never knew you noticed so much. (Act II, sc. i)

This revelation sets the scene for Victor's emergence as the
victor in more than name, suffering deeply but through that
suffering, and his love for his wife, establishing a situation in
which a painfully won degree of happiness is possible for all
three points on the triangle, husband, wife and lover.

Greene does not often allow himself even this degree of
bitter-sweet reconciliation; his more usual version of a happy
ending is the guilt-laden and secretive complicity of Arthur
Rowe and Anna Hilfe at the end of *The Ministry of Fear*. Even
this is a rare indulgence. As we think back over the novels and
their characters it does seem as if the sense of anguish is
inseparable from our experience of Greene's world. Carol
Musker, Minty, Raven, Pinkie and Rose, the whisky priest
and Scobie, the death of Hasselbacher, the destruction of
Castle's domestic life amount to a roll-call of hardly
surpassable pain. Greene's mastery of this desperate territory of
ordinary suffering is evident in even *It's a Battlefield*, one of his
less successful works, in the appallingly poignant attempt at
sexual comfort between Conrad Drover and his sister-in-law, a
passage that embodies incontrovertible proof of Greene's
command of the landscape of anguish:

> He felt no guilt at all; this did not harm his brother, this hopeless
> attempt to shield her, for she had not even been deceived; she was
> glad, she was grateful, she was his friend, but she didn't believe a
> word he said. Then she touched him with timidity, and his flesh
> stirred, and he felt a degree of guilt which only the bed and the
> tiring of his body and the forgetting of his love in the direct
> contact of skin with skin, the thrust of lust, could temporarily
> and in part assuage. When he felt her shudder, he had a dull
> sense of an irrevocable injury which one of them had done to the
> other. Love had been close to him, in the kitchen, before the
> glow and the hum of the gas, between chair and chair, which had
> escaped him now in the bed, in the dark. One of them had
> injured the other, but it was not their fault. They had been

driven to it, and holding her close to him with painful tenderness, it was hate he chiefly felt, hate of Jim, of a director's nephew, of two men laughing in Piccadilly. When he awoke in the night she was crying, and nothing that he could do would stop her tears. (Ch. 3)

NOTES

1. *Faith and Fiction*: *Creative Process in Greene and Mauriac* (Notre Dame, Indiana: University of Notre Dame Press, 1964), p.138.
2. *Twenty-One Stories* (Penguin, 1977), p.31. Hereafter page numbers following quotations refer to this edition.
3. *A Sense of Reality* (Penguin, 1975), p.65.
4. OM, p.173.
5. WE, p.177.
6. *Collected Essays* (Penguin, 1970), p.319.
7. George Woodcock, *The Writer and Politics* (London: The Porcupine Press, 1948), p.143.
8. 'The Novelist and the Cinema—A Personal Experience,' *International Film Annual No. 2*, ed. William Whitebait (New York: Doubleday, 1958), p.56.
9. Calder, *op. cit.*, p.367.
10. Francis Mulhern, *The Moment of 'Scrutiny'* (London: NLB, 1979), p.52.
11. *Television* (London: Fontana, 1974) and *Preface to Film* (London: Film Drama, 1954).
12. Raymond Williams, *Politics and Letters* (London: NLB, 1979), p.233.
13. *The Pleasure-Dome: The Collected Film Criticism 1935–40* ed. John Russell Taylor (Oxford University Press, 1980), p.7. Hereafter page references to this edition will follow quotations.
14. SL, p.11.
15. WE, p.46.
16. *The Nation*, November 10, 1945, p.179.
17. See WE, p.47.
18. *Ibid.*, p.50.
19. *The Confidential Agent*, Part Two, Ch. 1.
20. OM, pp.132–3.
21. *Ibid.*, p.120.
22. Kenneth Allott and Miriam Farris, *The Art of Graham Greene* (London: Hamish Hamilton, 1951), p.15.
23. Taylor, *op. cit.*, p.84.
24. T.S. Eliot, 'East Coker', Section 1 (in *Four Quartets*).

Bibliography

WORKS BY GRAHAM GREENE

All the books that Greene has chosen to reprint are available in the United Kingdom in the hardback Collected Edition (London: Heinemann/Bodley Head); unless otherwise stated they are also available in paperback (Penguin). The American Uniform Edition is published by Viking Press, New York. Greene's works are listed below with date of first publication.

Novels
The Man Within (1929).
The Name of Action (London: Heinemann, 1930. Garden City, NY: Doubleday, 1930). Not reprinted and not in paperback.
Rumour at Nightfall (London: Heinemann, 1931. Garden City, NY: Doubleday, 1931). Not reprinted and not in paperback.
Stamboul Train (1932).
It's a Battlefield (1934).
England Made Me (1935).
A Gun for Sale (1936). American title *This Gun for Hire*.
Brighton Rock (1938).
The Confidential Agent (1939).
The Power and the Glory (1940). American title *The Labyrinthine Ways*.
The Ministry of Fear (1943).
The Heart of the Matter (1948).
The Third Man (1950).
The End of the Affair (1951).
Loser Takes All (1955).

The Quiet American (1955).
Our Man in Havana (1958).
A Burnt-Out Case (1961).
The Comedians (1966).
Travels with my Aunt (1969).
The Honorary Consul (1973).
The Human Factor (1978).
Doctor Fischer of Geneva or The Bomb Party (London: Bodley Head, 1980).
Monsignor Quixote (London: Bodley Head, 1982). Not in paperback.

Short Stories
Twenty-One Stories (1954). First published in 1947 as *Nineteen Stories*.
A Sense of Reality (1963).
May We Borrow Your Husband? (1967).

Travel Books
Journey Without Maps (1936).
The Lawless Roads (1939).
In Search of a Character (1961).

Essays
British Dramatists (London: Collins, 1942). Not in paperback. Reprinted in *The Heritage of British Literature* (London: Thames & Hudson, 1983).
Collected Essays (1969).

Film Reviews
The Pleasure Dome: The Collected Film Criticism 1935–40. ed. John Russell Taylor (London: Secker & Warburg, 1972); paperback (Oxford University Press, 1980).

Plays
The Living Room (London: Heinemann, 1953). Not in paperback.
The Potting Shed (London: Heinemann, 1958).
The Complaisant Lover (London: Heinemann, 1959).
Three Plays (London: Mercury Books, 1961): *The Living Room,*

The Potting Shed, *The Complaisant Lover*.
Carving a Statue (London: Bodley Head, 1964).
The Return of A.J. Raffles (London: Bodley Head, 1975).

Autobiography
A Sort of Life (1971).
Getting to Know the General: The Story of an Involvement (London: Bodley Head, 1985).
Ways of Escape (London: Bodley Head, 1980).

Interview
The Other Man: Conversations with Graham Greene. Marie-Françoise Allain, trans. Guido Waldman (London: Bodley Head, 1983).

Biography
Lord Rochester's Monkey (London: Bodley Head, 1974); paperback (London: Futura, 1976). The book was written between 1931 and 1934, but not published at that time.

Pamphlet
J'Accuse—The Dark Side of Nice (London: Bodley Head, 1982).

Greene has also published four books for children with the London publisher Max Parrish: *The Little Fire Engine* (1950), *The Little Horse Bus* (1952), *The Little Steamroller* (1953), *The Little Train* (1957).

BIBLIOGRAPHY

Vann, J. Don. *Graham Greene: A Checklist of Criticism* (Kent, Ohio: Kent State University Press, 1970).

SELECTED CRITICISM OF GRAHAM GREENE

Allott, Kenneth, and Farris, Miriam, *The Art of Graham Greene* (London: Hamish Hamilton, 1951).
Atkins, John, *Graham Greene* (London: Calder & Boyars, 1957, revised edn. 1966).
Evans, Robert O. (ed.) *Graham Greene: Some Critical Considera-*

tions (Lexington, Kentucky: University of Kentucky Press, 1963).

Falk, Quentin, *The Cinema of Graham Greene* (London: Quartet Books, 1984)

Kunkel, Francis L., *The Labyrinthine Ways of Graham Greene* (New York: Sheed & Ward, 1959).

Lewis, R.W.B., *The Picaresque Saint: Representative Figures in Contemporary Fiction* (New York: Barnes & Noble, 1959).

Lodge, David, *Grahame Greene* (New York and London: Columbia University Press, 1966).

Stratford, Philip, *Faith and Fiction: Creative Process in Greene and Mauriac* (Notre Dame, Indiana: University of Notre Dame Press, 1964).

Wyndham, Francis, *Graham Greene* (London; Longmans, Green, 1955).

Acknowledgements

The author and publisher wish to thank Mr Graham Greene for his permission to quote extensively from his work. Extracts from the following titles are reprinted by permission of Viking Penguin Inc.: *Brighton Rock*, copyright 1938, renewed © 1966 by Graham Greene; *The Comedians*, copyright © 1965, 1966 by Graham Greene; *The End of the Affair*, copyright 1951, renewed © 1979 by Graham Greene; *The Heart of the Matter*, copyright 1948, renewed © 1976 by Graham Greene; *It's a Battlefield*, copyright © 1962 by Graham Greene; *The Ministry of Fear*, copyright 1943, renewed © 1971 by Graham Greene; *The Power and the Glory*, copyright 1940, renewed © 1968 by Graham Greene.

Index